CH

TEN TREES

AND A

TRUFFLE DOG

Sniffing Out the Perfect Plot in Provence

JAMIE IVEY

A Herman Graf Book
Skyhorse Publishing

About the Author

Jamie Ivey has written three books about the south of France: *Extremely Pale Rosé*, *La Vie en Rosé*, and *Rosé en Marché*, published by Phoenix (Hachette). He lives in Provence with his wife and daughter.

The *Daily Mail* has described Jamie as 'a younger Peter Mayle with a similar turn of phrase,' and *The New York Times Online* as 'great fun to read... particularly if you enjoy sticking your nose into little-known corners of France.' Jamie won the 2006 Gourmand award for book of the year on French wine.

Author's Note

Names, dates, and places have been changed. Some of the characters are composite.

Contents

Part 1

A Miracle in the Market

Chapter 1

It was a crisp December morning in Provence. Trails of smoke from the glowing barrel of a roast chestnut vendor streamed into the rich blue sky and the seared fatty smell of fried foie gras drifted in the air. Puddles from yesterday's storm had iced over making the pavement treacherous for the traders but even so an unbroken row of stalls lined the street.

The finest food from all over France was available – corn-fed chickens from Bresse, pungent charcuterie from Corsica, milk-reared veal, marbled Charolais beef, olives from Nyon, duck confit from the Dordogne and plump oysters from nearby Sète.

As my wife, Tanya, and I strolled slowly along we eavesdropped on excited culinary chatter.

'*Quel mélange, c'est magnifique.*'

'*Tout à fait – il faut le cuire à l'avance.*'

There was no mistaking the rapture in the voices as recollections of unforgettable dishes and historic recipes were shared.

'Rub a Sisteron gigot with rosemary. Slow bake, prepare the ratatouille with overripe tomatoes and courgettes, season with dried summer herbs,' rattled away an old lady, clasping an overflowing shopping bag in her bony fingers, 'and perhaps some winter leaves tossed in vinaigrette, then a peppered goat's cheese, and one of Monsieur Soggia's lemon tarts to finish.'

To listen was to salivate.

Provence has a food festival almost every week. If it's not the sweet melons of Cavaillon, then it's the spiky sea urchins of Carry-le-Rouet or the heat-baked wines of Saint-Rémy. The format is always similar – hungry crowds gather, enticed by seasonal delicacies and the sultry swing of a band. Before long the streets bleed pink with rosé.

There's a compère from the local radio station who fights his screeching microphone to interview the mayor and towards the end of the day a procession of food groupies. Cherries, strawberries, even the humble Provençal potato – each and every consumable has a society of admirers or *confrérie*. These plump men and women hide their ripe bellies under priestly gowns and measure each heavy step to a monastic chant. Deep, growling voices reverberate to the heavens. The melody seems serious, even moving, until you realise that somebody has spent long winter nights composing Latin odes to lavender bees.

My wife and I usually happen upon such festivals. Today, however, was the one exception: a gastronomic fair so unmissable that the date is marked in local calendars alongside all the national holidays. The village responsible for this *fête* among *fêtes*, Rognes, has no other culinary claims to fame – there's a decent enough butcher, an average baker and a couple of dodgy pizza parlours. Yet once a year this unremarkable commuter suburb of Aix-en-Provence is transformed into a Mecca for food lovers.

The fair always take place the Sunday before Christmas and people travel for hours, lured by the famed black diamonds (truffles) which are the essential ingredient in the region's Christmas celebrations. The price per kilo can reach €1,000 but from street sweeper to movie star everyone makes a little room in their annual budget, as if to do otherwise would be sacrilegious.

After just fifteen minutes at the *fête*, listening to recipes, browsing the delicacy-laden stalls, inhaling the rich mixture of aromas, I could resist no longer. I had to eat. Nearby, chefs in kitchen whites were handing out steaming bundles. Wrapped in greasy paper, the food – scrambled egg in a baguette – was the type that you might get in a roadside cafe but for the one secret ingredient. Tiny black flecks of truffle laced the golden mixture, elevating the experience to a totally different level and as the chefs' tray emptied people began to jostle for position. Luckily one of the hot parcels was pressed into my outstretched palm.

For me, this mid-morning sandwich was one of the gastronomic highlights of the year; no dish, not even one conjured by any of the local Michelin-starred chefs could elicit such simple pleasure. With the addition of the truffle the taste of the egg suddenly became deeper, more like a duck egg, and at the same time the earthiness of the truffle echoed the fleshiness of early season *cèpes*. I was halfway through the baguette before I remembered Tanya – eight months pregnant and exhausted from a sleepless night, she was clearly not enjoying the fair as much as me. Still, she had insisted on coming, anxious to make the most of the remaining four weeks until the due date.

'Do you want to sit down?' I asked belatedly, squeezing her hand.

'You buy the truffle and I'll wait in the cafe,' nodded Tanya.

From behind it was impossible to tell that she was pregnant. During the term she'd lost weight from everywhere apart from her tummy. Her blonde hair bobbed in the crowd, her slim-fitting jacket elegant amid a dense forest of fur coats. I watched her take a seat and then turned my attention back to the truffles.

At the far end of the market a close-knit circle of stalls was hemmed in by a collection of battered vans. It had been a bad year for truffles. Plenty of rain in the spring had provided early promise but the long dry summer and then a mild beginning to the winter had combined to stunt the growth of the tuber. Oak woods which usually produced plentiful supplies were said to be barren and reports in *La Provence*, the local paper, warned that prices were on fire. Demand today would be huge, so it was hard to see how I could grab a bargain, with the price likely to be €100 for a single truffle. Was it worth it? This was our third Christmas in Provence and previously I would have ruefully moved on. Somehow, though, the truffle purchase had become as emblematic as buying the tree.

To a man the dealers were short, scruffy and unshaven and together they smelled of the inside of a bar – a pungent combination of garlic, pastis and Gauloises. They sat at rickety tables covered in worn cloth. In front of them were cereal bowls containing a couple of earth-encased truffles about the size of golf balls. The overall impression was of terrible hardship. Clothes were worn through and patched up and the sole of one of the vendor's shoes hung loose like the tongue of a thirsty dog.

At least I was experienced enough to see through the charade. Truffle hunters are notoriously secretive about their profession. For tax reasons most of them deny being involved in the trade. If challenged by *le fisc* (the tax authorities), they might shrug and admit to finding a single truffle at the bottom of the garden.

'Look at my car,' they'd protest, as if a battered Renault was in itself proof of innocence.

However, in reality dealers make thousands of euros a year, competing furiously with each other to discover the best hunting locations. Historically they would have followed flies through oak woods, watching carefully where the insects chose to land and digging the soil in their wake. These days dogs have replaced flies and a champion truffle dog is a valuable possession. Sadly two or three dogs a year are poisoned as rival hunters seek to wreck each other's prospects.

Buying a truffle is complicated by a well-known sharp practice. Since finding truffles is so difficult, a few unscrupulous vendors sell Chinese truffles, which look similar to their Provençal cousins but have about 1/100th of the taste. Covered in mud and mixed in a bowl with the real thing it is incredibly difficult to tell the two apart. The odour of the Provençal truffles envelops their Chinese cousins, fooling all but the most experienced Gallic nose. Only once a truffle is cut open can you really discover its provenance. The white veins of a Chinese truffle are less tightly spaced and the skin pockmarked. To allay fears of fraud, each of the vendors in Rognes had a truffle sliced in half on the table in front of them. Other tricks of the trade include lacing the mud that always surrounds truffles with metal flakes and packing the natural indentations with mud. Both methods increase the weight of the truffle and hence the profit.

I chose the scruffiest, dirtiest, smelliest vendor, on the basis that his appearance meant he had the most to hide from the *fisc* and was therefore the most professional of the bunch.

'*C'est combien par kilo?*'

'*Neuf cents.*'

'*Huit cents?*'

'*Normalement, c'est neuf cent cinquante.*'

Comprehensively out-negotiated, I nodded and began examining the merchandise. In France it's almost rude not to touch and feel the food before purchasing. In the summer I've watched as shoppers in search of optimum ripeness have sniffed and re-sniffed up to twenty melons, and melons only cost a meagre five euros a kilo.

Flaring my nostrils like a horse before a big race I attacked the pile of muddy black balls before me. The odour was so strong that after examining just five truffles a dull headache began to develop. A professional buyer could easily sniff over a hundred truffles in a morning and still discern minute differences in scent. I, however, was already lost. The first truffle had smelt the strongest, and had felt nice and heavy relative to its size.

'I'll take this one,' I said, brushing the dirt away from the surface.

'Remember, wrap it in paper, keep it in a box and change the paper morning and night,' the dealer said as he weighed the truffle and dropped it into a plastic bag.

'Eighty-nine fifty.'

Two crisp €50 notes changed hands. Turning to leave I bumped into a man with flowing white hair and a deep wind-ingrained tan. In his arms he carried three cases of wine, of which he was struggling to keep hold.

'Can I help?' I offered, relieving him of one of the boxes.

'Set it down over there.' He nodded gratefully.

'Matured in the most expensive Bordeaux oak barrels for twelve months,' the vigneron told me, shrugging. 'And what do I get in return for twenty-four bottles? Three truffles – *c'est la folie*.' He grinned, clearly delighted with the exchange.

I made my way back towards Tanya, passing stands full of truffle liqueur (undrinkable), truffle oils, truffle-infused eggs, and sachets of dried truffle risottos, all with inflated price tags.

With the truffle purchased the fun could really start. Should we extravagantly grate it over the Christmas bird, or stuff great wedges in the cavities during the cooking process, allowing its aroma to permeate every mouthful? Better still, reserve it in a jar with eggs to make the ultimate morning-after omelette or slice it raw onto toast with a drizzling of the local olive oil? Tanya and I usually tried something different every year, plucking a new idea from a magazine article, but without fail we saved the last remaining slices to spike the festive brie. It's a divine combination and we'd been salivating at the thought since the first frost. This Christmas, though, things would be different.

The menu outside the local cafe had been infected by truffle fever: *pâté de foie gras aux truffes, homard* (lobster) *gratiné aux truffes, fromage aux truffes*. Even the green salad was treated to a grating of black diamond. Catching the waiter's eye I ordered a *café crème* and sat down next to a drained-looking Tanya.

'Well, I got it – nine hundred euros a kilo, but what can you do,' I chattered away excitedly. 'How about a *sauce aux truffes* this year?'

My coffee arrived and I took a deep injudicious gulp of the frothy mixture, burning the back of my throat.

'Jamie, I think it's started.'

'What's started?'

'The baby.'

I took another enormous gulp of coffee, still not quite registering what she had just said. The one job a father is totally responsible for is getting his wife to the hospital on time, practising the route, making sure the car is full of petrol, checking the oil level, the pressure in the tyres, making sure the bag is packed and generally that everything runs smoothly.

I'd heard stories of twenty-minute labours and births in the backs of cars, and was determined that it would never happen to us. Yet we were registered at a hospital near home over an hour away, through the sinuous Combe de Lourmarin, one of the last places you would want to negotiate with a wife in heavy labour: nothing but sheer cliffs and goat farms for miles.

'But it's not due for another month,' I protested, trying to hide the panic creeping into my belly.

'I know.'

'And we haven't got anything ready.'

'I know.' Tanya winced in pain.

'I'll get the car.'

I started at a fast walk, which somehow quickly became a jog and finally a run. I hadn't even asked how close together the contractions were.

'*Attention!*', 'Watch where you're going', 'What's the rush?' people called as I shoved through the crowds, fighting the flow of arrivals.

The engine started first time and I crawled down the hill in the slow-moving traffic. I could see Tanya waiting at the roadside, hands on knees, panting. Despite the cold she'd taken off her coat, which she'd handed to one of the many onlookers. Nothing attracts a crowd like a sick person in France. A grazed arm is enough to have yourself escorted to the nearest bar for a restorative brandy. Blame is apportioned, remedies shared, the doctor called out to stem the bleeding.

Perhaps twenty people had gathered around to offer their advice to Tanya. No doubt the majority of them were berating her imbecile of a husband. How had he allowed this to happen? Where was he now?

Please let one of them be a midwife, I prayed, burying my head in my arms as I waited for the traffic to move. Shoppers zigzagged between the cars, and the municipal policemen tried to bring order to the chaos. What would our baby wear when it was born? The hospital had stipulated about thirty essential items – but we had nothing with us. Would it be a boy or a girl? I really didn't care, as long as we got to the hospital. The pregnancy bible, *What to Expect When You're Expecting*, sat on the dashboard in front of me. The author certainly hadn't told us to expect this.

'Let's go.' Tanya slammed the door and a gap briefly opened in the traffic. A couple of bends later and the soft folds of the Luberon hills came into view. The panic was gradually replaced by an unexpected sense of calm. Finally it was going to happen, after months of waiting – a Christmas present to beat all Christmas presents. I'd heard good things about Pertuis hospital, which was much closer than Apt. We'd make for there.

'OK?'

Tanya nodded weakly. There was silence for a minute or so.

'There's just one thing,' she said tentatively. 'I left the truffle on the table.'

Chapter 2

Pertuis hospital smelt of strong detergent and overcooked food. The walls of the maternity ward were painted a crumbling pink and lined with arty black-and-white photos of semi-naked women with their babies. Strangely some of the mothers had chosen to wear their finest lingerie, giving the images an overtone of sexuality.

'Might as well look your best,' I joked to Tanya, but she didn't reply. Instead, she scanned the empty corridor for signs of a midwife. According to the local paper the service on offer was one of the best in France. People travelled up to two hours to have their baby in Pertuis, lured by its holistic approach – acupuncture, massages, aqua births, aromatherapy and, most importantly for Tanya, epidurals. Whatever the mother-to-be wanted, was provided.

Part of the reason for the hospital's notoriety was the French state's continual attempts to shut it down. The government wanted to concentrate resources on large birthing centres, cramming them with machinery and processing women like goods in a factory. Protest marches and fundraising failed to save the hospital but when the main local farmer threatened to stop supplying his famed asparagus to Paris, politicians finally took notice. Sitting together waiting for a midwife, we could not have been more grateful.

Nearby a tall man with three-day stubble and a shaggy mop of hair paced up and down, looking anxiously towards a distant door. He clutched a packet of cigarettes in his hands and judging from the plastic wraps over his shoes he'd come from one of the birthing rooms. Despite the heat in the hospital he wore a scarf wrapped tightly around his neck and a heavy woollen jumper. For some reason he looked vaguely familiar, but I couldn't place his face.

'*Ça va?*' I asked.

'*Oui, ça va*, you have to wait outside for the epidural,' he explained. 'The needle's big and sometimes the fathers faint.' With that thought he succumbed, placing a cigarette in his mouth and heading for the stairs.

'*Madame Ivey, venez avec moi.*' A slim elegant lady dressed in midwife green beckoned to us. She was perhaps our age, with warm nut-brown eyes, but her voice was stern and the hospital orderlies seemed to shrink away from her. Introductions were clearly not part of the service and I squinted to read the name stencilled on a badge on her chest – 'Lea'.

Tanya struggled to her feet and like the losing couple in a sports day three-legged race we hobbled into Lea's office. Inside the small room a large window looked north towards the Luberon hills. The evergreen pine and olive trees and the sumptuous blue sky combined to give the appearance of a summer's day.

'We've phoned for your records. Any trips or falls? Anything out of the ordinary?'

Tanya shook her head and the examination continued, with Lea writing notes slowly into a book. Outside in the corridor we could hear the wails of newborn babies and the odd piercing scream of a mother in labour, but Lea was oblivious.

'Do you smoke?' Lea's tone was that of an interrogator.

Once again Tanya shook her head.

'Drink?'

'Eat uncooked meat?'

'Unpasteurised cheese?'

All that was missing was a spotlight in Tanya's eyes. I could see her breaking soon and, to stop the incessant questioning, confessing to an invented orgy of wine, goat's cheese and Gauloises. Lea meanwhile sat unperturbed, reeling off an extensive list of prohibited activities, her single raised eyebrow suggesting all the time that she didn't believe a word of our responses. Something had to explain why our baby was premature and she would have her answer.

Inexplicably her attention then turned to me.

'Do you smoke?'

I shook my head.

'Drink?'

'A little,' I admitted, trying to figure out how my habits, unsavoury or not, could possibly be relevant. Rather than giving them the third degree, I'd heard of other French hospitals offering expectant fathers a wine list. Where was the touchy-feely holistic approach I'd been led to expect?

Sensing my disquiet, Lea's voice softened. 'It's for the baby – we like to get a picture of your home life.'

Turning her attention back to Tanya, Lea paused, perplexed at the lack of explanation for the premature labour. 'Truffles, perhaps?'

Provençal folklore was full of stories of the medicinal effects not only of lavender but truffles as well; to me, the idea seemed ridiculous.

'Did you eat any truffle?' persisted Lea.

Tanya shook her head. 'But I did sniff one.'

'It's often enough,' said Lea. 'In England, it's hot curries; for us, it's truffles.'

'The man outside,' I added in a flash of inspiration, 'who left for a cigarette – he was at the truffle fair too.'

'*Beh voilà*, mystery solved,' said Lea with great satisfaction, changing her demeanour completely now it was clear we were gourmands and not the chain-smoking, raw-meat-eating, pastis-swilling infidels that she'd initially presumed.

'You're in a stage we call pre-labour. Sometimes it can go on for days; for you, I'd say another three hours. Premature births can be a little complicated, particularly when they are truffle induced,' she went on, as if there were volumes of medical research on the subject. Her tone implied that as a father she expected me to be aware of the potential difficulties.

Just minutes ago time had been our enemy, as we fought shock and raced to the hospital; now, the clock on the wall ticked slowly by and Lea's pen scratched repetitively as she filled in form after form. My ignorance quickly bred a gathering paranoia. I imagined a library shelf full of learned discourses on pregnancy and truffles – perhaps a seminal book on the correct use of forceps in a truffle-induced birth, sitting side by side with the pioneering and definitive work: *The Father, the Truffle and Birth*.

Lea's pen came to the end of a sentence and a look of concern crossed her face. 'I am so sorry,' she stuttered, 'it's been a busy day, otherwise I would have noticed sooner.'

Glancing in the direction of her eyes, I saw that she was looking at the time – 12.15.

'Now, the best place is just down the road, they do a fantastic menu – twelve euros including the wine. Really excellent.'

Tanya shook her head in amazement. Was Lea really suggesting we leave, after all we'd been through to get here? 'But you said the birth could be complicated.' The sound of Tanya's voice was familiarly fragile. It was the tone she used when building towards one of our rare arguments.

'Yes, but you still have plenty of time. Count the minutes between the contractions and if you get to a regular four, come back as soon as possible.'

Over the preceding eight months I'd imagined plenty of questions that I might have to ask during the birth. My research had been meticulous, with lists of vocabulary learnt and relearnt: waters breaking, contractions, discharge, blood pressure, heart rate, epidural and umbilical cord – there was scarcely a situation I hadn't envisaged. However, never once, with all my first-time-father leave-no-stone-unturned gusto, had it occurred to me that the first serious medical problem to be overcome would be lunch.

'Is there anything she can't eat?' I asked in a concerned husbandly way, giving Tanya time to collect herself.

'She may not feel like much, but it's important to build up strength. Something light, perhaps a goat's cheese salad with a little toast, or they do an excellent *courgette farcie,*' confided Lea, looking sheepishly at the clock and clearly still angry at herself for forgetting such a basic need. Reluctantly, Tanya and I were ushered into the street.

On our return, after what I had to admit was an excellent lunch, we were led through a set of swing doors into the birthing area. I was instructed to put on the plastic shoe coverings and Tanya a hospital gown. Each of the four birthing suites had been named after local Provençal flowers and herbs – Lavande, Thym, Romarin and Mimosa – nice calming names which unfortunately did little to rein in my gathering anxiety. Historically births in my family were far from simple. One of my sisters-in-law nearly gave birth in the corridor in St George's, Tooting, due to a lack of available rooms; the other sister-in-law staggered over her front doorstep to give birth, having being wrongly sent home from Sevenoaks Hospital. The omens were not good.

'*Ça va?*' Lea asked, directing us through the door of Lavande, a spacious light room painted in a gentle purple.

'*Oui, ça va,*' winced Tanya, easing herself up onto the birthing chair.

Lea nodded and then moved on to more important matters.

'What did you have?'

Both of us looked quizzically back at her.

'For lunch,' chastised Lea.

'A little salad,' replied a bemused Tanya.

'Steak tartare, and a *pichet* of Côtes du Rhône,' I added.

'*Oh là là, c'est bon ça.*' Lea was momentarily carried away to her favourite little cafe, the upturned egg on top of the raw steak, and side helpings of finely chopped onions, capers and herbs. The waiters in their burgundy aprons, the white tablecloths and the rich blackberry smell of the house red. At any other time it was a restaurant worth daydreaming about.

I coughed politely to refocus everyone's attention.

Putting a hand across Tanya's stomach, Lea felt the strength of the next contraction. 'Good, not long now. Remember the various birthing positions, and if the pain becomes too much I'll call for the anaesthetist.'

Unfortunately there was little time to dwell on our discovery. Lea wired Tanya up to a machine that would measure the strength of her contractions and I was busy text messaging our parents when a pain shot across my stomach.

My muscles ripped taut, and then relaxed just like a contraction. I bent over and instinctively took the slow breaths I had learnt in the prenatal classes.

'Aaagh.' The pain came again, this time more severe. I collapsed to the floor, knees hunched into my chest. After twenty seconds I was able to sit up. Sweat poured from my brow and I was shaking.

Lea pressed a glass of water into my hands and I took small sips, fighting the next wave which I felt approaching. What was happening to me? I'd heard of animals having phantom pregnancies, could I be in sympathy labour, sharing the whole experience of childbirth with my wife?

'It's all my fault.' Lea held a wet cloth to my head.

'Truffles again,' I gasped, trying to maintain my sense of humour.

'No – food poisoning from the steak tartare.'

If there is one thing I have learnt about the French health service, they never do things by halves. All the taxpayers' money has to be spent somehow and the moment a possible illness is identified endless tests and medicines are prescribed. The patient is happy, the doctors are happy, and it's only the taxpayer who has cause to be upset. Lea picked up the phone and spoke to a doctor in another department and from that moment I was doomed. A bed on wheels arrived and I flashed through the hospital doubled up in pain, dizzy from staring at the strobe lighting on the ceiling.

'Tanya… my baby,' I muttered deliriously as a drip was inserted, a painkilling suppository rammed up my bottom and various needles and thermometers poked into me.

'One of the worst cases I've seen,' mumbled a doctor to a nurse.

'Should be all right in a day or so.'

From then on I drifted in and out of consciousness, vaguely aware of the incontinent farting patient who shared the room with me. In contrast to the maternity unit the room was scruffy and poorly kept. Paint flaked from the walls, the wooden window was warped and blasts of icy air periodically chilled my face. In rare lucid moments I remembered the hospital's wider reputation – 'It's good for births and deaths, but not much else.' People were admitted with minor problems and often developed serious complications. I had no idea where I was in the hospital, but it felt subterranean and claustrophobic. From the maternity unit there was a lovely view of the Luberon – a beautiful first sight for a newborn – but for me there was nothing but blank walls. The cycle of pain and painkillers was never-ending and time ceased to mean much. My condition worsened, the back of my throat was parched like a 5 a.m. hangover and the drip in my arm made it painful to move. The lights were turned off. Hospital orderlies paced the corridors doing their final rounds and my room-mate continued to fart.

A bright artificial light stabbed my retinas. Rubbing my eyes I displaced the catheter and winced in pain. I felt some dribble running down my neck and a blunt object poked in my ribs. My nose was tickled by a wisp of hair and warm breath fluttered across my cheek. Opening my eyes I saw my daughter Elodie for the first time. She had her mum's pretty button nose, bright blue eyes and a wail that had pierced even my drug-induced sleep. The feeling of happiness was quite overwhelming and a stream of my tears flowed onto the sheets. Since the truffle market, life had taken on a fearsome velocity with events tumbling over each other as if driven by some uncontrollable power.

'Welcome to the world, little one.' I took her tiny hand in mine. 'I've just one piece of advice: never eat steak tartare.'

Tanya laughed. She looked pale and the skin on her face was tighter than normal, as if it had been stretched, but there was no mistaking the delight in her eyes. She picked Elodie up and held her close to her chest, sighing with contentment.

'Quite a two days,' she said.

'Has it really been that long?'

Tanya nodded and a nurse gently ushered her from the room. The doctor had prescribed plenty of sleep for the three of us.

Chapter 3

The hospital released us late in the afternoon and the shadows were already lengthening as our car crunched up the olive-tree-lined drive. A dog howled from somewhere in the pine-clad hill and a shutter swung loose, clapping time against the stone walls of the farmhouse. The basin in the courtyard had completely frozen over and jagged icicles collected on the underside of the Roman fountain. The North Star was visible in the half-light and within moments all the other constellations unveiled themselves. The idyll was tempered by a line of newly sprayed car parts hanging from a washing line. Our landlord, who occupied the front of the farmhouse, had been busy at his retouching business.

Wrapped snugly in a blanket, Elodie slept. A hat was pulled down low over her eyes and apart from the occasional reassuring sigh she barely moved. According to Tanya the labour had been much easier than expected. After I'd been wheeled away she'd asked for an epidural and from then on the anaesthetist was able to carefully control her pain. In my absence the two of them sat discussing their love of France. He was on a temporary assignment in the south and owned a bed and breakfast near Dijon. Business cards were exchanged and promises to visit made; it was all so civilised that for a while Tanya forgot that she was having a baby.

She remembered a long conversation about the excellent patisseries of Burgundy, a minor disagreement over the overpricing of Gevrey-Chambertin and a shared joke about English tourists who would insist on putting milk in Earl Grey tea. Only the last twenty minutes of the six-hour labour were at all traumatic, with Elodie arriving in a breach position and two doctors being called to turn her, one of whom insisted on starting up a conversation about *Star Trek*, a subject far from dear to Tanya's heart.

Elodie safely delivered, Tanya had remained in hospital for three nights. During the day she learnt how to take care of a newborn with lessons on the correct washing and feeding routine. In-between she rested and enjoyed massages and if Elodie woke in the middle of the night, one of the nurses was on hand, thereby making sure Tanya caught up on her sleep. It was altogether one of the most civilised birthing experiences imaginable and, we both agreed, a tribute to the French health service.

Meanwhile, I'd endured an identical length of stay, in a draughty, dank room with a succession of unsavoury room-mates. Gradually my stomach returned to normal and the midwives judged I was strong enough to look after wife and child.

It was therefore with great relief that I pushed open the door to our house to be greeted by the stale musty smell of absence. We'd left the underfloor heating on, and inside it felt like the height of summer. Two half-full mugs of coffee waited on the sideboard, a magazine lay open on the table and the cushions on the sofa were a disordered mess. In the corner of the room the Christmas tree had rained brittle brown needles onto the presents below and on my desk there was a pile of invoices I'd promised to settle.

The unexpected heat woke Elodie and she regarded us with wide unblinking blue eyes. Setting her down, Tanya showed me the ritual she'd learnt in the hospital. First a sterile fluid to cleanse the eyes and nose, then an antiseptic wipe for the remains of the umbilical cord, a change of nappy and into new clothes. What surprised me was the speed with which I'd bonded with my new daughter. The elements of parenthood which had always terrified me – the screaming and the nappies – seemed incidental, an irrelevance. I fished a bottle of wine from the rack, uncorked it and poured two glasses.

'Cheers to Elodie,' we chorused.

Tanya took a small sip. 'Do you realise what day it is?'

I shook my head.

'Christmas Eve, and we don't have a scrap of food in the house.'

All across the valley French families would be sitting down to the largest feast of the year: platters of *fruits de mer*, the obligatory foie gras, a roasted capon (a large castrated rooster) with truffle gravy, salad, cheese, and then – wait for it – not one, not two, but thirteen desserts, representing Christ and his disciples. For once the wine would not be the local BIB (bag in box) but a fine red from one of the region's best vineyards. Then those that could still walk would drag themselves off to the village church for Mass, before returning home and collapsing into bed and, judging from the empty January streets, hibernating for a month.

Instead, Tanya and I made do with some bread from the freezer and some mouldy cheese. Afterwards I was overcome by a sudden sense of guilt. Elodie's room lay empty. I'd cleared it out in preparation for decorating in January. The walls were a sterile white, the floor bare and the place musty and unsuitable for a baby. Leaving Tanya asleep on the sofa, I mopped the floor, retrieved children's posters and paintings we'd picked up in local attic sales and arranged them as best I could on the walls. Suspending a mobile from the ceiling took an annoying half an hour as all the string became entangled, but I worked with a blinkered determination.

It was either the electric screwdriver or my wails of despair that finally woke Tanya. She peered round the door frame to find me on the floor, amid the infernal combination of nails, screws and an incomprehensible instructional booklet printed on cheap white paper. I had reached diagram 13A of 15 and discovered one misplaced screw at step 2B. I was exhausted and there was no way Elodie's cot was fitting together unless I dismantled everything and started again.

Tanya came over and ruffled my hair. 'It's very sweet,' she said, kissing my forehead, 'but she's sleeping in the Moses basket.'

Late on Christmas morning a blue Citroën 2CV came dipping down the track towards our house.

'It's Madame Grimaud,' Tanya said excitedly, smiling.

Madame Delphine Grimaud was our fairy godmother. Born in Paris, she made a career in television before retiring to the region and buying a vineyard. Eccentric but adorable, she'd somehow managed to create one of the region's best wines – a boutique 100 per cent Cabernet.

When we'd first moved to the area we'd been summoned to her château. A perfumed envelope with a pink satin tie had contained a handwritten invitation – she'd heard of the English couple selling rosé in the French markets and wanted to meet us. For some reason she took to us and the presents never stopped flowing after that – care packages of olive oil picked and bottled on her estate, or lavender essence to ward off the scorpions. Scarcely a week went by when there wasn't a little something on our doorstep.

'My darlings, how are you?' A long Armani-jean-clad leg swung out of the car. 'I heard all about it – terrible, simply terrible. How did you survive all that ghastly hospital food?' Next out of the car was a lit Gauloise, then another leg, until finally Madame's face emerged, wrinkle free and ageless thanks to the attention of

Paris's best plastic surgeon. Trailing as much ermine as a monarch on state business, she swept towards us, extending a gloved hand. Poking out from the heavy folds of her fur coat were the wet inquisitive nostrils of her tiny white pet dog, Fifi, a bichon frise. Brown-eyed, with delicate features and exquisitely coiffed, Fifi was the canine mirror of his mistress. To strangers he was a snarling ball of fanged anger, but with us these days he was docile and friendly, eagerly licking my outstretched hand.

'Now, where is the little *crevette*?' Delphine said, employing the familiar French name for a baby.

'Happy Christmas, Delphine,' said Tanya, warmly embracing our friend. 'Come on in for a drink.'

'*Bah non*, I've come to whisk you away to the village, for the annual drink – *c'est le vin d'honneur. Mais* first – the presents.'

Opening the boot of the 2CV Delphine clasped a huge carrier bag, branded with the name of the most expensive baby shop in Aix. Inside there were little bonnets, Babygros, dresses and trousers.

'I grabbed a little of everything. One must always look one's best, even if one is only a few days old.' In a single movement she stubbed out her cigarette and whirled Elodie into the air. '*Eh ma crevette, comme tu es jolie.*'

As usual it was proving hard to get a word in, with Madame sweeping us along with her *joie de vivre*. Following the baby clothes from the boot of her car was a feast to dwarf even the one we'd planned. Home-made foie gras – although we were never sure whether it was Madame or one of her legion of servants who was responsible – a slow-cooked daube, half a salmon baked with fennel, a Hungarian goulash and a tarte Tatin for eight.

'With a new baby you are not going to have much time,' offered Madame by way of explanation. 'The daube is from Olivia, the salmon from Pierre; we've all pulled together. Oh, and the tarte Tatin from the *traiteur* – I just couldn't resist.'

Together with Tanya she arranged the food neatly in our fridge and before long it was replete, a proper Christmas larder. I have to admit I was pathetically grateful; our bland desolate lunch had metamorphosed into a gourmet experience, and the prolonged hug I bestowed on Delphine made the old pro blush.

It may not be comfortable (in fact it's anything but), it may not be environmentally friendly (and judging from the cloud of diesel that erupted from the exhaust, it wasn't), but undoubtedly quite the best way to arrive for a Christmas drink in a rural French village is by 2CV.

The narrow country lanes are free from bullying 4x4s, and there's just the cinematographic stream of the countryside passing slowly through the rattling windows, a glimpse of a church spire here, an isolated old farmhouse there, an olive grove, and the white giant of Mont Ventoux in the background.

The engine prattles along, with each gear change inducing a geriatric chassis-shaking spasm and each hill a hacking wheeze reminiscent of a forty-a-day smoker. All this grease and grime, the low-slung brittle floor, the tin thin doors, somehow makes you part of the journey. Distance is still something to be conquered, and safe arrival to be celebrated.

Unless, of course, you happen to have a four-day-old baby, in which case I warn you that such a journey may induce mild hysteria.

Shaken and stirred we arrived in the Provençal village we'd come to cherish. The bedraggled hairdresser's which doubled as a *coiffure chien*, the *boulangerie* with its erratic opening hours and the rickety old Bar du Centre, which stirred from its slumber in the summer and doubled as a restaurant. Apart from these three gloriously decayed businesses there was little to go to the village for – perhaps a walk to enjoy the shade of the tight cobbled streets and the mellifluous play of the fountains, or a stolen hour in the shade of the plane trees taking on members of the *club de boules*.

There was a reassuring sense of timelessness to the village; the world could whirl ever onwards, but here a blackberry would always be something picked in the hedgerows.

The crowd at the bar erupted with applause as we arrived. A champagne cork popped, flying in a celebratory arc over Elodie's makeshift carrycot, and a fountain of fizz flowed into mismatched glasses. Agricultural labourer and vigneron, cleaning lady and homeowner; all stood together saluting the new arrival.

'Santé!'

The women quickly surrounded Elodie, each in turn asking to hold the little *crevette*. It wasn't a flattering name but even I had to admit she was just like a little prawn, all pink and curled up.

'How much does she weigh?' asked Madame Parmentier, the wife of the *boulanger* and the source of all gossip in the village. 'How long was the labour?'

'Two and half kilos, and it took six hours.'

'You look back in shape already,' added Vivienne, the owner of the bar, who was overdressed as usual, notorious for taking her sartorial cues from Cannes rather than rural Provence. She rested a curious hand on Tanya's belly. 'I know an excellent place for *rééducation*.'

'*Rééducation?*' queried Tanya.

The women glanced at me and led Tanya away to a corner of the bar.

Ange, a local builder, slapped me on the back with a disproportionate amount of force. It was the sort of blow appropriate for ramming a stone plinth into place, but no way to greet a human. My bones rattled along with the village bells, which were just striking midday.

'Heard you had a bit of a problem with the steak tartare,' he said, handing me a large pastis to replace the empty champagne glass. 'My advice to you – have another one as soon as possible.

You have to kill the enzyme that caused the problem; leave it too long and you'll never be able to eat the dish again.' Despite the somewhat dubious reasoning Ange looked genuinely distressed – as if my bout of food poisoning was somehow more significant than Elodie's birth.

'It was terrible,' I confessed, playing along and enjoying the attention. 'Still, you're right, best to give it another go. A life without steak tartare…' I left the sentence hanging, enjoying the Gallic shrug of agreement.

'Best one I ever had was in Paris,' confided Ange. 'Rich client wanted to discuss an extension. The meat was diced at the table, you could choose more or less of each herb, an extra twist of the pepper grinder, an additional squirt of Tabasco – you get the idea. *Magnifique!*'

The Christmas drink in the Bar du Centre was one of my favourite events of the year. There were plenty of other occasions when residents got together to celebrate their communal life – Bastille Day, the end of season *fête*, the women's association's annual pesto soup – but typically they were more formal, with temporary tables positioned across the village square and seating plans posted outside the *mairie* for people to sign their names on. The same groups always stuck together, meaning the opportunities to make new friends were fairly limited.

However, the Christmas drink was an altogether different occasion. Our chauffeur Delphine, perhaps the richest and most well-known resident of the valley, was sitting at the bar, regaling anyone who cared to listen with stories of her TV-presenting days – her favourite being the moment the president tried to proposition her.

'His hand was halfway up my skirt and we were live.' She smiled and patted Fifi on the head. 'No man has ever looked so happy discussing the fiscal deficit.'

As always, the mayor had put some money behind the bar, and the rest Vivienne the owner donated as a thank you to her clientele. There were even nibbles; a bowl of garlic cloves marinated in oil to take away the edge, some spiced chickpeas dusted with parsley and, rather incongruously, a huge bowl of popcorn. There is nothing like free food and drink, and the bar bubbled with different conversations.

'I'm telling you, she's twenty years younger.'

'Bah non!'

'Bah oui!'

'I've never seen him so sprightly, even hunting again.'

The theme switched. 'Twenty boar already this year. They've even been sighted at the basin.'

'Not been there for a decade.'

'Bah oui.'

'It's the drought.'

One of the pleasures of being a foreigner was that nobody particularly expected me to contribute. I could sit, sip on my drink, occasionally nod my head and take everything in; the smoke-stained mirror, the flaking paint on the chairs, the smell of once-a-year Christmas aftershave, and the lingering odours of the hunting dogs.

Three years ago when I'd first walked into the place, heads had swivelled, conversations stopped and I'd felt about as welcome as a vampire at a convention of virgins. These days a drink was poured without me even asking. Somehow I'd graduated to the status of semi-local.

Tourists drank beer out of huge litre mugs, second homeowners out of pretty 25-cl branded glasses and regulars out of wine glasses or whatever else was to hand. There was a set price for the first two drinks; for the third you just handed over whatever you thought appropriate. Sitting at the bar for an hour or so with a copy of *La Provence* was one of my pleasures in life. I hardly read an article; instead I just drank in the atmosphere, eavesdropping on slices of local gossip and revelling in the odd piece of theatre, such as the day two live chickens got loose and emptied the place.

The only downside to the bar was Serge, an unpleasant man who usually occupied a seat in the corner. Ignoring the ban, he smoked the occasional cigarette, letting the stubs smoulder between his fingers until his flesh began to burn. Always unshaven and wearing the same pair of dirty jeans and a jacket, he stared at the rest of the patrons with eyes that never seemed to focus. Even when I looked directly at him he refused to avert his gaze. I'd once enquired what was wrong with him and been told that a decade ago foreigners had bought his parent's house. The sale took place before the stunning growth in prices and Serge had been embittered ever since. Thankfully, he was absent on Christmas Day.

Ange had by now moved on to the delicate subject of the best egg to bind the steak tartare with – Bresse chicken, goose or quail.

'The flavour of the quail is definitely more subtle. The problem is you need so many of them. Goose, on the other hand, has something of the richness of quail, but chicken is definitely the poorest.'

I was halfway through my second pastis and Ange and I had switched to the dilemma of whether to use shallot or onion in the mix, when Tanya signalled that it was time to get Elodie home.

Delphine took a long final draw of her drink. 'Come on, my young ones,' she said, putting a protective arm around both our shoulders and leading us into the crisp air.

The journey home was an uncomfortable one for me, and not just because of the suspension.

'*Il faut le faire,*' Delphine said with surprising urgency, reviving the exclusively female conversation from the bar. 'You know men – eyes for anything in a skirt, and those muscles aren't going to come back magically.'

I blushed.

'Ignore those women in the bar, you should see my man in Paris, go shopping at the same time. We'll make it a double date – I'll have a refresher session and we'll lunch at Bofinger, it's just round the corner.' Delphine roared with laughter and nearly crashed into a plane tree, swerving across the road and temporarily losing the rear end of the car.

'Is *rééducation* what I think it is?' I asked as we pulled to a stop on our drive.

'Absolutely, and a hundred per cent funded by the French state. We are a nation of great lovers and we have a reputation to uphold,' said Delphine, enjoying my discomfort as she said goodbye.

Gathering Elodie in our arms, we retreated inside for our gourmet lunch, happy in the knowledge that the only education to be discussed for the rest of the day was our daughter's.

Chapter 4

January is a tough month in Provence. It's bitterly cold, windy, overcast, damp and generally unpleasant. Stone-fringed basins freeze and snow blocks the mist-cloaked mountains. The weather saps the spirits and the lifeless landscape grinds on the mind. Skeletal rows of vines dominate a desolate panorama. Fingers of discarded growth lie limp on the muddy ground and the wire trails, usually hidden by the verdant summer foliage, call to mind a battlefield rather than a vineyard. In almond orchards, discarded husks hang from leafless branches. Even the silvery leaves of olive trees are blighted by withered reminders of the long-forgotten harvest.

Dogs kicked out into the cold bark occasionally but their cries dissolve in the pervading stillness. Carrion hawks sit in eager, wind-blasted vigil but only the wild boar, driven by hunger from the hills, move below. Cicadas hide deep underground, the combined heartbeat of millions causing barely a tremor.

In the villages the majority of businesses are boarded up with vague promises of a return pinned to flaking shutters. Anyone with sense disappears to the Alps. The remainder huddle next to wood-burning stoves, unplug the telephone, eat preserved food and do their best to deny the existence of the outside world. It's a miserly, frugal, grudging existence that quickly makes the feasting of Christmas appear like a dream. People who once spent €900 a kilo on a truffle will now hesitate at the indulgence of fresh vegetables. Occasional tourists, cameras slung redundantly over their shoulders, pace the streets, scanning guidebooks in frustration as they search for whatever induced them to book their holiday at this time of year.

As new parents we were immune to the January blues that inevitably beset everyone around us. The local paper, *La Provence*, proclaimed doom and gloom: flooding in Cavaillon, rioting in the slums of Avignon and the inexorable rise of the cost of living. A survey found that the Provençaux were the most depressed people in France. Nobody disputed it. Yet our bonhomie endured.

When a simple standard format letter arrived from the *mairie* of Pertuis congratulating us on the birth of our daughter, we quickly had it framed.

'Where else in the world would the mayor take the time to write?'

'Where indeed,' I agreed.

We both stood back and admired the embossed letter, hanging from the newly painted pale pink wall of our daughter's bedroom. To us, drunk on the joy of our firstborn, it represented incontrovertible proof of the superiority of French society. The rest of Europe was going down the drain, consumed by capitalism, but here in France, the mayor still cherished every birth. Visits to the paediatrician induced similar gushing praise. Appointments were readily available, there was no waiting and each week the doctor spent forty minutes with Elodie, charting her minute progress and prescribing a seemingly endless list of preventive medicines which the state was all too happy to subsidise.

'What a marvellous country, what a marvellous way of life,' we agreed.

Even the avalanche of new year tax bills, the receipts from which helped pay for such administrative niceties as the mayor's letter and the inexhaustible supply of medicines, failed to shake me from my good mood. Two weeks with my mother-in-law passed without incident. A local vigneron offered to bottle a jeroboam of wine to celebrate Elodie's birth. An artist cast her feet in clay and we hung the result in the bathroom. Cards and presents arrived on a daily basis and well-wishers deposited more casseroles and confits, assuring us that we were too busy to cook. Momentarily this was true. My power drill was on permanent charge as I assembled the cot, rebuilt the mobile, took down a bed and put together a replacement futon. Nightly sleeps were almost always interrupted and catnaps during the day became a necessity.

When the squeaking new wheels of Elodie's buggy bumped along the cobbled streets of the village, heavy wooden doors swung open letting plumes of precious heat escape into the icy street. The excuse for such inexplicable largesse was not just a baby but a blue-eyed baby. Women would knock on neighbours' doors, imploring their *voisins* to come outside with a sense of pious urgency more usually reserved for a minor religious miracle.

'*Regardez les yeux.*'

'*Ils sont magnifiques.*'

'*Oh là là, ils sont beaux.*'

Gradually we came to appreciate that any eye colour other than nut brown was as rare as a comet here. Even field-hardened labourers would press their hands to their hearts and swoon at such alien blueness. As a consequence each trip out ended like a procession, with a line of admirers waiting for their turn to peel back Elodie's blankets.

A more disturbing habit was an obsession with Tanya's body. Hands were pressed to her tummy to check the speed with which it was returning to normal. A hello kiss became an intimate experience as arms were wrapped around her waist searching for the remaining signs of her pregnancy – was she carrying weight on her bottom, or water on her thighs?

This all too intrusive interest perplexed me until I overheard a conversation standing in the *boulangerie* queue.

'Attention, c'est chaud!' The baguettes were still fresh from the oven and the homely aroma of soft dough pervaded the small shop. Condensation traced its way down the windows and beads of my breath coalesced on the furry inside of my jacket. It was the most popular time of the morning and at least ten people were pressed into the room. Turning around was difficult so instead the customers, most of them wearing fur coats, shuffled forwards with their arms clamped to their sides, rather like a queue of penguins preparing to launch into the sea.

The different breads waited in a sentinel line. The fridges to the right held a collection of sumptuous tarts: raspberry, strawberry and fig, together with the speciality of the house – layered caramel on a crunchy biscuit base. Customers with less voracious appetites needed to turn left where there were rows of individual pastries, fruit tarts and chocolate concoctions. This early in the morning every minute spent in the shop was a temptation; sugar levels were low and the oven was constantly churning out new delights.

'Sunflower bread and a multi-cereal.' The features of the next customer were shrouded by the hood of her coat.

'Sliced?' asked Madame Parmentier, the baker's wife.

'No thanks. It's such a cold rain.' The conversation opener was always the weather.

The *boulangerie* was widely recognised as the centre of all gossip. Its effectiveness was multiplied by the French willingness to travel to buy different types of bread. The common consensus was that it was impossible for any baker to perfect all elements of his art. Thus, some bakeries were renowned for their speciality breads, others for their croissants, and some for their skill with the humble baguette. People therefore frequented not one but all the local *boulangeries*, depending on their requirements for that day, spreading news as they went.

The queue stalled as Madame Parmentier revealed the details of a botched perm and my mind ranged over the options for breakfast: buttery croissant, rich enough to work with a strong black coffee; *pain au chocolat*, one of the finest in the region, laced with two thick seams and presumably, like the baguette, still warm; *croissant aux amandes*, simply sublime but too indulgent for a weekday; and finally my daily temptation, the *feuilleté saucisse*, the closest the French got to a cooked English breakfast. A tray of pizza emerged from the oven, filling the shop with the smell of thyme and overripe tomatoes. I couldn't... a pizza for breakfast?

'Just a month and her tummy is already tight.' The two women in front of me had found the space to wait side by side. From the quality of the fur coat and the tiny wet canine nose poking inquisitively from its folds, one of them could only be Delphine. I hesitated before saying hello, waiting for her to buy her bread.

'I was always too terrified to have babies; the thought of what it might do to these.' Delphine somehow delved into her coat and hoisted her no doubt surgically enhanced cleavage skywards, revealing a lacy bra in the process. 'Maybe I was wrong, I mean, her décolletage is still firm, lucky girl.'

Filling in the gaps, I suspected the décolletage they were discussing was Tanya's. Nice as it was to have one's wife's breasts complimented in public, I didn't think Tanya would be happy. Yet it seemed too late to intervene. The conversation had achieved a critical momentum and I was powerless to stop it. Instead I shrank into my coat and pretended not to listen.

'Legs are in good shape.'

I thought of Tanya, busy at home sterilising bottles for expressed milk, and folding baby clothes. The immediate manic aftermath of the birth had passed – the hapless clothes-wrecking first nappy changes and baby-dropping baths, as the physical impossibility of holding child and soap at the same time became apparent – and life had settled down into an enjoyable semi-peaceful rhythm. And yet inexplicably we were the news on the bakery semaphore.

To the French female mind Tanya's struggle to regain her pre-pregnancy shape was, I realised, a race against time. Men were feckless wandering souls to whom monogamy was anathema. From politicians to pool boys we were all the same and so when Delphine looked at me, rather than seeing a doting father she must have seen a philanderer. From her perspective, the only way Tanya could ensnare me into a life of loving servitude was a tight butt and flat stomach.

'Look at what happened to Claudine,' continued Delphine. 'Husband insisted on night harvesting, said it was to stop fermentation in the field, but every morning he came home as clean as a whistle, and the resulting wine tasted worse than ever.'

'How dare he?'

'If that was me, I'd hire a hitman.'

The *rééducation* that Delphine had so strongly advocated was, I now understood, core to the French woman's sexual psyche. The sooner after giving birth she could get her man back into bed the less likely he was to start 'night harvesting'. Temptation was all around. The swinging sixties had never left our corner of remote Provence. At a local road-restaurant-cum-nightclub, two villages away, couples checked in and the ladies picked a set of car keys at random as they left, and only this summer, according to gossip, a hotelier had tried to persuade a couple in the honeymoon suite to order some extra entertainment.

We were now near enough the front of the queue for Madame Parmentier to spot me. Quickly picking up the topic of the ongoing conversation, she raised her eyebrows at Delphine in warning.

'Charming couple, though, sure they will be fine.' Delphine turned and greeted me with the warmest of grins. Not a moment's surprise registered on the old pro's face.

'*Bonjour, ça va?*'

'*Ça va, merci.*'

'*Et Tanya, et Elodie?*'

'*Tout va bien.*'

We exchanged farewell kisses and I shuffled forwards, trying to comprehend the consequences of such a heightened sense of insecurity. Society was promiscuous. Like loving food and wine, having affairs had become an intrinsic part of being French. However, far from living in a permanent state of euphoric ardour, French women, theoretically the world's greatest lovers, appeared to exist in a state of terror, ever fearful that they would lose their man. This daily agitation seemed to explain another until now unsolved enigma of life in France – the abundance of lingerie shops.

There was scarcely a street in a town where the plastic nipples of a mannequin didn't protrude through a lacy embrace. Until this moment I'd assumed that Provençal men had insatiable appetites and that after a hard morning picking pumpkins or pruning vines, they rushed to spend their hard-earned wages on the very latest edible thong, crashing through the door to their home in a fit of raging passion, wolfing down a daube and spending the remaining hour of their lunch licking an *île flottante* from their wife's heaving breasts.

Instead, I now appreciated lingerie was a defensive female purchase. It might never be worn, but it was there in a drawer, ready and waiting, a threat and a temptation. And the beauty of it all for the lingerie shop owners was that a woman could never have enough. These shops fed an insatiable arms race between wives and mistresses, each faction desperate for the reassurance of another pair of suspenders, just in case they were ever needed.

Madame Parmentier slipped the pizza into the bag and the warm topping immediately clung to the paper.

'*Merci beaucoup, bonne journée.*'

We parted company. For once Madame Parmentier sheepishly averted her eyes.

Back at home Tanya was busy trying to reassemble a breast pump and Elodie was lying on her back in her cot, wailing with hunger. My mind was still turning over the eavesdropped conversation as I placed breakfast on the table. The photos at Pertuis hospital with the mums in their finest underwear now also made sense. They were a timely reminder to the husband of what he'd been missing and a warning not to stray. Imagine the hassle, though; you've just given birth, you're tired and exhausted, all you want to do is sleep and yet instead you commission a photographer and put on your finest bra, posing artfully to reveal a heavy post-pregnancy cleavage. Such dedication took a special kind of distrust of one's husband.

'It must be exhausting being a French woman,' I said without thinking.

Tanya's raised eyebrow said it all – gave birth three weeks ago, up every night breastfeeding, the pump which you were supposed to fix doesn't work, I'm still doing all the washing and the cooking and you want to discuss the plight of French women.

Chapter 5

By the beginning of February I was back at work selling wine. In the corner of my *cave* (wine cellar) I came across a box of rosé from a'Beckett's vineyard in Wiltshire. I'd ordered some out of curiosity following a lunch the previous summer with the wine expert and *Decanter* columnist Steven Spurrier, and now this English pink gave me an idea.

In 1976 Steven had organised a blind tasting of the best French wines against the best American wines. The premier tasters in the world had lined up, sniffing, swilling, tasting and pontificating over the lingering finish of Cabernet on the tongue. Then, in a result that shocked oenophiles everywhere, the tasters scored the American wines higher than the most famous French clarets. The sporting equivalent of this result would be the Faroe Islands beating Brazil 5–0 at football, in Rio de Janeiro with a Brazilian referee, and with the Faroe goalkeeper having been sent off in the first minute. According to the French mindset, the second coming of Christ was more probable than their best wines being judged inferior to foreign muck. And yet it happened.

The tasting became known as the Judgement of Paris and at the time caused outrage in the wine industry. Steven was temporarily ostracised by major vineyards, who criticised the methodology employed, and such was the legacy of the event that there are now two Hollywood films in production on the subject.

Much of the rest of the lunch with Steven had been spent discussing the nascent English wine industry. Steven's new project was the creation of a vineyard in Dorset. He'd had experts over from Champagne and Chablis to examine the soil and they'd pronounced his prospects to be good. Global warming had led to longer hotter summers and the UK climate was now similar to that of northern France a decade ago. The same band of chalky soil that gave rise to the steely whites of Chablis and lent the finesse to champagnes resurfaced in the UK as the North, South and Dorset Downs. Technically there were no obstacles to the UK beginning to produce fizz, whites and even reds of the highest quality and Steven was determined to be one of the new generation of growers.

These memories returned as I regarded the box of Wiltshire rosé. I needed an event to create a buzz and it would be fun to find out whether Steven was right about English wines. Why not organise a mini Judgement of Paris and see whether in a blind tasting the locals preferred English or French pink? At the very least the tasting would garner some much needed publicity for my business and gain me a few new customers.

As always, it was best to check any new idea with a local.

Born in the house we lived in, Manu, our landlord, was a typical Provençal peasant: dark hair, dark eyes, and arms like anvils. I'd watched him labour for hours unaided by machine, picking olives in the bitter December cold, or harvesting lavender in the heat of July. His body had the durability of an ox and he used his vast bulk to eke money from the land in whatever way possible. Deeply distrustful of strangers, he'd at first refused to allow us to rent the other half of his farmhouse. Our worlds were just too different. To him we were effete intellectuals selling a luxury product (bottled as opposed to pumped wine) to the region's second homeowners. Such people, in Manu's eyes, had the social status of leeches and he would love to have stuck a lighter up their Parisian derrières.

However, once the estate agent had suggested doubling the deposit, Manu's moral stance weakened and finally he relented. Now, after three years living next door to each other, we'd developed a mutual friendship, sharing occasional drinks of the moonshine liquor he produced and talking about politics. Manu was the archetypal French socialist: an ardent advocate of the poor, supporter of strikes, of working shorter hours, retiring early and higher taxes for the rich. In his eyes Tanya and I were the political enemy, capitalists whose belief in profit would bring the world to its knees. A hundred or so years ago he would probably happily have seen us guillotined; these days he had to be content with the occasional dramatic gesture of disgust and some more shared moonshine.

As well as being a reliable barometer of local opinion, Manu was also a vigneron. He'd reclaimed the field of old untended vines outside our kitchen window. The rows now stretched neatly towards the horizon. French winemakers have a saying, 'the wine speaks of the people', implying that the most important element in a wine is the love and care of the person who makes it. By dedicating himself to the land, the winemaker becomes at one with his terroir. I'd never fully understood the concept until I watched Manu work, monotonously, unyieldingly bending his back to the elements harvesting whatever the land offered. If I wanted to know whether the local producers would submit a representative wine to my blind tasting, Manu was the person to ask.

The sound of metal grinding against metal meant that our landlord was at home. Whether it was a hobby or a business I was never quite sure, but Manu spent days dismembering and then reconstructing old cars. They wheezed up the drive or arrived on the back of trailers and a line of vintage Renaults and Citroëns now awaited his attention. Some of the cars had been around for so long that they had become part of the garden. In the summer wild flowers grew out of the windows, in the winter just weeds. I'd persuaded Tanya to view them as art installations, the type of stuff the Tate Modern would pay thousands for – a retrospective on the role of the car in French society.

As I approached, Manu lifted his visor and extinguished the blowtorch. He did most of his mechanical work in an old barn which divided the two sides of the farmhouse. Various pieces of equipment hung from the beams – a yoke for a donkey, heavy iron chains and a plough. In one corner there was a rusty tractor and the barn as always smelt heavily of diesel. Nails, screws and other pieces of metal covered every surface. Rakes, hoes and a scythe fit for the Grim Reaper rested in a bundle against the wall. A severed finger or toe was only a misplaced hand or foot away.

'*Bonjour!*'

'*Bonjour.*'

'*Tout va bien? Est-ce qu'Elodie est toujours sage?*'

Having a baby in his house hadn't been part of Manu's thought process when he rented it out to us. Although the walls were thick and the division between the two sides of the *mas* well constructed, he was still paranoid about Elodie's crying. Hence the first question every time we met these days was, '*Est-ce qu'Elodie est toujours sage?*' – 'Is she still behaving and sleeping well?' Only once his mind had been put at rest could we continue.

'*Toujours sage,*' I reassured, catching a strong whiff of garlic, a foodstuff which Manu insisted was '*très bon pour la santé*'. The smell was sometimes so overpowering that I wondered whether, in private, he chewed on raw bulbs.

We moved outside into the bright sunlight. A small stream had sprung up outside our house. After years of drought this winter's rainfall had exceeded all records. Rocks in the hills wept and water played along forgotten riverbeds. Jumping over the stream, Manu opened the door to his chicken coop. Ten birds immediately huddled around his legs, clucking hungrily. As Manu tipped seed to the ground I explained my idea for a tasting. Ducking into the hen house he began collecting eggs; only the odd grunt reassured me that he was still listening.

'And so that's it – a blind tasting of an English rosé against a local French one. We'll hold it on market day for a bit of fun.'

Thousands of small white snails clung to the fence which enclosed the chickens. Manu casually plucked them and tossed them to the birds. He still hadn't said a word.

'What do you think?' I prodded.

Ten more snails met their end.

'You'll be wasting your time,' Manu finally confided. 'The people here know their own wines.'

'But you don't object.'

Manu shrugged his shoulders, indicating indifference or perhaps even a little hostility to the idea. After the chickens it was the turn of the hunting dogs. Manu kept three of them in a large cage. In the season he would depart before dawn, and I often saw him returning home in the misty half-light, gun cocked over his arm, dead game slung over his shoulder and dogs circling adoringly around his ankles. Such was his command of the animals that he could silence them with a glance.

'We'll enter Christophe's wine,' Manu grunted as he forked leftover meat into the dogs' bowls. 'It won a silver medal at the Orange Concours des Vins.' He might not have let it show but secretly I believed Manu was looking forward to the tasting, hence the sudden change of mind: rugby, football, tennis – beating the old enemy was always amusing and here was an opportunity for the Provençal vigneron to add to the glory of France.

At just before midday on the following Wednesday morning I stood in the village square. Underneath my jacket my woollen jumper had absorbed the water from the air and the knitted cloth was wet against my skin. I shivered with the cold. The plane trees that bestowed a dappled effect on the marketplace in summer had been pruned back, and now the stunted branches reached heavenwards in supplication, like the upturned fingers of a penitent. Puddles from the previous night's rain dotted the gravel and forgotten Christmas decorations creaked in the wind. The breeze shifted and the smell of burning damp leaves replaced wafts of strong tobacco. The morning was drawing to a close and the agreed hour for the tasting approaching.

On the table in front of me were the two competing wines, French and English, both shrouded in tissue paper. When poured, one had the colour of ripe cherries, the other vibrant pink coral, but neither showed that well against the grey sky. The two were notably different in taste. The a'Beckett's estate rosé from Devizes in Wiltshire was light and fruity and relatively low in alcohol at 10 per cent. Made from a mixture of Pinot Noir and Reichensteiner, its closest comparator in France was a Marsannay rosé, which many in Burgundy regarded as the country's finest. The Côtes du Ventoux by contrast, a Syrah and Grenache mix, was a much more robust wine, more aggressive on the palate and a better accompaniment to food. Choosing between the two should have been easy.

A group of local vignerons, including Manu, had gathered around my stall to watch. Their faces were red and stained with grime, their hands raw from a morning sawing last year's excess growth from the vines, but their mood was upbeat and expectant.

'I wonder who will vote for the English,' said one.

'Only people with colds,' Manu chirped up and the group dissolved into laughter.

The members of the *cave* cooperative had every reason to be confident. Typically a French child has his first glass of wine at the age of five. Perhaps a little Sauternes to go with some foie gras, a sip of a buttery white with some smoked cheese. From that moment on the child's taste buds are educated with more fervour than his brain. Can't add up? Never mind. Can't tell a corked wine? Go to bed and as a punishment memorise each of the 472 different appellations.

By the time they are young adults, the educated French will have typically sampled wine from each of the major producing regions, and they'll know in which shape of glass, at what temperature and with what food to serve it. For this reason, not one member of the *cave* cooperative committee had countenanced the possibility that the local wine might lose.

At random I'd asked a group of twenty shoppers at the market to participate in the tasting. One by one they began to sample the wines, sniffing, swirling and finally drinking.

'*C'est plus riche...*'

'*Plus sensuel...*'

'*Plus capital...*'

'*Très sincère.*'

French is a wonderful language with which to describe wine. Elaborate phrases rolled off the tongue, nobody contented themselves with simple flavours – instead, the wines were imbued with human characteristics, so the tasting almost felt more like meeting a friend. In this case an English friend. Amazingly, the first four tasters selected the Wiltshire wine.

Looking at the gathered vignerons, I realised I was in trouble. These men spent all year toiling across endless fields, pruning, training and finally picking from thousands of individual vines. The enormity of their task was daunting; row after row, with no help, just them and the elements, the wind, the cold, the rain and finally the beating summer heat. Their reward: producing a wine that the local people called their own. How terrible if the villagers actually preferred the English wine.

'That's another vote for the English, and another one,' I advised, trying to prepare them for the worst.

'Probably been gargling,' quipped a vigneron referring to the latest taster.

'Sea-salt spray up the nose,' Manu added.

'Anaesthetic throat lozenges,' said another, joining the sport. It seemed that they were going to list the whole contents of the pharmacy.

As the tasting continued the French wine enjoyed a minor resurgence, but even so the Wiltshire rosé stayed ahead and continued to attract votes. Why were people getting it so wrong? Well, the first and most obvious answer was that it was more suited to what people wanted to drink on a cold wet February morning. Perhaps being from England it coped better with the lack of sunshine, and the lower alcohol percentage made it more palatable. However, even wearing a blindfold, I would have expected the villagers to recognise their own wine and vote for it for patriotic reasons. That they hadn't been able to identify the Côtes du Ventoux was interesting.

Educating a palate is relatively simple; keeping a palate educated takes a lifetime of dedication. Think of what happens to a heavyweight boxer when he gives up his sport. His physique quickly becomes flabby and heavy. It's the same with wine tasters. Contrasting wines need to be tasted every day otherwise the skill quickly disappears. Sommeliers will often tour vineyards trying hundreds of different wines a day. Their taste buds are their living and the only way to keep them in top condition is to work them, exhaustively. Stop drinking and the carefully collected archive of thousands of different flavours becomes a confused indistinguishable mass. And that is what had happened to the French as a nation. Collectively they'd stopped drinking. Government health campaigns, when combined with a Frenchman's obsessive concern for his health, had led to a dramatic decline in consumption.

The sickly smell of petrol from the departing van of a trader drifted across the square and the village clock chimed the hour, signalling the end of the agreed time for the tasting.

'Come on, who's won?' Manu slapped me on the back. 'It's lunchtime.'

'Perhaps we'll let a few more people taste. The more the merrier,' I responded.

'Can't hurt.' Manu took a swig of the French wine.

The *coquillage* merchant was vigorously quartering lemons and sowing them like seeds among rows of yawning seashells. Unlike me he was busy with several customers – men with hardened constitutions happily sucking the innards from sea urchins. Their fridges were presumably full of veal's head pâté, pig trotters and tripe, and to them a dozen oysters before lunch was a stomach settler. Surely they could be tempted into a glass of wine?

'*Une dégustation de vin rosé d'Angleterre,*' I shouted again.

A shopper turned to face the *dégustation*, the head of a king prawn poised between his teeth.

'*Vin anglais – ça existe?*' He dropped the shell of the prawn in horror. Life was uncertain enough without the English starting to make rosé.

'It's down to global warming,' I explained. 'Same soil and climate as Chablis.'

Chasing an oyster on its way with a glass of sharp Picpoul from Sète, the shopper showed no interest in tasting England's finest. 'Soon they'll have cicadas,' he muttered, as he shuffled away, no doubt looking forward to a nice lunch of cow's testicles fried in garlic.

'*Allez goûter…*' Finally I managed to attract another taster – an unshaven workman in a luminous jacket. Bald head, jowly, jaundiced eyes, yellow complexion of an inveterate pastis drinker – just the wrong type of person.

Like a child offered medicine the man grimaced as he put the glass to his lips. How bad could English wine be?

'An excellent nose,' he declared with the formality of a sommelier. 'Soft and subtle to drink,' he continued, his demeanour emphasising that although he might wear the clothes of a workman, he was in fact a connoisseur. Did I have a real expert?

I poured the second wine. 'It's not well balanced. The first was much better, and definitely French.'

I nodded in relief. A few of the vignerons had already left, the call of their stomachs proving hard to resist, particularly since in their eyes the result was a foregone conclusion.

Apart from an old lady huddling under an umbrella struggling with the weight of a basket full of vegetables, the square was empty of potential tasters.

'*Venez goûter le vin,*' I cried one last time.

The old lady paused and looked up before pulling the umbrella low over her eyes. Putting her bags down, she readjusted her grip and then continued on her way.

It was over. I rechecked the score and called the vignerons over. The least I could do was keep the result as private as possible. Pouring everyone a glass I prepared to make the announcement. A cough stopped me.

'*Je veux bien goûter.*' Unable to turn directly around, the old lady had prescribed a large circle, ending up behind my tasting stand. I now recognised her as Miriam, the octogenarian head of the village *fête* committee. If there was a *soupe au pistou* to be made, or an aioli, then she would volunteer, and just that morning I'd had some of her excellent apricot jam with my morning baguette. As always her eyes were bright and alert.

Gratefully I poured two glasses of wine for her to taste.

'My husband was a vigneron,' she declared, raising my hopes.

With an expert swish she transformed the contents of the first glass into a vigorous pink whirlpool. As a heavy drizzle set in there was a sigh of contentment, and a scarcely audible murmur of appreciation. The process was repeated for the second rosé: a swish and a swirl, a plant of the nose, a sip and suck as she churned the wine through her teeth.

'And?' I asked anxiously, aware of the watching vignerons.

'*C'est difficile, mais*' – Miriam was obviously enjoying the attention – '*je préfère le deuxième vin.*'

'*Égalité,*' I declared. '*Vive l'entente cordiale.*' In gratitude I put corks in the remaining wine and slipped the bottles into her basket. The final result was eleven all.

The uproar was immediate. I was pressed backwards against my table, until I could retreat no further.

'Which wine did you taste first?'

There was no chance to answer.

'What temperature was the wine served at?'

'Did you check it wasn't corked?'

'Everything was done properly,' I reassured the vignerons. 'Tasting glasses, refrigerated for the same length of time...'

'Well, that proves it,' Manu interrupted, 'we were right in the first place – it's the flu, the whole village has got it.'

'Have you seen the queues at the doctor's?' Another took up the theme.

'Can't get an appointment for a week.'

'What do we pay taxes for?'

Gradually the crowd dispersed. Face had been saved. Just.

Chapter 6

March began with a shock of heat, blue skies and an impatient sun. The land blistered with ant hills, bees pollinated the first wild flowers, and a plague of black centipedes marched into every house. South-facing fields of almond trees blossomed first, dressing the land white, pink cherry followed, and on the rare windy days a stream of confetti drifted in the air. Rivers bubbled with energy, swathes of marshy grass erupted along their banks, and broken branches from the winter storms lodged in the riverbeds, creating peaceful pools.

Shutters in the village were thrown apart, welcoming fragrant air into houses. Dormant businesses slowly reopened, one day at a time, so as not to shock the systems of owners or customers. The chairs outside the cafe which had been stacked and chained together once more populated the pavement. Relief rippled through the streets. Everybody agreed it had been one of the toughest winters in memory. Rosé orders for my wine business started to arrive and pink wine once again winked from tables in the weekend sunshine.

A sign for the village *vide grenier* appeared by the roadside. These attic/car boot sales were a relatively new concept when we'd first arrived in Provence. Since then they'd been embraced by nearly every local village. Rather than carting unwanted stuff into cars and driving to a distant field, the Provençal way was to set up outside the front doors of their houses.

Whole villages were transformed into emporiums of Provençal tat and just occasionally a piece of valuable *brocante*. The locals loved the *vide greniers* for the opportunity to sit in the fresh spring air and exchange gossip with their neighbours. Kids swapped toys for a couple of euros and parents scoured the second-hand clothes rails. To the expat community a *vide grenier* was a chance to outwit the professional antique dealers who often charged extortionate prices for items as simple as a set of copper kitchen pans. Our flat was small and already furnished so we scarcely bought anything, but we always went, welcoming the opportunity to chat to people who'd vanished Elvis-like during the winter. Invites to drinks parties usually followed and a whirl of social activity began as people tried to see each other before the arrival of the hordes of tourists.

With the improved weather came a new found enthusiasm for work, even in the estate agencies. The euphemistic *'en visite'* signs came down, lunches were curtailed and cold calls to everyone on the books began. 'Thinking of buying, thinking of selling? Do it with me.'

The agent who called us was Eric Serep.

If *agents immobiliers* are judged by the value of houses they sell, then Eric belonged to the bottom division. His home doubled as his office and he pasted property details onto his living room window. Eric's clients were the locals whom he'd grown up with. In his distant teenage years he'd midnight drag-raced with most of the men and kissed most of the women. Nearly all these old *copines* had their houses permanently on the market. None of them particularly wanted to move; however, they'd heard stories of people who'd hit the jackpot with a foreign buyer. As a result prices were always inflated and there was absolutely no room for negotiation.

A year ago, in a brief, misguided foray into the Provençal housing market, Eric had treated us to a melange of falling down walls, cracked foundations, leaking roofs, ladders doubling as staircases and termite-infested beams. Owners had greeted us in an obsequious manner, pressing bottles of wine and olive oil into our hands, and almost bowing as we looked around. In all we saw ten houses with Eric. Occasionally there was a view, sometimes a swimming pool, and usually there was a large amount of scrubland which offered the potential for development. The price was always shocking: little short of six figures for a collection of stud walls and peeling plaster, most of it built without planning permission. Not a single one tempted us to go back and have a second look.

Yet the hopes of Eric's clients were not completely forlorn and some of the houses we'd seen did gradually come off the market. A single viewing by a misty-eyed summer tourist was often enough. With the lavender in bloom, the golden glow of sunset on a crumbling wall could look quite beautiful to a wealthy wife in need of a project. Thus, another paysan would hit the jackpot and the long property boom would continue.

Our tour with Eric had concluded with his promise to give us a call should anything more interesting come on the market. Nothing had, until now. Eric promised a must-see property with views across the whole valley, in walking distance of the village – he'd heard we'd had a baby and was doing us a favour showing us first. Once the summer came foreign buyers would be snapping off his hands. How could we resist?

The answer was: quite easily. However, curiosity overcame us and I booked the rendezvous. The appointed day was an estate agent's dream. Clear blue sky, warming but not hot sun, birds singing in the trees, terraces of cafes full, canvas roofs on 2CVs rolled back, and the first new leaves on the plane trees providing just a hint of shade. It was a day to fall in love with Provence, to sit and marvel like a painter at the folds of the distant hills. On such a day a house could easily steal the heart of the uninitiated.

'What's he going to show us now?' I giggled with Tanya as we followed Eric up a dirt track, 'A pigsty with development opportunities?'

The car ahead slowed as Eric negotiated a particularly vicious looking pothole. The track then took a sharp turn around some oak trees and we arrived on a high plateau above the village. In the distance I could see the spire of the church and the heavy bell of the clock tower suspended within a dome of ironwork. A patchwork of fields sloped away from us: fresh-leaved vines, lavender showing just a stirring of colour, and sunflower seedlings bursting through the earth.

I'd seen the multicoloured summer view before on postcards and in artists' paintings. The setting was perfect and there was even a glimpse of Mont Ventoux, the white giant of Provence. Tanya squeezed my hand. Both of us knew that we couldn't afford this location.

Eric threw open the door of his battered Peugeot and beamed at us. He looked as dishevelled as ever. Just the sort of person you'd fear trusting with your money: jacket stained from a decade of partying, three-day stubble, and a slogan T-shirt that smelled like it had never been washed. He did, however, have a horribly smug grin on his face. For some bizarre reason he believed he was going to make a sale.

'*Regardez,*' he said, sweeping his hand along the panorama. '*C'est magnifique.*'

'You're right.' I nodded.

'Five-minute walk from the village, south facing, large but manageable plot.' Eric was enjoying his spiel. 'Imagine yourselves here, glass of wine in your hand, sun dipping over the hills, children playing in the meadow, perhaps a dog at your feet. Oh, it will be perfect for you. I'm so pleased.'

'We might as well see the house,' sighed Tanya, all too aware of the no doubt horrendous price tag.

'House?' queried Eric, doing his best to fake genuine surprise.

'Yes, the house.'

'But there is no house.' Eric was still smiling. For some reason he was confident his pitch was going well.

'What do you want us to do?' I asked. 'Camp?'

'With Elodie?!' Eric laughed, ruffling our daughter's hair, 'No, no, no, who do you think I am?'

'Mobile home?'

'No, no, no.' Eric swept his arms out expressively. 'You are going to build a house, Jamie, right here, and every morning you are going to say a little thank you to Eric: the man who found this slice of heaven. Eh?'

'There's a right to build?'

'Yes. A hundred and fifty square metres, plans have already been submitted and approved by the *mairie*, you could be in by next spring. There's already an old well for water.'

I looked at Tanya. She raised an eyebrow. Eric had both of our attention.

'There's more, follow me.'

Eric led us up a dirt track which ran along the tree line. An embankment climbed away on one side, while on the other there was a muddy field of arable land. We headed into the mottled shade of an avenue of pines, and the path turned to our right at a steep gradient, making me struggle to carry Elodie. Eric was panting by the time we reached level ground. The wood thinned and we emerged into a prairie filled with wild flowers. Cool spring air tickled my nose and a flurry of blossom induced a heavy sneeze. I removed my jumper, enjoying the sensation of freshness as the breeze stirred the hairs on my arms.

Planted in two rigid lines across the field was a series of trees, spaced equidistantly. Most of them appeared to be oak, but there was also a shorter variety, perhaps olive. It would certainly be a lovely place for Elodie to play, to build camps and to come and make as much noise as she wanted. We might even be able to harvest enough olives to earn our own label at the mill. However, the field of trees was far from the selling point Eric's demeanour had promised. If anything, I felt slightly deflated.

Eric continued his sales pitch. 'Lavender fields, plenty of them, olive groves, everywhere, vineyards, too many to count. Bet you've never seen one of these before, eh?'

'Are we missing something?' whispered Tanya.

'Must be,' I replied.

Eric crossed his arms and stood in silent contemplative awe. Eventually he broke the confused silence. 'Usually they're kept secret, but I've found one just for you. And of course, all that rain – it's going to be a fantastic year.'

I smiled. It all began to make sense. The trees I'd mistaken for olive were in fact oak as well – just the evergreen local species. Then there was the precise spacing, to allow plenty of sunlight through to the earth below. And Eric's reference to the importance of rainfall had clinched it. From Tanya's grin I could see she had reached a similar conclusion.

'It's a *truffière*,' we chimed in unison.

'*Beh voilà!*' Eric couldn't contain his glee. 'Last year the owner harvested five kilos.'

'That's a lot of truffle risottos,' whispered Tanya.

'It's also a good earner.'

Eric slapped one of the trees like a long-lost buddy, and then wrapped his arms around another with the beatific smile of a hippy communing with nature. Perhaps we had to be French to understand. We loved eating truffles, and we'd certainly happily collect an income from selling them, but they weren't going to make us buy a house. Yet Eric seemed to think the papers were already signed and the commission in his pocket.

'And a watchtower as well.' Eric gestured to a conical pile of stones hidden among the trees. There was a small rotting wooden door, which swung loose on its hinges. With a little renovation it might have made a happy home for a hobbit, but a watchtower? Judging from the size of the walls I would barely be able to stand up inside. It was, of course, a *borie*, one of the thousands which had been built by Provençal peasants in which to store their tools while working in the fields. It was certainly an attractive addition, but not Eric's elusive deal clincher.

'Is it part of the sale?' I asked suspiciously.

'Might as well be – there's no one else up here to claim it,' came the evasive reply.

On our return to the lower field we discovered a white van parked next to our car. My immediate thought was that competing buyers had heard of the sale. The door swung open and I was relieved to see Ange, the local builder with the penchant for steak tartare, step out of the van. We kissed on both cheeks, Ange's stubble grating like sandpaper. He smelled of lunch – a pungent mix of red wine, coffee, cigarettes and garlic.

'What was on the menu?' I asked.

'*Magret au poivre*, dauphinoise and tarte Tatin for dessert. Come on, let's see the plot,' he winked at Eric.

'OK, she's south facing, best to orientate the house for the village views, plenty of shade in summer, plenty of sun in winter, no reason why eventually you can't put a pool in over there, soil's a bit dodgy so you'll have to think about foundations, monomur construction's the way to do it these days, nice and speedy, you can have the shell up in a couple of months, and once the roof's on, the whole thing is easy.'

Both Tanya and I had given up on the dream of owning a property in Provence. We'd concluded that we just didn't have the budget. Now our future was open again. The two of us strolled across the land, marking the territory, admiring the view from as many different angles as possible. Without thinking I knelt down and crumbled some of the soil between my fingers. Truffles or no truffles – what an opportunity. We walked hand in hand back to the car, where Eric and Ange had spread some plans out on the bonnet.

'Three bedrooms, two downstairs, one upstairs with a sun terrace,' Eric explained. 'Open-plan living downstairs, three arches dividing the living room, sitting room and kitchen, all approved and ready to go.'

'Anything you don't like, you can speak to the mayor and can probably change,' said Ange. 'Cost-wise, you've got to be careful – plenty of criminals out there, worst sort will take your money and not even complete the job. I'll manage it myself and introduce you to everyone else you'll need – electricians, plumbers, plasterers, painters.'

'Keep the plans,' beamed Eric, as he started the ignition on his car, 'and I'll be in touch in a couple of days.'

'And I'll give you a call with a rough price,' Ange added helpfully as he stepped into his van.

The two of them bumped off down the track, leaving Tanya and I standing, a little stunned, admiring the view.

'Best not get too excited,' Tanya counselled.

'You're right. Hard not to, though. No more of Manu's banging, loads more space, a garden as big as a country estate and the truffles.'

'Why do I feel like I've just been ambushed?'

'Probably because Eric planned it so carefully.'

There's something about seeing a house that induces a buying fever. As I've grown older I've become more and more conservative in my shopping habits. A jumper has to have been practically destroyed by a plague of moths before I'll consider buying a new one. And yet within moments of Eric leaving I was thinking about calling him to check whether other parties were interested. This was Provence, remember, where the average house takes well over a year to sell. But there was my heart, pumping away as if a pack of competing buyers was prowling in the surrounding woods.

'Play it cool,' advised Tanya. Gradually the urge to reach for my mobile dissipated. We took one last look at the view and jumped into our car.

As we headed back to the village the radio station was playing a show called *Les Bonnes Affaires*, a Provençal labour and goods exchange. Listeners phoned up to swap things, such as a bike for a sofa. The idea was that no money changed hands. We loved the show because the proposed swaps were always so unequal that they were comical.

'I am looking for a girl to come and do two hours' cleaning a day.' The voice was female and quite old. 'Ironing, making the beds, cleaning the floor, generally helping out around the house, and in return I am prepared to teach the girl the basics of home economics, budgeting, making ends meet.'

'Remind the listeners of your phone number.' The presenter's voice was weary. The morning had been full of people trying to swap caravans for houses, and bunny rabbits for horses, and here was another chancer with no realistic possibility of a swap. Still, the show aired for two hours a day and there was never any shortage of people trying their luck.

Chapter 7

There should be some sort of obligatory oath sworn by all foreign buyers in Provence – a type of wedding vow to their new house. Hold your hands up and repeat after me: 'A property transaction is not to be taken in hand lightly or thoughtlessly but reverently, soberly and in the fear of God.' Perhaps friends and relatives could be invited along to the signing of contracts and the *notaire* could ask them to show their support for the couple by chiming in 'we will' at the appropriate moment.

Reverent and sober were certainly not words that could describe us in the weeks after seeing the plot. We were giddy with excitement, in lust with the idea of finally achieving our dream. At every opportunity we visited the *terrain*. We joked that it was like a courtship. Each day a new delight was unveiled to us, a hitherto undiscovered plum tree or a hidden corner filled with wild herbs. We were being teased and seduced by the thought of owning a tiny part of the countryside we loved so much. In the past we'd always laughed at wide-eyed tourists who could be duped by a whiff of wild thyme into a lifelong relationship with an old whore of a house. Now we were behaving exactly like them.

Sensible thoughts like whether we could afford to take on such a project only fleetingly entered our heads. Instead, we sat down on a daily basis and drooled over pictures of cast-iron doors, distressed kitchens and antique baths. We annotated the plans – a larger opening here, a utility room there – and took them off to the *mairie* for approval. We visited ongoing *chantiers* (construction sites) and watched artisans create gleaming polished concrete floors, recessed alcoves and drystone walls. Somehow we convinced ourselves that we were special and that we'd manage to build the house within budget and on time.

Our weekends were spent raking *vide greniers* for furniture for our new house. We fooled ourselves that the prices quoted were so cheap, it didn't matter if the purchase fell through. However, a quick inventory of several days' hard shopping showed that all the small items had added up. Our cellar was crammed with rash purchases such as: an old sewing table (in need of repair), an eel catching net (we thought we would convert this into a light), a wicker table and chairs (believed valuable, later identified in an IKEA catalogue), a set of large glass bowls with tapered necks (to decorate new kitchen), a fireguard (so cheap we had to purchase it even if it was the wrong size) and finally a set of truffle digging tools.

Other than this final impulsive purchase, we'd given little thought to the truffles or the practicalities of finding them. A little further investigation had shown that the *borie* and the *truffière* formed part of the *garrigue*, or wild countryside, but as Eric had explained the current owner harvested the truffles, so why not us?

As a result, given the price per kilo of the black diamonds, there was an unspoken assumption that we'd probably, rather reluctantly, get a dog, but no more than that. At least my grasp of truffle technicalities was helped by an article in *La Provence* about the Ménerbes *mairie*. Rather than devoting funds to such mundane things as rubbish collection, the mayor had decided to plant a communal *truffière*, gambling that the way to secure re-election was through his constituents' stomachs.

The article went on to explain how truffles were a fungal disease carried by some oak trees, rather like you or I might have athlete's foot, but tastier. The truffles were attached by a gossamer-thin thread to the trees and grew by sucking nutrients from the oak. Take an acorn from a diseased oak, plant it, and the chances were that you would one day have a truffle tree. Plant lots of acorns and you'd end up with a *truffière*, just like the one we were going to purchase.

Our buyers' ardour couldn't be dented. Local records showed the *terrain* had previously been used as landfill for the village clay works and Eric advised us to consult engineers about reinforced foundations. This was a startlingly honest revelation, even romantically dressed by Eric's story of rows of women sitting in the shade of the trees casting roof tiles on their ample thighs. Yet instead of heeding the warning that the clay soil would swallow any normal construction like a horror-movie child snatched into hell, we discussed names for our house. To stabilise our proposed humble three-bedroom family house we'd apparently have to build the type of concrete foundations more commonly used for office blocks in earthquake zones and yet, such was our optimistic state of mind, we settled on the name 'Le Paradou'. To the English ear the word sounded like paradise, hence our choice, but in fact a *paradou* is something much more prosaic: a type of watermill.

Eventually the misty-eyed courtship came to an end and financial reality impinged. I asked Eric for help and soon a plague of advisors were on the phone trying to sell us mortgages, life insurance and even pensions. Our application headed off to all the respectable banks and a coterie of dodgy, far-flung institutions. The latter offered ridiculously low interest rates teamed with default clauses so punitive they could have been drafted by the mafia. The results, when they came back, were all the same – unsuitable for finance. We might have only missed out by the tiniest margin, but it didn't matter – there was no more money.

The realisation that the project wasn't going to happen brought us back to our senses. Like patients waking from a coma we shook our heads, looked around and demanded to know what had happened over the preceding weeks. Life gradually returned to normal. Even the news that Manu had filed for planning permission to develop more of the farmhouse and that we would effectively be living on a building site didn't jump-start the purchase of Le Paradou. We sold wine, we looked after our child and we barely gave a thought to the plot we had loved so much. Then Delphine phoned. 'There's someone I'd like you to meet. Take him to lunch, he's a gourmand.'

The person in question was Philippe Raimbaux and as Delphine explained he was a retired mortgage broker who still had excellent relationships with all the local banks. His passion was truffles. During his working life he'd discovered just how hard *truffières* were to finance. Harvesting the black diamond is a cash business and there are rarely accurate records of income for banks to lend on. And so in his retirement, through his contacts, Philippe had chosen to ease the path of select loans in return for a small payment in his own favourite currency – truffles. Delphine finished her summary with a warning: 'And a word of advice: choose a good restaurant – for Philippe it makes all the difference. And know your subject – you're going to have to convince him you can find the truffles to pay his fee.'

Selecting a venue perplexed us for a while. The south of France was full of great chefs who had no idea how to run a restaurant. Recently a new bistro had opened in a nearby village. Miraculous creations emerged from the kitchen, plates were dressed as sexily as Carla Bruni, and the resulting festival of flavours was enough to turn even a swinging local's head away from the nearest brunette. Two months later, though, due to soaring overheads, poisoned customers and the restaurant manager having had an affair with the chef's wife, the restaurant was out of business. Mortgage brokers, we reasoned, were reassured by stability and track record, and on this basis Tanya and I agreed to discount flashy newcomers. We also ruled out the established Michelin-starred restaurants – at nearly €100 a menu we'd hardly be displaying financial prudence, even if sampling lavender-infused ice cream would send us all home with smiles on our faces.

Philippe was based in Saint-Rémy-de-Provence, the uber-chic capital of the Les Alpilles area, and, trying to make his job as easy as possible, we finally decided to travel to him and chose the friendly local brasserie – Le Bistrot Découverte. The restaurant had one of the best cellars in the area and we'd met the owner Claude through our wine business. Like a fine sauce, the menu at the bistro had been reduced to a series of intense yet simple flavours.

We met to discuss our loan one sunny lunchtime in March, on the type of day that makes the locals sigh that their home is a corner of paradise, while the second homeowners hide their smug satisfaction behind a pair of oversize designer shades. The terrace was filled with early diners sipping on the remains of their red wine, toying with their coffees and showing absolutely no sign of vacating their tables. On the road opposite, the driver of a Porsche with Parisian number plates struggled to wedge his car into a small space. In the end he casually shunted a battered Citroën out of the way.

Our reservation was inside, but since Philippe had yet to arrive, we decided to wait for a place on the terrace. The more longingly we looked at the tables the more the residents – it was as if they'd set up home – reclined, and nonchalantly soaked up the sun. Even a crying and clearly hungry Elodie failed to dislodge the patrons. Bills arrived, but unlike the customers they didn't lounge indolently around. Credit card machines – which in France you wait for as long as for a train in England – were pressed into slightly unwilling hands and we had our table.

Like students swotting for an exam we pulled out note cards and did some last-minute revision, staining the cards with baby food as we read through them. The last thing we wanted to appear was ignorant but now some of my jottings from the night before appeared totally irrelevant. The fact that Madame Pompadour relied on a diet of truffles to heighten her libido in order that she could assuage the sexual demands of Louis XV was hardly the type of titbit to casually drop into a conversation. Worse still was the rumour that some of the Marquis de Sade's most notorious orgies followed truffle-laced banquets. Philippe could easily get the impression I was more interested in finding my inner sadomasochist than in the construction of a family home. Listing the different varieties of truffles – Burgundy, Perigord, Italian white, Oregon, even Kalahari – was surely safer ground. As was a probing question on the catastrophic effects of the two world wars on French truffle production: rather than passing on the secrets of the trade on their deathbeds, truffle hunters died on the battlefields, taking their knowledge with them.

I flicked to the next card and tried its contents on Tanya:

'According to the prophet Muhammad, truffles were a gift from Allah.'

Before she could respond Philippe arrived.

'And Emperor Nero called them the food of the gods,' he interjected as he sat down, shaking our hands enthusiastically and sliding his briefcase – which was of the battered academic type – under the table. He was dressed in a checked jacket and open-necked shirt and looked more like a university professor than a banker. His hair was grey but still thick and his tan the leather of a man who spent the summer in the south and the winter in the Alps. Menus and glasses of house wine – a lazy Côtes du Rhone – were placed before us.

'Isn't she beautiful?' said Philippe as we slid Elodie under the table for what we hoped would be a long sleep. A minute of gurgling protests followed, then some high-pitched screaming, which provoked disapproving clucks from nearby tables, but then finally there was silence.

'So, what are an English couple doing hunting for truffles?' asked Philippe.

'Where shall we begin?'

Philippe shrugged and relaxed back in his chair. 'We've plenty of time, we can start with where you were born if you like.' There was genuine interest in his voice and over the course of the lunch we found ourselves telling our story. How we left England determined to experience a better quality of life. How we built a wine business around rosé and how it had expanded to encompass wines from all over France. We described the little farmhouse we lived in and how with a growing family we felt that it was time to move on.

The food was perfect, complementing rather than overpowering the conversation. Starters were simple, but the quality immaculate. Thin slices of Iberian ham from a pig which had grazed exclusively on a diet of acorns were nutty and – perhaps the sun was getting to me at this point – almost truffley in flavour. The smoked salmon was from Scotland; it was fleshy, as peaty as a good whisky, and served with chive cream and toasted bread. I'd expected Philippe to eat with the kind of mechanical fastidiousness I've observed in 'foodies', who tend to concentrate intently as they dissect dishes. Far from it; instead, he crammed great mouthfuls onto his fork, eating with the hunger of a starved dog, and calling for more bread to mop up traces of olive oil.

The early signs were good. Philippe nodded approvingly as the plates were taken away and then searched for his briefcase under the table. 'The tests for your trees have come through. You must remember they are indicative rather than conclusive. However, it seems possible that you may find truffles.'

Tanya and I smiled triumphantly at each other and I wondered whether this might be the moment to order a little champagne.

'However, I'm worried that you may not be the right type of people. You've never had a dog, you grew up in the city.'

'But, but, but…' Tanya and I began to protest simultaneously.

Philippe waved our resistance away. 'It's a secretive, unpredictable, sometimes dangerous business – even the professionals who come from generations of truffle hunters struggle to maintain a constant income. Are you sure you want to do this?'

'We're sure,' answered Tanya.

'We're sure,' I added supportively.

'Tell me about your village.' Philippe changed the subject. 'How have the residents reacted to foreigners?'

Tanya chatted away about the warm welcome we'd received while I fidgeted uncomfortably as we waited for the main course. There was the loan to worry about and also my choice – *le steak tartare*. I'd followed Ange's advice and ordered the dish again at this, the first opportunity, but just the thought of the pain I'd endured made my stomach cramp.

I needn't have been concerned. Rather than the cheap mince which had so recently poisoned my whole system, my steak, when it arrived, had been entirely chopped by hand into the finest slivers, with the seasoning already mixed in. On top, however, were parboiled quails' eggs: salmonella on a fork, I thought, as I turned them into the meat. After each mouthful I waited for a reaction – the first painful tightening of my stomach that might have indicated the contractions were about to begin again. Instead, there was just the bliss of sitting in the sunshine, munching on a perfectly seasoned meal and knowing that I had successfully conquered a fear. Philippe and Tanya both had *faux-filet*.

'*Frites*,' Philippe explained as he tucked into the juicy sirloin and the side order of golden-brown chips, 'have to be tended to and nurtured. In a busy kitchen it's all too easy to turn out something with the texture of an old leather jacket.'

I couldn't work out whether this was a real compliment or just a platitude. Had Philippe been expecting more? Here was a broker who could pick and choose his clients and apparently pleasing his palate was everything. My fear was that despite the professionalism of the staff and the chef's concentration on detail, the meal was a little too simple, a little too polished. Where was the potential for disaster or moments of culinary genius? Still, Philippe seemed relaxed enough, enjoying the sun on his face and ignoring the queue of customers still looking for a table (it was past the witching hour of 2 p.m.). We ordered some coffees, which came accompanied with freshly baked miniature chocolate cakes and finally got back, somewhat obliquely, to the subject of the loan.

'Just one question,' I interrupted Philippe. 'Delphine said to choose our restaurant carefully – why?'

Philippe smiled. 'By letting you choose the restaurant you told me a lot about yourself. Firstly, you were kind enough to come to Saint-Rémy. Secondly, you sensibly avoided the name restaurants – quite wrong for a business lunch – and thirdly, you chose somewhere that serves great food at a decent price. By doing so you showed me you knew the area.'

'And the fact that we grew up in the city and don't know the first thing about dogs?'

'You can always get a pig instead,' Philippe joked as he rose from the table and held out his hand. 'I'll be in touch when I've agreed everything with the bank. The gap in your finances is only small. Plus, there's the truffle income. Don't worry, it won't be a problem.'

It should have been perfect: my wife and I sitting in the spring sunshine about to realise our dream. The warmth on our skin was uplifting and neighbouring tables bubbled with bonhomie; bottles were upended in glistening ice buckets, and waiters summoned to provide *digestifs*. Parisians taking long weekends passed by, their stride as jaunty as that of the designer dogs trailing in their wake. As Philippe left us we began analysing our lunch, what had been said, how we'd managed to convince him. Finally, we moved on to the daunting topic of building the house – when would we begin, which materials to use, the precise positioning of the house on the plot and, of course, which builder to choose.

Our mood was still upbeat as we left the table and walked through the cobbled streets, pushing Elodie's pram under the Roman arch, following the path of the summer bull run to the central square. There we sat on a bench underneath an ancient plane tree which was just coming into bud. The *tricolore* extending from the nearby *mairie* fluttered above our heads. Chicken turned on a rotisserie outside the butcher's and an assistant was busy dressing the window of the nearby art gallery. The surrounding buildings cut off the sun and the drop in temperature was immediately noticeable. I shuddered and edged closer to Tanya. Suddenly the spectre of winter had returned.

Perhaps had we stayed in the sunshine we could have managed our doubts but in the cold shadows the nervous feeling which had been building, and which at first I had put down to excitement, finally crystallised. What if Philippe was just a foolish old man and the collective finance departments of the ten or so banks we had originally applied to were right? Our wine business was profitable but it was still young and relied on the goodwill of numerous small clients. Any decline in sales would see us quickly struggling. Then there was the question of finding truffles. Philippe had been right to challenge us. What real hope did we have of learning the secrets of a shadowy profession? It wasn't as if we could walk into the village and ask the nearest truffle expert to show us their trade.

'Are you sure we should go ahead?'

Tanya was gazing into the sky. 'Funny, I was just thinking the same thing.'

Had it been just the two of us there would have been no question. Together we'd left London and set up our own business in a foreign country. Buying the piece of land was a risk; however, both of us believed that opportunities should be taken. We had always wanted a life less ordinary. But our first daughter, without us noticing, had changed this. Just a glance at her face provoked an overwhelming desire to protect her.

'If we ever needed to sell, it could take years.'

'I agree – Elodie's education, our parents, the wine business going bust…' Subconsciously I started scratching the back of my neck. 'There are plenty of reasons we might have to go back.'

'And yet?' Tanya's words were loaded with a subtext. If we walked away, there would always be regrets. Somehow, we would find a way to make it work. We always had in the past and we always would in the future.

'And yet,' I agreed. We sealed the deal with a kiss.

Part 2

A Lion in the Lavender

Chapter 8

It was the end of August and Provence sweltered under intense blue skies. The summer scents of lavender, thyme and rosemary evaporated under the punishing sun, fruit in the market shrivelled before the shoppers arrived and the locals barricaded themselves behind thick walls, draping wet towels over whirring fans.

The land rippled with heat and emergency wards filled with seared dehydrated tourists, their skin as raw and bloody as the steak served in the village cafes. Olive trees withered, fridges combusted with shuddering sighs, wells ran dry and armies of ants marauded across the cracked ground. People prayed for a storm and bickered over whether the heat was as severe as 2005.

Temperature readings were held to be inconclusive; instead, shoulders were shrugged and fingers were pointed at the earliest ever grape harvest and the greedy village Labrador who'd continued to gorge himself in 2005 and now scarcely twitched when thrown juicy remains. The debate was finally settled when the owner of the notorious key-swapping *resto* cancelled the regular Thursday night get-together. Only then did the residents of Provence nod sagely and declare themselves to be in the midst of a *'vraie canicule'*, grateful that there was nothing wrong with their libidos after all; it was just too hot for sex.

On the final day of the month Tanya and I called a summit meeting of all the artisans who had been so studiously avoiding our calls for the past sixty days. Granted it was July and August in Provence, but quotes that had been promised in April still hadn't arrived. Our righteous indignation somehow prevailed and miraculously, incredibly, a meeting took place before 1 September. Perhaps everyone had heat stroke and had simply forgotten the date, but here they all were: builder, electrician, plumber, window fitter, door fitter, painter and, of course, Ange, the project manager.

As bait we'd invited them all to lunch and we sat in the heavy shadows of our dining room. There was no question of eating on the terrace. Slowly, imperceptibly, our English instincts were leaving us. For a week's holiday the blinding furnace of the outside world was enjoyable but day after day, week after week, the heat began to test nerves. Even barricaded inside there were constant reminders of the season. The trees throbbed with cicadas, their incessant song occasionally interrupted by the drone of cumbersome firefighting planes circling the distant hills, belching water onto the chargrilled forests. The acrid smell of Manu's grapes, which had begun their fermentation on the vine, crept into the house. Earlier that day the first tractors laden with grapes had snaked their way towards the *cave* cooperative. At least the intense heat pleased the vignerons – starving the vines of water concentrated the flavour, and made for a great vintage.

The men ate with their faces low to their plates, occasionally muttering to each other, but essentially concentrating hard on their food. They shared the same dark, slightly shrunken eyes, and wind-burnished, sun-cracked, skin. Hidden from the outside world, clustered in the shadows, it was as if we were planning a crime, rather than trying to organise building a family home.

Ange had his weathered baseball cap pulled low over his head, and only when he occasionally removed it to mop his brow could I catch his eyes.

'So what's the latest?' I asked as he cut himself another large slice of goat's cheese and onion tart.

'Soil survey has arrived – five metres of clay,' Ange clucked in disapproval as I turned down an extra helping of tart. 'You'll have to send it to the engineers, but it's not going to be cheap.'

The sound of Elodie crying carried from the bedroom. The *canicule* had destroyed any hope of a routine. Our daughter wore only a nappy and still woke drenched in sweat. Sleep took place when she was too tired to cry.

'Her teeth are arriving, poor thing,' announced Tanya as she clasped Elodie to her chest. As was his habit, Ange rose and kissed Elodie on the forehead. 'Isn't she beautiful?'

We nodded, proud as ever, oblivious to the less than aesthetic blotchy red heat rash which covered her body. The rest of the men also rose from their seats and clustered around.

'Have you tried ginger?' asked Ange as he bit into the slice of tart I'd rejected. 'Smear a little on her gums, it's a natural anaesthetic.'

'Lavender rub on the chest before she sleeps,' added the plumber.

'Homeopathic suppositories worked for us,' said the electrician, who was several years younger than us.

Tanya was already searching in the fridge for some ginger, but I was determined to continue the progress update.

'Any firm prices yet?'

I looked around. Eyes fell to the floor.

'It's August.' Ange's raised eyebrows implied I should have known better than to ask.

'Clack.'

The noise came from the driveway. Whoever it was, they weren't worth sacrificing the bubble of cool air trapped in our house.

'Clack, clack.'

The sound was vaguely familiar, like metal on metal, reminding me of the camaraderie of the regulars who sipped pastis in the shade of plane trees and rattled their boules together as they waited for their turn. However, at this time of day the square in the village with its wooden sleepers and members' bar was a barren dust bowl. In any event, the sound had never carried before.

'Clack, clack, clack.'

After five years of living in Provence I'd learnt that from the beginning of June to early September you never ever opened the shutters between midday and midnight. In fact, a Provençal would prefer you to proposition his wife or poison his prize truffle dog rather than fling open his windows. The reward for this obstinate determination not to let the light of day into houses was that the cold air remained trapped and in the eyes of the locals there was no real contest between having a view and being able to sleep at night.

However, curiosity overcame me and I opened a window to take a look.

Strange sights are not that rare in Provence. Only the previous week a local butcher had chopped the heads off two pigs, placed sunglasses on their eyes, cigarettes in their mouths and hung signs around their necks saying 'Sarko and Carla'. The display proved an instant hit with Japanese tourists, who tended to huddle in excited groups before one of their number was propelled screaming hysterically towards the pigs for the obligatory photo call. Ever enterprising (but of course avowedly socialist) the butcher made space beside the pigs and started charging 2 euros a snap.

I am still not sure which was more alarming – the sight of one Japanese woman kissing a dead pig's head or the view that confronted me as I poked my head into the sunshine, so bright it momentarily seemed white. Briefly I considered phoning the *pompiers*. These jacks of all trade were responsible for dealing with everything from fires to hornets' nests. If I made the call, then ferrying deep-fried boules-playing tourists to hospital could be added to the list.

'Clack, clack.' The two young men continued their game, oblivious to my stunned gaze. Both of them dripped enough sweat to drown a swarm of flies. They wore Bermuda-style swimming trunk shorts with colourful polo tops tucked in behind their bottoms like horses' tails, leaving their bare chests exposed to the brutal sun. One of them had the dark skin of someone who tans easily, the other was cursed with freckles, and welts of sizzled skin covered his body, giving the appearance of an extreme case of measles.

'Come here,' I urged our lunch gathering.

Despite their obvious exhaustion the players remained blithely cheery, sharing a bottle of rosé between shots as they rested their hands on their knees and panted like athletes at the end of a marathon. Stranger still, they were lobbing their boules over the old pig shed at the bottom of our garden. Tiles could easily be snapped or windows broken but the potential for damage didn't seem to worry the two intruders; instead, they whooped with delight as their boules disappeared from view.

The two men finished their shots and walked around the back of the pig shed. There was a shout of delight and when they reappeared moments later the light-skinned one was kissing the *cochonnet* – the little wooden target ball at which the larger boules are aimed.

'You little beauty,' he exclaimed as he planted another smacker on the wood, before tossing it into the shadows adjacent to Manu's carefully cultivated lavender bushes. In a shower of purple confetti the first shot of the next game sliced the heads from one of the plants.

'*Oh là là, le gibier d'été*,' exclaimed Ange as if nothing else was to be expected. *Gibier* is French for game, anything that can be riddled with lead in the winter – boar, hare, partridge; in fact, anything that moves and isn't wearing a hunter's fluorescent jacket. In the summer months, the word is used to describe tourists. Fortunately for my visiting *gibier d'été*, Ange didn't have a gun.

'Are they still alive?' ventured the electrician.

'They're twitching,' added the painter helpfully.

'Boars convulse for minutes when shot,' said the plumber, who had strange emotionless eyes.

'They're covered in rosemary,' Tanya observed.

'What do you expect?' quipped Ange. 'It's like a rotisserie out there.'

I coughed loudly to get the players' attention.

'*Bonjour*,' the lighter skinned of the two men called back, dragging his sweaty mop of hair away from his steamed-up glasses, and holding his hand up in a signal of friendship. Looking like they did, doing what they were doing and with their appalling accents, the two could only be my fellow countrymen.

'Good afternoon.'

They grinned broadly and one replied: 'We're a little lost. We started a game and just kept going. We're renting a house over there somewhere.'

He pointed to the far side of a distant hill and smiled again, disarmingly, as if he appreciated the madness of what they were doing and was welcoming me into the comedy of their endeavour.

'You do know boules is usually played on a pitch?' I couldn't help but like them.

'And in the shade,' grunted Ange under his breath.

'By Frenchmen,' whispered the plumber.

'Yes, yes, but it's much more fun this way.' They were still grinning inanely.

'Can I offer you a lift back to your villa?' I said, dreaming of the air-conditioned interior of my car.

'Wouldn't want to put you out,' said one, with a crisp accent. Impeccable breeding had clearly taught him to refuse all offers of help. A surgeon trying to save his life would doubtless only be given the go-ahead 'if it wasn't too much trouble'.

'We'll manage,' lied the paler of the two as he collapsed in a heap, throwing a crop circle of sweat into the gravel.

I beckoned them into the house and poured a couple of chilled beers while they excitedly explained how they'd become hooked on a roaming version of boules.

The gathered ensemble of artisans regarded them with suspicion, as if to speak to them would be to humanise a species they were all too happy to regard as alien.

'It's a bit like golf – you never know what terrain you are going to come across. Olive groves, vines, hills, valleys; sometimes you need lob shots, sometimes you have to throw it flat, and there are even water hazards.'

'Water hazards?' I raised an eyebrow, determined to be supportive.

'Yeah, yeah – it turns out the boules don't break the tiles. We always dive in anyway, just to make sure they make a soft landing.'

'You play in the swimming pool?'

They nodded vigorously. 'Yeah, it's really extreme.'

The four Brits laughed. Even Elodie reacted by banging her hands happily on the table and rocking backwards with a toothy cackle. Ange, who was a well-respected local boules player, pushed back his chair, took off his cap and excused himself. Taking his cue, the artisans did the same.

'Call me when you've heard from the engineers,' said Ange and shook his head. Perhaps he'd be motivated to write a letter to the

French Boules Federation seeking to ban such bastardisations of his favourite game.

'What about your quote?' I asked, remembering the purpose of our meeting.

'Let's wait and see what the engineers say. I'm not going to take your last *bonbon*.' Ange pulled his cap over his head and braved the sun. The rest of the group filed away, and each and every one of them leapt on the excuse of the missing engineers' report. Quite what the concrete content of the foundations had to do with how many electrical sockets we wanted in the bathroom, or the finish on the doors, I'll never know, but since I wasn't in the trade, and was momentarily distracted by my compatriots, I just accepted the answer.

Our new English friends followed the artisans out the door. I watched as they restarted their game, zigzagging down the drive, stumbling painfully over stones wearing just their flip-flops, shredding lavender, trampling over wild thyme and finally disappearing into a drainage ditch. Their antics made me feel strangely patriotic. A verse of 'God Save the Queen' wouldn't have been out of place – only it was too hot to even consider singing.

Chapter 9

Over the summer we'd somewhat grudgingly accepted that we were going to have to get a truffle dog. The problem was that neither Tanya nor I were great dog lovers. My family had always had cats and during my childhood my parents were more likely to invite a Satanic emissary into their house than the neighbour's retriever, Jerry. Swearing in the house was only allowed when the target of my parents' wrath was this dog. The fact that Jerry stank and defecated on our lawn at every opportunity – seemingly storing up his daily efforts for maximum impact – provided them with an inexhaustible supply of ire and me with a vocabulary far too spicy for my age.

I remember an entire summer when Jerry's preferred hobby was chasing our cat up a tree, so high that only my father on a ladder could get her down. Dad worked late, and could think of better things to do at 2 a.m. than sway, 20 foot up in the air, trying to grasp a panicky stranded moggy. To his credit he always managed the rescue before retiring to bed, plotting a slow death for Jerry. Shipping him to China and turning him into a burger was the preferred solution.

Then there was my grandfather's Jack Russell. It's hard to imagine a more vicious, unfriendly little beast than Sally. My brothers and I nicknamed her The Rat for the way she scampered across the furniture gnawing at everything in her path. The main problem with Sally, though, was her hair. Every surface was thickly coated from her annual moult. As a result, the moment I entered the house it felt like I was wearing a boa constrictor for a scarf. Within minutes my airways had seized up. No matter how hard I inhaled only a whisper of oxygen made it to my lungs. By the time Granddad had made tea and demonstrated his latest ballroom dancing step, I was usually ready for a trip to casualty.

Dogs and my family just didn't mix. In fact, when my parents retired they'd specifically sought out a housing development that banned pooches. Some of their antagonism towards dogs must have rubbed off on me, because as an adult, while I tolerated other people's canine addiction, I could never for one moment imagine having a dog in my house.

Fortunately, I married someone with a similar mindset. The story of Tanya and dogs is much briefer. When she was nine her pet guinea pig, Pacer, was eaten by a stray. The sight of his torso slowly disappearing down the throat of a terrier has, as you can imagine, stayed with her for life.

However, the income from the truffle plantation was not something we could afford to turn down. To begin with we'd discussed our other options.

Fly truffling appealed for its simplicity. The idea was to approach the trees with the sun in our faces. This way we wouldn't cast a shadow. Using a stick we would then gently disturb the ground in front of us, watching for any of the flies that habitually gravitated to ground where truffles were buried. The practice, though, had all but died out. It was time-consuming and inaccurate and relied on the presence of the required species of flies. Both Tanya and I agreed that it was too much of a chance to take.

We spent a long time discussing getting a pig. Pigs were cute in a, well, piggy sort of way, plus they lived outside, required little attention, and were incredibly cheap to feed. Sows in particular are naturally attracted to truffles because the tuber emits a steroid similar to the one produced by boars in pre-mating rituals. Selecting a pig would be simple – find a farmer with a litter, hide a truffle in our hands and see which pig approached first.

Once a pig had tasted truffle it apparently developed a voracious appetite for the tuber and would hunt all day. Best of all, unlike a dog, if a pig didn't work out as a sniffer, we could always eat it. On the flip side, several truffle hunters had lost fingers, even entire hands, trying to swipe truffles away from the mouths of hungry sows. More often than not the lost digit ended up as an accompaniment to a truffle feast.

Following the anything-but-a-dog approach, we briefly considered a goat and even a bear – cubs were used in Russia to hunt truffles. However, the more we turned the problem over in our minds, the more we realised that we would have to get a dog. Surprisingly, once the decision was taken, we started to really like the idea. We talked about appealing thoughts such as our pet curled up by the fire, or running gaily across the fields with Elodie. When I was away from home it would be the perfect companion to Tanya and a fierce protector of the family.

All we needed was some advice on breeds and naturally we decided to consult Delphine. Her annual *fête des vendanges*, the celebration of the grape harvest, was one of the biggest events in the village calendar, and took place, as always, in the final week of September. The guests consisted of the twenty or so labourers who spent their days hand-picking and sorting the grapes and most of the residents of the village. Long tables stretched the length of the imposing terrace of the château and plates of canapés slalomed amidst bottles of wine and ordered legions of glasses. Fairy lights looped between the trees and they flickered into light as dusk fell, attracting the last of the season's mosquitoes.

A jazz band played on a small stage, and a ripe moon shone overhead. People wandered arm in arm exploring the extensive formal grounds – the rose garden, the herb garden, and the old water basin which had been converted unobtrusively into a swimming pool. Stirred by the lingering smells of the surrounding *garrigue*, memories of the summer hung in the air: the terrace of the village cafe filled with a multilingual, multicoloured pastiche of tourists, market stalls stacked high with ripe melons, peaches splitting from their skins, and the rippling thunder of an August hailstorm which had shredded entire fields of vines.

Under an iron *treille* (arbour) draped with vines, Vivienne, the owner of the village bar, appeared to be conducting a line-dancing lesson. Dressed in a white sparkling cowboy hat, matching boots and a frilly sequinned skirt, she was whooping and whirling away with a succession of unwilling partners. Sitting on a nearby wall, watching and laughing, were Ange and a coterie of local tradesmen. Tanya and I nodded hello, but this evening wasn't the time to discuss business.

Well, at least not for us. On the far side of the party, Fabian, the geothermal millionaire, responsible for introducing environmentally friendly heating systems to the area, saw us, waved and immediately began making his way over. He'd heard we'd bought a plot of land and had been pestering us ever since. It wasn't about the money, he insisted – although he had recently installed a helipad at his otherwise traditional Provençal *mas* – it was just that he was evangelical about saving the planet. Even a wake wouldn't stop him in his mission to convert all the houses in Provence to his system. To Fabian, a dead relative was to be celebrated rather than mourned, because his old boiler could be sent, with him, to heaven.

To escape the familiar spiel, Tanya and I ducked through the open door of the *cave*, absent-mindedly shutting it behind us. A line of bare light bulbs hanging from cords illuminated large vats of wine and the metal gangways that zigzagged between them. The air was pleasantly cool but dominated by the acrid smell of the harvest.

'Open the door or you'll kill us all,' shouted a worker, busily pulling rotten grapes from a conveyor belt.

Fermenting wine emits carbon monoxide and for the health of the workers all *cave* doors in vineyards are kept open immediately after the harvest. Centuries ago, deaths from carbon monoxide poisoning were not uncommon – wine was aerated by men plunging in and out of the wine vats, and if they lost hold of the rope they were trapped in a gas cloud. I always thought it would have been an appropriate way for Bond to kill off a villain.

'Sorry,' we apologised, opening the door, and heading deeper into the safety of the *cave*.

Delphine's vineyard was biodynamic, with all important work taking place according to the cycle of the moon; hence the frantic activity this evening. Nearby, a destalking machine churned grapes out ready for the press. Men heaved hoses running with grape juice between the vats, marking the varieties on little blackboards. And through all this noise and activity Delphine materialised, sweeping towards us in a flowing white gown, magically untouched by grape juice. Trailing behind her, as always, was Fifi.

'Darlings, you found me! Such a shame to miss the party, but as you can see I have my hands full.'

'How many more days?'

'Two, maybe three – just the sweet wine to go.'

I bent down to caress Fifi. 'Did you know we're getting a dog?'

Momentarily, Delphine appeared horrified. It was as if we were a couple of celebrities poaching an African child from his or her loving parents. Then the look was replaced by a benign smile.

'Why don't you come and see me tomorrow?' Delphine swept imperiously away, followed by a trail of workers. 'Let's put the rest of the Cabernet in there.' She gestured at a large vat and was gone.

Back outside there was thankfully no sign of geothermal Fabian. Instead, we chatted to a lovely Parisian couple who had a second home in the region and a penchant for our Pouilly Fumé, a young vigneron who invited us, presumably for corporate reasons, onto his yacht, and an expat Englishman, former gynaecologist to the royals, who'd given Tanya occasional advice during her pregnancy and now wanted to hear all the details of the birth. At the end of the evening we danced to jazz under the stars and returned home over an hour late for the babysitter.

The following day, as requested, we dropped over to Delphine's vineyard. It was just before lunch but the terrace was already immaculate. The long tables had vanished and every last cork had been collected from the floor. We knocked on the heavy door but there was no answer; instead, on the doorstep, we discovered a DVD entitled *Wolf in the House*.

Watching it before bed that evening stopped me from sleeping. The advice of the presenter, a former Foreign Legion dog-training specialist, was as follows: if you have children do not even consider getting a dog; buying a dog is like inviting a wolf into your house; at some stage the dog-come-wolf will get hungry and eat your children; if you are lucky it will just be a minor appendage, but some of the bigger breeds can sever a toddler's head.

I am exaggerating, but the basic scaremongering tone was the same and for a while Tanya and I were put off the idea, oscillating back to the pig. Common sense eventually prevailed. Plenty of people with children had dogs. Granted, having a baby and a puppy was not going to be ideal but given time, surely the two could learn to live happily with each other? We'd raised

Elodie for nine months, learnt how to change her nappies, read her moods and adapted our lives to hers. How hard could it be to manage a dog?

Delphine's unexplained absence did, though, leave us with an immediate problem. We had no expert with whom to discuss breeds.

In the end Eric Serep, our estate agent, recommended a former client, Pascal, who might be able to help.

We arranged to meet Pascal in a walkers' and climbers' hideout near Buoux. The lodge was hidden at the bottom of vertiginous cliffs and accessed via a chassis-wrecking dirt track. The swimming pool fed from a mountain stream doubled as a watering point for wild animals and the surrounding hills were so full of boar, hare and game birds that the owner never needed to visit the *boucherie*. Instead, first thing every Sunday morning he simply trained his gun on the basin and collected enough food for his restaurant for a week. The surrounding hills that had once sheltered Protestants fleeing Catholics and Jews running from the Nazis now embraced recluses who wanted to spend their lives communing with nature.

Pascal, the man Eric had described as the best truffle hunter in the valley, was already nearly an hour late, but we had little choice but to sit and wait. Still, it was a pleasant place to idle away time. An early September storm had revived a lush field of grass and we sat letting the sun warm our faces as Elodie crawled in a circle around us. The Aigue Brun river bubbled away nearby and a couple of birds rode thermals until they were enveloped by the endless blue sky. Occasionally the smell of a slow-cooked stew emanating from the kitchen of the auberge reached us, and I swallowed involuntarily with misguided anticipation. We were here for a meeting, not to eat. A couple of ramblers waved from the top of the Fort de Buoux, which guards the entrance to the valley. Another day we would have to return and make the ascent.

I lifted Elodie onto her feet and supported her as she made hesitant stumbling steps.

'She'll be walking soon.'

I turned to find a bearded man sitting on the grass beside us. His relaxed posture was that of a person who'd been lounging around for hours but neither Tanya or I had heard him approach. His feet were crossed and the soles of his weather-beaten trainers faced towards us. Their uneven bottoms had been repaired with what looked like the remains of old car tyres. The rest of his clothes were in a slightly better state: combat trousers with green patches across the knees and a sun bleached T-shirt inexplicably bearing the logo 'Aqua Land'.

'Pascal?' I asked.

The stranger nodded in agreement. We smiled and shook hands a little awkwardly. Pascal's eyes drifted off to the horizon, and momentarily we sat in silence.

'We've come to find out about truffle dogs,' volunteered Tanya.

'So Eric explained,' Pascal shrugged. 'Understand that it is not the dog that finds the truffles, it's the man.'

What could we say? We'd travelled an hour into the hills to find out about dogs only to be told we didn't need one.

Pascal stared at the horizon again. A climber halfway up a distant cliff face shouted a command that echoed down the valley. There was a clatter of pans from the kitchen and the auberge's cat meowed with hunger. I signalled to Tanya that we should go. Elodie would be getting hungry and the sky was still fascinating Pascal.

'Anyone can smell a developing truffle,' Pascal finally offered. 'Once you have the scent, you must watch the ground, observe the small daily differences, chart the path of the cracks, note where the vegetation dies, leave a stone as a marker, smell the underside to see if you are right. How can you begin to teach a dog to find truffles if you can't find them yourself? Patience is the key, Jamie. Are you a patient man?'

I nodded in agreement, only too aware that the older I got, the more impatient I became. Sudoku puzzles frustrated me after just moments and the first clue of a cryptic crossword was enough to have me reaching for the TV remote. Adding to my problems, a childhood accident had left me with only one functioning nostril. If anyone needed a dog to find truffles it was me, and yet Pascal insisted canine help was unnecessary.

His spiritual view was that 'the man doesn't find the truffle, the truffle finds the man', that there was some sort of hidden force that would guide us to the black diamonds. However, rather like characters on a quest, he believed we had to be pure of heart to stand any chance of success. 'Finding truffles is about the spirit of *la chasse*. People who just want money never succeed.' Our teacher nodded sagely, pressing his palms together and rocking backwards and forwards as if entering a trance.

'Bravo Elodie!' Pascal clapped his hands as our daughter's attempt to walk once more failed spectacularly and she tumbled towards him.

'How did you know her name?'

'I overheard you speaking as I approached.' I was beginning to think the man had superhero powers: enhanced hearing, heightened sense of smell, the ability to appear out of nowhere – had he, like Obelix, fallen in a pot of magic potion when he was younger?

'Now, let's talk about dogs,' Pascal continued. 'First you have to decide who's going to be head of the pack. If it's you, Jamie, you must get a bitch; if it's you, Tanya, get a boy. That way the dog will obey better.'

'And the breed of *chiot*?' Tanya asked.

Pascal laughed, which immediately relaxed him and robbed him of his distant intensity. He gathered himself but then started laughing again. At the time I couldn't understand what was funny, but later we learnt that by not dropping the 't' at the end of the French word for puppy, Tanya had in fact enquired what breed of toilet she should be getting.

Once Pascal had regained his composure, he continued, 'Breed? You don't want a breed. What you need is a one hundred per cent mutt. The more different dogs in him or her, the better. Don't ask me why, but homeless bastards make the best truffle dogs. Perhaps it's the need to please.'

Confessing a weakness is never easy; confessing a weakness to a man who has only just recovered from a convulsive giggling fit is doubly hard. I could hear the question in my head before I asked it, and looking at myself through Pascal's eyes I saw a town dweller who didn't deserve to be the owner of a truffle plantation. Still, I'd gone to the trouble of looking up the correct vocabulary in the dictionary and so I pushed ahead.

'We need to get a hypoallergenic dog; you know, one that doesn't drop its hairs. I get asthma you see,' I prattled on, realising just how pathetic I sounded.

Over the years I'd observed that the Provençaux were not the world's greatest dog lovers. Owners tended to set their pets loose in the garden, but, of course, instead of sitting serenely under a tree munching a bone and looking at the view, the dogs headed off to explore the countryside, chase cars, scavenge in bins and bonk on street corners. Roadkill carcasses piled up, but nobody really believed that neutering was worth the expense and so the puppies kept on coming. The answer I expected was therefore an obvious one: keep the dog outside, and if it runs off, get another one.

Pascal, though, surprised me. 'And of course you have Elodie to consider. A pure breed is more predictable, a poodle is probably best.'

I winced. Visions of overdressed, over-made-up French women, the latest designer bag on one arm and a poodle trotting daintily from the other, came to mind. Having a poodle would be just so emasculating. Part of me thought that Pascal was enjoying a personal joke.

'They're very intelligent, excellent noses, obedient, good with kids – you could do a lot worse. You could even get a big black one, much better for men,' he said, showing an uncanny ability to anticipate my objection.

'Training is simple. The younger you start, the better. Get him used to the smell of a truffle. Put a slice in an old sock and let him sleep with it. Hide some more around the house, under the legs of furniture, under beds – wherever he has to work a little to find the truffle. Then make it a little harder – slightly higher up, but at a level he can reach. Make it fun. Once he's really enjoying it, go outside, hide the truffle under a stone, then some earth, then some more earth. He'll be ready for the real thing in a month or so; take him for a walk in the woods, and he'll be off following his nose. Be careful, though – after dark only. Having a dog with you in these parts makes you a target. Someone once shot at me with an Uzi, bullets rattling the trees, all because they thought I was after their truffles.'

Now Pascal was on to his subject he really seemed to be enjoying himself. 'That's when I started going hunting with the chief of police. The landowners thought he was out on patrol, protecting their land, and letters of praise for his diligence even arrived at the *mairie*, when in fact he was out with me, acting as a bodyguard while I dug up the truffles. Night after night, village after village, we performed the same scam. Ah, that was a great year. Not that you'll have any problems; you've got your own trees. Just watch out for police cars in the middle of the night.'

'The police are poachers?' exclaimed Tanya.

Pascal looked away into the distance, aware, perhaps, that he'd said too much. He shook his head, rose, brushed himself down, said the briefest of farewells and headed off towards the trees. I took my eyes off him for a second, glancing at Tanya, and when I looked back he was gone. Trotting along the line of trees, though, was a white wolf-like dog.

'You don't think?' I joked with Tanya.

'What?'

'The sense of smell, heightened hearing, arriving silently…'

'Only if dogs have a sense of humour – you with a poodle!' Tanya smiled.

I think she was secretly content with our choice of breed. On the other hand, my only consolation would be the phone call to my parents to tell them that we had a dog.

Chapter 10

The more I thought about it, the more I disliked the idea of getting a poodle. A poodle was more of a fashion statement than a dog and I just wasn't sure how well one would complement my Primark T-shirts. Tanya didn't help the matter by showing me pictures of coiffed pooches with pink ribbons in their hair, wearing pearl-encrusted tiaras and coats studded with diamonds. Only oligarchs' wives, Parisian princesses and Hollywood honeys had poodles.

I had a recurring nightmare about the village bar. As I entered the Bar du Centre all heads swivelled towards me and jaws dropped cartoon style to the floor at the sight of my prancing poodle. Pulling up my seat I nodded to the barman and opened my copy of *La Provence*. Then when I reached for my drink I discovered that instead of my regular beer, I'd been served a Babycham in a Martini glass with an iced cocktail cherry. 'Anything for the dog?' the barman asked and all the other customers burst out laughing. Above all the noise I could hear one particularly unpleasant cackle – it was Serge, the man with the fixed eyes, whose bad mood always seemed to form a shadow in the corner. In my dreams Serge's area of the bar was so dark that all I could see were his mirthless eyes boring into my skull. At this point I always woke up in a cold sweat.

Internet searches revealed any number of poodles waiting for a new home. There were two breeders within a thirty-minute drive with recent litters and yet I prevaricated. We weren't just choosing a dog, we were choosing a new member of our family. Pascal had stressed how successful truffle hunters were at one with their dogs, thinking together, moving together, existing, if only on the hunt, in a state of synchronicity. How could I ever achieve this with a poodle?

An alternative briefly presented itself in the form of the labradoodle, a cross-breed from Australia first bred in the 1980s, which promised the temperament and size of a Labrador with the hypoallergenic non-fur-dropping characteristics of the poodle. I was sold and immediately checked the Internet for local breeders. There were none. I changed the search to the south of France, only to get the same answer. Finally, I checked the whole of France and discovered the website of one breeder near Paris. The next litter wasn't due for six months and there was already a waiting list for the puppies. Even in England there were no labradoodle puppies immediately available. Short of flying one in from Australia, the breed simply wasn't an option.

Meanwhile, time passed and it became increasingly likely that my poodle obstinacy was going to cost us the first season of truffle hunting. Fields of vines turned a ripe robust gold, the streets emptied of tourists, pumpkins replaced melons in the fields, and falling leaves lay on the surface of the local *étang* (pond) like pieces of an unfinished jigsaw. Progress on the build was non-existent but finding our first truffles was within our control – if, that is, I was prepared to sacrifice my manhood and get a poodle.

I was one click away from ordering a whole new poodle-matching wardrobe when I came across a breed called petit chien lion. The dogs grew to just below knee height and appeared to be bundles of fur, not the tight curl of a poodle, but rather long and shaggy, like a fireside rug in a bad porn movie. Descriptions of the breed were positive: the dogs were loyal, excellent with children, fierce defenders of their owners and – most importantly – hypoallergenic. When displayed at shows they had their hind legs shaved, which made them look ridiculous, but otherwise for a small dog they carried an air of rough toughness which appealed to me.

A further click pulled up a photo of a twelve-week-old pup being offered for sale by a breeder in Cassis. His kennel name was Flairer. We'd never heard the word before and looked it up in the dictionary – 'to hunt with one's nose; to snuffle', read the definition. 'Snuffle the truffles,' I said under my breath. It had to be fate.

In the photo, Snuffle's eyes were invisible, even his legs were invisible; in fact, all that could be discerned was a black blob with a flash of white across the chest. It reminded me of the type of painting a three year old would bring back from nursery. I called Tanya over.

'What do you think?'

She laughed. 'What are we buying, a rug?'

'Shall I give the breeder a call?'

'Why not.'

Moments later I was on the phone to Veronique, hearing all about Snuffle. Her description made him sound more virtuous than Mother Theresa; never had she had a dog like him; he was calm, wise, caring, attentive, clever and gentle. The adjectives just went on and on and the praise was limitless. Finding truffles was child's play for Snuffle; he could sniff out a black diamond at over one hundred metres. Encase it in kryptonite and he would still find it.

When I had the temerity to enquire whether Snuffle was house-trained, Veronique's indignant tone implied that here was a puppy so domesticated that he would cook us a three-course meal every night, uncork the wine, make the beds, do the hoovering, sweep the terrace, keep Elodie amused, make a fortune shorting the stock markets and enable us all to retire in a year. A price a little shy of 600 euros was not much to ask for such a dog.

In fact, it was not really a question of whether we wanted the dog, of course we did, rather whether Veronique would allow Snuffle to come and live with us. What type of people were we? Could she see photos of our house and the room where Snuffle would sleep? Would we agree to send her photos of Snuffle every six months? Would we update her website with a blog about Snuffle's life? If the accommodation was suitable and the answer to all these questions was yes, then she would consider selling him to us. However, before taking her final decision she would have to sleep on it.

Veronique phoned again the next morning. She'd looked at the photos of our apartment and felt that it was a little small for a dog such as Snuffle. However, she'd also examined the designs for the place we were building and noticed a little corner under the staircase that could be adapted just for Snuffle. No major structural alterations were necessary and it would provide the perfect refuge for him when he needed some peace and quiet.

Had this been any normal transaction I would have politely told Veronique where to go, but I already felt out of my comfort zone. This was the doggie world, about which I knew so little. Perhaps such overbearing concern for the welfare of puppies was normal. I was reluctant to contradict Veronique: she was the expert and I was the novice, and to object to her suggestions would be to show a callous disregard to the needs of Snuffle. And so instead I agreed a pick-up time the following morning and was reassured that Veronique would sell me, at what she insisted was a large discount, everything one could ever need for the health and happiness of a dog. Apart, that is, from the pick-up truck to bring it all home.

Cassis out of season is a gem of a seaside town. Pastel buildings surround a crescent-shaped bay. Boats gently rock at anchor and stairs wind away into pretty cobbled backstreets. The port is fringed by endless restaurants offering carnivals of *coquillage* piled high on mountains of crushed ice. Our favourite was a cafe which allowed its customers to purchase direct from the fisherman. Sea urchins were heaped in the corner of an old wooden boat. As the orders came in, a man wearing oily yellow gloves shovelled the spiky balls into bags and handed them to his partner, who split open the urchins and placed them on a paper plate. It was the freshest seafood available and once the purchase was made diners retired to the cafe, where for a cover charge of a couple of euros they were provided with bread, napkins and an accompanying glass of sharp white wine. Our plan was to pick up Snuffle at around 11 a.m. and then head to the seafront and lunch under the arching cliffs of the port.

Veronique's *domaine* (estate) was in the hinterland behind Cassis on the way to Roquefort-La-Bédoule. The countryside was dominated by vineyards making the sophisticated white for which Cassis is famed and also heavier, tannin-laden reds that echo their more illustrious neighbours from Bandol. As a result I'd assumed Veronique was a vigneron with a sideline in dog raising. The *domaine* I'd visualised was pine fringed, with rows of vines falling away from a country *mas*. The marketing symbol Veronique used on the Internet was the silhouette of a dog under a palm tree, and so my mental image also contained a long drive guarded by two ancient palms, forming a natural bridge over the road. It was all rather idyllic and peaceful. Perhaps we would share a coffee in the shade of some ancient stone walls, and the trickle of a fountain would provide the background music to our first meeting with Snuffle.

Instead, the directions took us to a piece of scrubland sandwiched between the *autoroute* and the *route nationale*. As our car rattled up the track, Veronique emerged from one of a number of portable buildings. She was wearing riding boots and jodhpurs, a ragged shirt and a dirt-stained body warmer. Her hair was tied back, although a couple of strands had escaped and dangled in front of her eyes. A loose horse ambled over and nuzzled her face and she reached into her coat and produced half an apple that had gone brown in her pocket.

We waved apprehensively and got out of the car. My shoes disappeared into mud and water soaked through the thin leather, drenching my socks. The sound of cars and juggernauts rumbled in the background and the smell of manure and heavy animal rugs brought back memories of the riding stables my mother had insisted we visit when we were young. Lifting Elodie from her car seat, we crossed the boggy land to Veronique.

'*Venez, venez!*' She beckoned us over to the far side of the field, where a series of gates led through to a large enclosed pen with another Portakabin in the corner. Our arrival prompted a cacophony of barking and the cabin shook with the combined might of all the dogs throwing their weight against the door.

'Wait here. I'll go and search for the babies,' she said, paying not the slightest attention to our baby. Without thinking, I set Elodie down. She'd just started walking and at every opportunity we were encouraging her to take wobbly steps. I glanced at Tanya, aware that she was as uncomfortable as I was in this environment. At that precise moment Veronique opened the door to the cabin and unleashed a ferocious torrent of yapping, jumping dogs that came tumbling out, devouring the distance between us in seconds.

The dogs noticed Elodie and like a school of piranhas honed in on her in a slathering, over-excited mass. I was only metres away but before I could hook my arm around my daughter she was enveloped by the lion dogs. Her screams for help were drowned by the barking.

Plucking Elodie from the melee I held her aloft to check she was OK.

'*Mais alors!*' I protested.

Veronique was unperturbed and called over and kissed each of her babies.

'Micha, *bisous*… Arthur, *bisous*.'

I was overcome by a strong urge to leave, with or without our new puppy.

'Play with my babies,' said Veronique, unaware that I would have rather put my hand in a cage full of tarantulas than once more expose my daughter to the crazed rabble. An uncomfortable five minutes of growling, barking and licking followed as Tanya and I tried to simulate enjoyment while continuing to hoist Elodie into the air to avoid the fangs of the yelping pack. Was it too late to confess that the whole idea had been a terrible mistake?

'And now let's introduce you to Snuffle.' Veronique ushered the dogs back into the cabin, which once more rocked like a fairground ride. 'I'll be back in a moment.' She headed out of the enclosure towards another temporary building.

Tanya and I looked at each other with panic in our eyes.

'It's only because there are so many of them,' I said reassuringly.

'Exactly, it's pack behaviour.'

'The book said they were fantastic with kids.' I tried to soothe the disquiet we both felt. 'Still, if we are going to leave, now's the time.'

Tanya shook her head. 'Think of the truffles.'

Veronique was on her way back. Two dogs followed her.

'Sure?'

'Sure.'

'Last chance,' I joked.

'Sure,' said Tanya definitively.

As Veronique approached, I began to have a dreadful feeling. I squinted to make sure my first impression was correct. However, the dogs walked in a tight file behind her and it was difficult to see. The closer they came, though, the more convinced I became. I'd only known Veronique for a few days but already I appreciated that this was a big moment for her and her dogs. So far everything had been stage-managed: meeting the other dogs and then leaving us alone to anticipate the arrival of our new pup. We were part of a pageant, a parade put on to mark Snuffle's departure from the *domaine*, and of course at parades people always wear their best party outfits. In the case of a petit chien lion, I realised with horror, this meant shaving the hind legs.

Veronique opened the gate to the paddock, and Snuffle's bare bottom and Twiglet legs followed quickly afterwards. It was anything but love at first sight. Snuffle looked like a cross between a cat and a dog. One half of him was scrawny and bare, the other fluffy from a recent blow-dry. Of all the thousands of breeds in the world, we'd ended up buying, at extortionate expense, this mismatched mistake. Unbelievably, I wished we'd got a poodle instead. Following the aggressive pattern of the other dogs, Snuffle's mother, who'd also had her legs shaved for the occasion, bared her teeth and let out a deep rumbling growl.

'Ah, she knows he's going, poor darling. Go on, play with your puppy for the last time.'

We sat down at a wooden picnic table and began to fill out the required paperwork. As usual in France this was exhaustive and in triplicate. Fetching one of the other dogs, Veronique showed us how to groom Snuffle properly, demonstrating how to comb the hair away from the eyes and how to clip the nails. Photocopies of the various forms were made, to be sent to a multitude of government agencies. The clock ticked towards midday and thoughts of our planned lunch in Cassis crept into my head. At least Snuffle's shaved legs would be admired by the Marseillais divas who strutted up and down the seafront.

'It's time for Snuffle to say goodbye to all his friends,' announced Veronique, preparing to let loose the dogs which, behind the thin walls that separated us, were baying for our blood.

'A little lunch?' She dropped the question into the conversation with a barely disguised subtext of emotional blackmail – did we want to deny Snuffle the opportunity to say a final farewell to his family? My face is not good at hiding emotions and only a sharp kick from Tanya restored a faux grin to my face.

'Of course we'll stay.'

And so rather than munching on sea urchins and watching the waves roll in, we ate mixed leaves and dry cheese, trying to ignore the overwhelming odour of horse manure. A crisp glass of Cassis winking in the sunshine was replaced with a stained coffee mug filled with tap water. Instead of enjoying the warmth of a blow heater on a sheltered seaside terrace, we endured icy blasts that swept down the slopes of the surrounding hills.

Elodie began to cry but Veronique was oblivious to our discomfort, opening another file from her office. This one contained rosettes and pictures from various dog shows.

'Here's his father in Monaco,' she said, pushing a photo under our noses, 'and in Barcelona,' another photo arrived, 'and Nice.'

We did our best to appear interested, but one photo of a dog show looked very much like another. I couldn't avoid noticing that Snuffle, who was supposed to be saying his tearful goodbyes, spent the whole lunch playing with a football. Still, Veronique was doing her best to make it feel like a wake, telling us how Snuffle was the last of the litter to depart and how because of his adorable character, boundless good looks and charm he held a special place in her heart.

Finally at the end of an interminable lunch, during which Veronique appeared determined to enter the *Guinness World Records* book for slow eating, it was time to go. With Elodie still in tears, Veronique led me over to her in-house shop. There were three items on my list – a dog cushion, some food, and some bowls – and with Tanya strapping Elodie into the car I was determined to be quick.

Here's the list of items I came out with half an hour later:

- 1 lead
- 1 comb
- 1 tick twister
- 1 bone chew
- 1 waste bag holder
- 2 waste bag refills
- 1 dog seat belt
- 1 Christmas bone chew
- 1 plastic crab toy
- 1 plastic Dalmatian toy
- 1 plastic blue ball
- 1 can of hairspray
- 1 bottle of Oh My Dog shampoo
- 1 dental snack
- 10 chews
- 1 vet bed
- 1 dog house
- 1 exercise harness

At each stage Veronique made me feel I would be betraying Snuffle unless, for example, I bought the very latest chew toy for him to rip apart. There were no farewell gifts from Veronique. Instead, she sat and methodically added up the cost of the whole ridiculous list. A staggering 300 euros. More prolonged goodbyes followed and Veronique walked alongside our car as we bumped away, practically kissing the windscreen.

Two and half hours after we first arrived, we had a dog, and neither of us could quite believe it. His dark eyes were deep and trusting and he trembled on Tanya's lap as we got onto the motorway. He was quite cute really, even if he did have shaven legs, and we couldn't possibly blame him for his lovesick owner. Next week it would be December, and the first of the season's truffles would begin arriving.

Now all we had to do was train our dog.

Chapter 11

Ask anybody: having a puppy is a nightmare. They wee, they poo, they bark, they bite, they hurtle around the house like pinballs. And all this goes on for nearly a year. Yet for the first glorious forty-eight hours we thought all the scare stories had been made up. Snuffle did very little but sleep and eat and he happened to be outside when he needed to wee or poo. Looking after Elodie was far more demanding and sleep depriving than caring for our shaven-legged friend. The new member of our family could not have been less trouble.

Then things changed. Snuffle recovered from the trauma of leaving his mother, regained his strength, and decided to treat each corner of our house as his personal toilet. Veronique, as it turned out, had sold us everything Snuffle could ever need but had omitted to consider our requirements. Hence, we had a puppy with a million and one toys but no cage with which to house-train him.

Desperately we manufactured temporary solutions from toddler playpens but Snuffle invariably escaped and by the time we finally bought a cage a week later, our little puppy was not so malleable. He'd been granted his freedom and he wasn't about to give it up. Advice on the Internet stated that caging puppies was kind and the best way of introducing them to life with humans. Young dogs rarely barked for more than ten minutes when caged, said the website, and yet we endured hour upon hour of an enraged Snuffle.

Driven crazy by the noise we binned the cage and instead kept him on the lead at all times. Wherever we went, Snuffle went. This was fine when Tanya and I were together, but the moment one of us left the house, the balance of power shifted dramatically in Snuffle's favour. Changing a nappy while restraining a dog determined to sniff, lick and yes, even eat the faeces, is a difficult trick to master. Snuffle's nose was almost a thousand times more powerful than ours, and the pack member he associated as his immediate contemporary, Elodie, was busily leaving her scent all over the house. Quite naturally Snuffle simply followed her lead and deposited his own markers.

Meanwhile sleep deprivation began to set in. At night Elodie, teething, screamed and woke the dog. Snuffle in turn barked and fidgeted and demanded to be let outside. A typical night would see Tanya pacing inside with Elodie, while I walked up and down in the garden waiting for Snuffle to empty his bowels. Elodie falling asleep and Snuffle finally obliging didn't often occur at the same time, and so, as we desperately tried to claw our way back to sleep, one or other of our babies inevitably woke the other, and the whole process started again.

After two weeks Tanya and I were so tired we were arguing incessantly with each other. Smug dog owners said that the reason Snuffle was behaving so badly was because he had yet to identify a new head of his pack. Doing my best to right this situation, and on the basis of advice in a dog book, I started growling at Snuffle. The noise I made was deep and guttural and alarming enough to make Elodie toddle away. If Snuffle did an inadvertent pee on the sofa I would bear my fangs and snarl like a geriatric hunting hound.

This new policy worked in a way. Certainly, Snuffle began to fear my displeasure, and so instead of peeing in front of me, he picked his moments, waited until I was distracted and sneaked off to a corner of the house. Meanwhile, all the growling began to have a debilitating effect on me. Naturally I was a happy person – in fact, my nickname from university was Smiley – but the new, growling me, was miserable. And yet it was the only training tip that worked, and so I continued to growl and snarl my way angrily through days.

However, when instead of 'Mama' or 'Dada' Elodie's first words came out as a deep and guttural growl, I realised something was wrong.

'She's becoming like those children raised by wild dogs,' pleaded Tanya.

Yet once I stopped growling I lost the small semblance of control I'd begun to exert. I'd devoted hours to walking around outside in the freezing night air, so that my dog had every opportunity to be a good boy. I'd rewarded him liberally with small pieces of cheese, patted and praised him throughout the day and still that most basic of skills – house-training – was beyond our *chien*. Most people achieved in seven days what still eluded me after a month of ownership. What hope was there of us ever achieving the synchronicity of mind and movement necessary to find truffles?

The sense of despair was heightened by the small size of our farmhouse apartment. When we'd first rented the place, we were a young childless couple. The open-plan living area, with kitchen, dining room and sitting room all crammed in a 30-metre-square space, had echoed the urban flats we were used to, as had the small bedrooms which fed off a narrow corridor. When Elodie arrived we'd had to reorganise our lifestyle but ultimately we'd achieved a balance, where I could work undisturbed and, when needed, Tanya and I could find space from each other.

The addition of Snuffle destroyed this balance. One of us always had to be in the room to check that he wasn't pushing Elodie over, and that Elodie, with her prods and pokes, wasn't inciting him to bite. By early December, with the cold weather returning and all of us cooped up inside the flat, Tanya and I began to suffer from an acute sense of claustrophobia. We had to get out, and yet with the onset of winter there was nowhere to go. Instead, our days were filled with barking, and screaming and rowing. In-between the shouting, the only thing we could agree on was that we should never, ever, have got a dog.

It's hard to place precisely when my throat began to seize up. I remember feeling tight-chested at the breeder's in Cassis. At the time I dismissed it as a combination of the horses and the sheer number of dogs. On the way home in the car I was still wheezing slightly but the spasms passed. For the next week there was nothing and I relaxed, but ever so gradually the symptoms reappeared and I noticed that the more Snuffle misbehaved, the more I wheezed. My self-diagnosis was that these attacks were not allergy related, but rather psychosomatic. Although I felt terrible at the thought of having to find a new home for Snuffle, subconsciously the allergy reappearing gave me the perfect excuse.

At least somebody was pleased by the new addition to our household: Delphine. The bag full of designer clothes she'd purchased on Elodie's arrival appeared a mere trifle when compared with the daily gifts for Snuffle. In a way, I could understand her fascination. Our new *chien* was the son of champions, he pranced rather than walked and his demeanour, the way he carried his head, his general comportment, all spoke of an inbred elegance. Next to Tanya he seemed a naturally chic accessory; next to me he looked ridiculous. By mistake we'd purchased one of the rarest and therefore most desirable companion dogs in the world.

And like an expensive motor car our little pooch took some maintaining. Veronique had raised him on a diet of poached free-range chicken fillets, and Snuffle refused to eat anything else. When I substituted battery-reared meat he went on hunger strike for two days, became thin and lethargic, and refused to move until his nose told him all was right with his chicken again. The hypoallergenic non-fur-drop nature of the breed meant that daily grooming was necessary to remove all the twigs, insects and burs he picked up. If his toilette wasn't carried out on time then Snuffle began to bark, with the yelps picking up in volume until he got the attention he felt he deserved. I'd always dismissed people who said that dogs, just like humans, had complex and involved personalities but now I agreed. Snuffle, I decided, was a prima-donna princess who, if human, would live in a Manhattan penthouse apartment and run some kind of bitchy blog about celebrity mores.

Even so, despite everything, and almost against my best wishes, I began to like him. Perhaps it was a certain admiration for his determination to reorder our lives to suit his, or perhaps it was his undeniable need for love and companionship. In any event my hostility was gradually worn down and I developed, if not a love, then certainly a sense of fondness for Snuffle. As these feelings developed so my breathing eased. The fur grew back on his legs and the sight of our little black ball playing so gently with Elodie was heart-warming to watch. If she pulled his hair, stamped on his feet, or stuck her fingers in his eyes, Snuffle reacted in the most mild-mannered way, retreating to his den, before minutes later returning to play again.

All these positive developments in my relationship with Snuffle nearly dissipated just days before Christmas when I dropped into the vet for Snuffle to be microchipped and have his rabies jab administered. Our arrival in the waiting room generated the type of hysteria usually reserved for teenage pop stars. Snuffle was mobbed by humans and dogs alike.

'Isn't he beautiful?'

'What breed is he?'

'Look at the paws!'

'Oh, I could take him home now.'

During my first few visits I'd found this type of response hard to understand; however, in the dog world Snuffle was something of a rarity. One old lady explained that the breed had nearly been wiped out during World War Two and only now had petit chien lion numbers started to recover. I'd begun to take pride in the admiration in which he was held. I'd even given him a special brush-up for this visit to the vet's.

Once the acclamation died down, I sat and waited and Snuffle pottered around indulging in the unattractive habit of sniffing the bottoms of other dogs. Pinned to a noticeboard were cards from numerous dog-related businesses: training schools, hairdressers, clothing and collar makers, even a *traiteur* (caterer) offering a five-course festive dog menu. To pass the time I made conversation with the old couple sitting next to me. The man wore a threadbare tracksuit, the lady a thin flowery dress covered by a dirty overcoat. Unlike the rest of the clientele they'd shown little interest in Snuffle; instead, they sat holding each other's hands and glancing anxiously at the clock on the wall. Unusually, they didn't seem to have a pet with them.

'Where's your dog?' I asked. Immediately I felt the question had been a mistake.

'In the other room.' The man motioned to the swing doors.

'What's wrong with him?' I blundered on.

'Old age – he was eighteen last week.' The woman wiped a tear from her eye and the realisation dawned on me that their pet was being put down.

'I'm sorry,' I said and the room returned to silence.

The mood in the room lightened with the arrival of a mother, daughter and cage containing a writhing, hopping bundle of rabbits. It was hard to estimate but there could easily have been twenty of these babies. I eavesdropped as the mother talked to the receptionist.

'We need to have them sexed.'

'They look a little young,' said the receptionist, pulling one from the cage. 'What's the rush?'

'A month ago, we had two male rabbits – now look!'

'Ah, it's always difficult to tell the sex.'

'Well, Zing is now Zingella, and we're anxious to divide this lot. Otherwise we'll soon have a hundred rabbits.'

'Still, it's too soon.' The receptionist paused and examined the rabbits again. 'There is another option. They're the right breed. You could keep them together and set up an *élevage*. I know butchers are always looking for good suppliers.'

At this point I expected the rest of the clientele to show some discretion. The girl, who could only have been seven, was looking anxiously at her mother. They'd come to the vet's for help, not to be told to sharpen their carving knives. However, the empty bellies all around me were rumbling.

'They're delicious roasted with a little rosemary.'

'Always dust the skin with sea salt first.'

'Try a champagne and cream sauce.'

'*Magnifique.*'

'Mr Ivey?' One of the vets, Matilde, a woman in her mid forties, called me through. This was our third appointment and gradually Matilde had correctly formed the view that I didn't have a clue what I was doing. The failed house-training, the fact that Snuffle still insisted on play-biting, his skittishness and excitability were all blamed on me. I closed the door behind me, just catching a final recipe:

'Stewed with olives, tomatoes and Provençal herbs.' The prospective chef, quite unbelievably, was the mother of the little girl.

The vet's room smelt of chemicals and strong detergent. Clean, reflective surfaces amplified the over-bright lighting. Posters warning of the effects of worms and ticks lined the wall. A credit card machine and invoice book sat expectantly on the desk. Snuffle whined, twisting in my arms. He was panting heavily.

Matilde expertly took Snuffle from me and placed him on the brushed metal examination table. Forcing her hands into his mouth, she examined his teeth, then she picked up each paw and pressed for tenderness. Running her hands through his fur she encountered several of the burs which Snuffle collected with such regularity that I swear they were breeding in his coat.

'He's not in bad shape; teeth need a clean, paws could do with some wet-weather wax, the coat needs more grooming, but overall healthy.' The verdict was delivered in an emotionless tone which made me feel incredibly guilty.

'Have you bought the rectal thermometer yet?'

I shook my head. Taking Elodie's temperature was one thing, but sticking a thermometer up my dog's bottom was just too unappealing. Snuffle had yet to be prescribed any suppositories but given the French proclivity for administering medicine in this way, the day was surely coming.

'Right, hold him tight, I'll do the injections – rabies and microchip, you said.' I watched as Matilde took the first syringe. Snuffle began to shiver with fear. He'd been to the vet's enough to know what was coming. As instructed by Matilde I held him steady, trapping him with my forearm and bracing him for the injection.

'Here we go – number one.' Snuffle whimpered as the needle pierced his skin.

'And number two,' Matilde announced, unmoved by my ongoing struggle to hold Snuffle. His legs kicked vigorously against my chest and I grappled with my other arm to quieten him. The needle approached and Snuffle's eyes rolled to the ceiling and his whole body bucked in anger. There was a whimper and then I felt a sharp prick on my forefinger.

'Ouch!' I let go of Snuffle and shook my hand. 'You caught me.'

'It's not possible,' said Matilde, ignoring my claim until I held my finger under her eyes. There was a small glistening red pinprick of blood.

'*Merde!*' Matilde was flustered. She crossed to her cabinet, knocking some bandages to the floor as she went. She needn't have been so worried, it was barely a scratch, and I could joke with my friends about having a dog microchip in my finger. Matilde emptied copious quantities of a brown antiseptic onto a sterile wipe and pressed it to my finger.

'Are you feeling all right?' She looked genuinely concerned, as if she feared I might swoon and faint. Until this point I hadn't realised what lily-livered, pathetic patients most of the French were: a drop of blood and it was like they'd had a limb blown off.

'Perhaps we should get you to the hospital for a check-up.' Matilde reached for the phone and I laughed at the ridiculousness of it all. Jingoistic World War Two humour was dated, but sometimes too relevant to blot from the mind. No wonder they needed our help to beat the Germans. Only the Italians, with their fastidious love of shiny-buttoned uniforms, could compete on squeamishness.

As these thoughts passed through my head, logic took over from humour. Something was wrong. What if Matilde had injected the microchip first? That would mean the second jab was rabies. Millions were spent keeping England free of rabies. A whole pet passport scheme had been instigated to prevent the spread of a disease which, as I understood it, could be fatal. I pictured myself on a hospital bed, foam bubbling viscously from my mouth, saying a final farewell to my family. And all because we'd got a dog.

'What was it?' I blurted out, suddenly concerned.

'I thought you knew.' Matilde looked surprised. Her grimace seemed to confirm the worst.

'What's going to happen to me?'

'Maybe nothing at all,' said Matilde. 'Maybe you'll bleep at the airport.'

Chapter 12

New Year's Day dawned bright and crisp. The fields were covered by a frost that crunched underfoot and wisps of mist still slept under the overhanging branches of trees. As the sun climbed so did my feeling of well-being. A trip to the village *boulangerie* reinforced my new sense of purpose, as I was stopped and kissed in the street by nearly a dozen different people. The conversation was always identical.

'*Bonne année, bonne santé, plein de bonnes choses, mais le plus important c'est la santé. Bisous aux filles.*'

Translated this meant: 'Happy New Year, I hope it's filled with loads and loads of wonderful things but most of all I hope you are healthy. Kisses to the girls.'

In the *boulangerie* I bought a slice of *gâteau des rois*, a marzipan-based cake, symbolic of the gifts the wise men gave to Jesus. It tasted rather like a deluxe *croissant aux amandes*, and I ordered myself a strong black coffee in the cafe as an accompaniment. On the second bite my teeth hit something solid and I pulled a little plastic figurine of a king from my mouth. Each cake had one such figure baked into it, and the person who found it in their slice was guaranteed good luck for the entire year.

It was warm enough to sit outside. I placed the figure on the table and relaxed back into my chair. Snuffle panted happily at my feet and the occasional villager hurried by on their way to buy bread. Absent-mindedly I studied the faded flaking paint on the shutters, and the sun-bleached writing above the shops, proclaiming the names of the proprietors and their trades. Many of them were alien occupations which had long since died out in England, for example *'Menuiserie'* (repairing all the wooden windows which had *'descendu'*), or *'Ébénisterie'* (custom making furniture).

A sign in a nearby window advertised the services of a *'Nounou'* – a kind of impromptu nursery, set up by a mother looking to make some extra cash. Another handwritten sign offered jams for sale. On a daily basis my eyes filtered out these little fragments of Provençal life. A knock on a door, and within moments I could be feasting on plum jam. I could even see the branches of the tree arching over the garden wall. I finished the final sip of my bitter black coffee, dark, viscous and heady. Another resolution for the coming year would be to appreciate, as if for the first time, the place in which I lived.

Back at home my new resolve was tested almost immediately. There are many pleasant ways to spend the morning of New Year's Day: a long leisurely lie-in, breakfast with the paper, perhaps a conversation with a loved one full of gentle reflections on the year that has just passed and hopes for the one to come. Alternatively, one can just treat it as any other morning. Manu, our landlord, favoured the latter option, and the banging began soon after ten. For a couple of hours there was the usual amount of noise. Then at midday, suddenly silence.

Manu appeared at our door, coated in a layer of white dust, looking like an actor who'd overdone the zombie make-up.

'Didn't realise there would be so much dust,' he beamed, clearly happy that work on the conversion of the rest of the farmhouse was beginning. 'You're going to lose water for a couple of hours.'

'*Bonne année, bonne santé, plein de bonnes choses, mais le plus important c'est la santé,*' chimed Tanya and I in unison, managing to behave as if Manu's appearance was an everyday occurrence.

'*Bonne année, bonne santé, plein de bonnes choses,*' echoed Manu, although how a man who was about to turn off our water supply could wish us a new year full of good things was beyond me.

'It'll be the electricity next week; always be back on by dusk.'

For the rest of the day we were treated to a master class in how to get work done in Provence. A lorry load of labourers arrived and the men cut, hacked and pulled away at everything in their path. Manu strode through the billowing dust, cajoling and persuading the workers, heaving bricks, stones, boilers, bathtubs and cookers from the back of the truck. Quite where he got all the parts and the workers from on a public holiday was beyond me.

All this activity only served to highlight our own lack of progress. When the engineer's report had finally arrived just before Christmas I thought the final excuse not to price our job had disappeared. I was wrong. All that had happened was that the explanations for the missing quotes became more colourful, with the Provençal D-roads suddenly sounding as dangerous as the trunk route out of Basra.

'Someone drove into my van.'

'I hit a wild boar.'

'I was clamped.'

The last excuse made me spit out my morning coffee in disbelief. Provençal parking is an art form, a piece of theatre, a concerto of crimes. A street corner, a raised curb, backwards, sideways, practically upside down – no matter how small the space the Provençaux will manage to ram their car into it. Once

I'd even seen a 4x4 with its rear wheels hanging off the side of a bridge. Encouraging this creative approach were the police, who considered that they had far more important things to do than hand out parking tickets, like wearing reflector shades and looking intimidating.

Imagine the time and effort that went into affixing a clamp, all that heaving of metal and wrangling with chains, and for what purpose? Simply to take it off again. The Provençaux might be tight with their money but they were even more parsimonious with their work. Hence, clamping has never and will never exist here; in fact, I was surprised that the artisan in question had even heard of the practice, let alone ventured to offer it as an excuse.

Late on New Year's Day, when the drilling had finally stopped, Tanya and I tried to reason our way through the web of half-truths we were being offered. On the one hand we had to trust these people. We'd selected them to build our house, we'd dined and laughed with them. They all seemed good, honest, hardworking men. They had families like us, and they knew how important it was to get our house built. Equally, we'd understood when we took on the project that Provence was a notoriously difficult place for a foreigner to get work done.

For three years we'd lived with the local habits, adapted to them and embraced them, and now was no time to lose patience. However, there was also the creeping feeling that we were being taken advantage of. The speed with which Manu had started his renovation showed what could be done. Yet here we were, having waited for nearly a year, and not a single brick had been laid. Plus, we also had only the vaguest idea of how much the whole project was going to cost. Our sense of helplessness was exacerbated by the fact that there didn't seem to be anybody else we could employ. Normally we might have asked Delphine for a recommendation, or other people within the village community, but everyone knew we were working with Ange and therefore to ask advice could be interpreted as sacking him behind his back.

Our problems came to a head the following week. We'd been looking around some houses with Ange, trying to determine what type of wall we would like. The plans Ange had been working with assumed a simple monomur construction, with the insulating material built into the brick, which he was going to soundproof with a layer of special material. After a lot of walking around, banging, knocking and shouting, we decided to opt for a thicker, traditional brick wall. No more was said until I received a phone message from Ange explaining the plans would have to be resubmitted to the engineers, to check that the foundations could take the extra load. There would be a charge of an additional thousand euros, and of course a further delay in Ange producing his final price. Bearing in mind the engineers had taken three months to produce their first report, it was a major setback.

As a result, I sent a carefully worded email to Ange explaining how upset we were at all the delays. Somehow he interpreted it as a direct challenge to his professional competence. Half an hour later his car crunched up the drive and he entered our house, waving a handful of files. There was no kiss for Elodie, no time to offer the customary beer and if Tanya had suggested nibbles, I suspect they would have been flung back across the room.

Ange had clearly not had time to clean up. His work overalls were stained white with paint and plaster and the grime of a day's hard labour clung to his face and in the calluses of his hands. I noticed that he was shaking as he pulled up a seat.

'Do you know what these are?'

I shook my head.

'All the projects I've worked on in the last five years. Look at them: big jobs, bigger than yours. My clients are important people; Parisians, Americans, the English, financiers with millions to spend and they trusted me. Why? Because I am honest. I do what I say I am going to do, and that's a rarity round here, and then you send me this,' Ange slapped a printout of my email down on the table, 'insulting my competence. Tell me what to build and I'll get it built. That's what I do, but not for you anymore. I'm here to resign. I don't want your work.'

Tanya diplomatically left the room. I sat listening, not quite believing what I was hearing. Perhaps when translated into French the language of the email had not been as neutral as I'd imagined. Even so, the aggression and chest beating was inexplicable. If Ange was like this now, how would he be when we encountered problems later on in the build? As he ranted I sat calculating our options. We'd come a long way with Ange and we were nearly ready to start. If we stuck with the existing walls, then the diggers could start rolling soon.

Alternatively, we'd have to find a new builder, new electrician, new plumber and so on. There were a few other names we could try, but the local tradesmen operated a little like a cartel; once one of them had their teeth into a job, the others wouldn't take it.

Despite the unfairness of Ange's reaction I rationalised that it was better, if possible, to stick with him rather than start all over again. There was also the fallout in the village to consider. We saw Ange almost on a daily basis, in the bar, *boulangerie* or *tabac*. On the roads he'd hoot his horn as he passed and Elodie had even learnt to recognise his blue van from the distinctive large roof rack. If we were going to work with someone else, we should have chosen to do so from the outset. Now, circumstances made him almost un-sackable.

'I am sorry you misinterpreted my email, it was never meant to be critical,' I began, but Ange quickly interrupted, shoving more photos of his work under my nose.

'See this villa in Saint-Rémy? We did this for a sheikh. Look at the curve on the balcony, look at the finish, the attention to detail. And see this *maison de ville* in Nîmes, totally renovated in just a couple of months, all the old stone work exposed.'

I nodded along. The pictures were impressive. I also realised that Ange wasn't behaving like a man who wanted to resign. If he'd really wanted to give up his job, he could have just phoned or not bothered to return my call. Instead, he'd come and put on a show. I'd hurt his pride and he wanted me to know it.

'I've never doubted you do excellent work.'

'Then why the email? There's nothing I can do if you change your mind about the walls. And the engineers, these intellectual types from the city – it's not my fault if they sit on their hands for a couple of months, blowing figures out of their arses.'

'As I said, I am sorry if you misinterpreted the email, you have to appreciate that we're in a difficult position – we need to get started, we need to move house.'

'Well, you also need to find yourself another project manager.' Ange made a show of gathering his papers.

'Come on Ange, we can still work together. I've apologised, let's move on.'

Ange stood by the door. His head turned towards his car and then back to us. I've often thought our lives would have been much simpler if he'd walked out at this point, but he didn't. Instead he said, 'If you can live with the walls, we can start in a week.'

Tanya re-entered the room with Elodie in her arms. She'd been listening to every word.

'We can live with the walls,' she said definitively.

'I'll call you Monday.' Ange tipped his baseball cap and departed as if nothing had happened. His jaunty gait needed only to be complemented by a whistled tune and the picture of the carefree labourer would be complete.

Tanya and I were too tired to overanalyse. We were simply delighted that the house would finally get going. Stud walls were better than no walls. Our happiness would have been complete but Snuffle chose this moment to trot over and urinate at my feet. Almost without thinking I let out a rumbling growl of anger. Elodie laughed and copied me. Snuffle fled outside.

Chapter 13

There is a moment every morning when the countryside takes a pause. The sun has yet to fully warm the land but there's enough heat to dissipate the night's moisture, and banish the lingering scents of rooting animals and decaying vegetation. The exact timing of this moment changes every day. Sometimes the interlude is too short for a man to identify but animals always sense it, ceasing their activity and holding their noses quivering to the air, confused by the absence of smells. The birds stop singing, the dogs choke back their barks, and cats pause mid stride. Everything waits. It's in this vacuum that a man working alone has the best chance of finding truffles. Momentarily his sense of smell is heightened and with the help of the flies, it's theoretically possible to do away with the need for a dog or a pig. Or so the experts said.

One early January morning I tested this theory, waiting until I felt the moment was approaching, when the last trails of mist vanished and the first whisper of warmth appeared in the air. I rushed to our plot, parking the car against the fringe of the trees and clambering up the path towards the oaks. Amid the trees everything was pleasingly still. I stood for a while, watching, acclimatising before breaking through the barrier of silence that area the size of my hand, probing deeper and deeper into the soil. Nothing but roots and earth and a woody smell which made it impossible to distinguish the scent of truffles. I widened my search and worked quicker, tearing at the soil, until I had prescribed a semicircle around my knees.

My arms ached from the unaccustomed motion, and yet still I dug, sure that somewhere nearby I would find a truffle. The flies and my nose had pointed me to it, but I'd already searched the immediate area and to probe anymore would be to risk next year's harvest. I'd read that Italians had once harvested truffles like potatoes, churning the soil with heavy machines until the tubers were unearthed. For one year it was incredibly efficient, but the following year no truffles were found.

I rose to my feet, and started to move forward with my stick. The sun was just that bit higher in the sky, and the black shadow of a hawk speared towards the earth. There was a rumble of traffic noise from the distant village, followed quickly by the crack of a hunter's shotgun and the bell of his hound. A gust of wind sent the leaves chasing around my feet. I sniffed the air and smelt nothing but the first puffs of smoke from the hearths of the nearest houses. The moment was gone. Quickly I began to doubt whether it hadn't been a fantasy – me so at one with nature that I could smell truffles. One of my nostrils had been crushed in a rugby accident as a child. Wave smelling salts under it and I wouldn't recoil. Yet foolishly I'd believed that I could smell a truffle buried under inches of soil.

For some time I'd been asking advice on the best method of training a truffle dog. The information should have been easy to find and there was no shortage of amateurs keen to offer their opinion. Market traders in particular were full of tips and suggestions.

had held me transfixed. I walked slowly between the truffle trees, sun on my face, stick twitching in front of me. The only sounds were the brush of denim against denim and the crunch of my footfalls. The smell of truffles was ingrained in my mind. At this time of year the scent was always on the air, drifting through the markets, churning from the fans of restaurants, lingering in the dusty boots of labourers' cars. The problem was isolating it.

Now, in this otherwise odourless moment, I imagined I could smell truffles amid our trees. My eyes followed the cracks in the ground, charting their mazy progress, looking for unnaturally large openings that might hint at the development of a tuber. Amid the dusting of crumpled brown oak leaves I searched for bare areas, where grass no longer grappled to reach the sunlight. These telltale burns or chicken feet, as the Provençaux called them, were the quickest way to locate a truffle. I scattered the leaves with my stick, hunting for an absence of growth, squinting for the dizzy flight of flies in the weak sunlight, and sniffing, always sniffing, pulling the air in quick snorting gasps like an addict in need of a fix. I was convinced I smelled the rich earthy smell of truffles. They were tantalisingly close.

The wind shifted and for a short time I lost the scent. I stood still, waiting, pleased by the absence of sound; another snort of air and there it was again, weaker but distinguishable, somewhere ahead of me. I moved forward, snapping the stick this way and that through leaves. The heavy tools of my new trade clunked at my side – a miniature trowel and pitchfork with which to careful dislodge the earth from around the black diamonds.

Two flies snapped into the air, one piggybacking on the ot in a mating dance. Quickly I squatted down, scattering ac and dead foliage until I reached the bare earth. I fumbled a drawstring which fastened my tools in their bag and they tumbling to the ground. I began to dig, slowly at first, cleari

'Hide slivers of truffle in a saucisson,' offered Rene at the charcuterie stand.

'Any particular type?'

'Donkey; it's the hardest for me to sell.'

And so it went on – the honey lady advised dipping a truffle in honey, the sock salesman insisted that his pure fibres would pick up and hold the scent of the truffle, and the hat man suggested a small doggie cap soaked overnight in truffle oil, so that wherever Snuffle went he would be accompanied by the hum of the tuber. The most impartial advice we received came from the vegetable vendor. His father had had several truffle dogs and always maintained that the most economical way of training them was with a tennis ball.

Back at home I prepared the ball, cutting the outer casing and inserting the slivers of black diamond. Evolution, at least, was on my side. Truffles were essentially highly developed reproductive organs creating the spores that spread the truffle fungus. Unlike other mushrooms, truffles survived not by releasing their spores but by encouraging animals to eat them and then deposit them in a distant place. To do so truffles had to ensure that they were found; hence, over the years they had developed an overwhelmingly powerful smell – the Chanel No. 5 of the animal kingdom, supposedly irresistible to any scavenger.

'Fetch,' I cried as I tossed the ball towards the distant vines. One bounce, then another and the ball ducked out of sight. Snuffle looked up at me and then settled down on all fours, rolled over onto his back and barked at me to tickle him.

I collected the ball. This time I held it in front of Snuffle's nose. He sniffed and quickly lost interest. 'Fetch!' The ball came to rest in the same area. Snuffle looked after it, looked at me, and rolled over on his back and barked.

Perhaps, I reasoned, I needed to throw the ball into the sunshine rather than the shade. Once more I held the truffle ball out for him to sniff. I noted a little more interest this time. 'Fetch!' I threw it with a gentle high lob, the ball landing no more than 10 metres away. Surely even the most lethargic of dogs would be suckered by the seductive odour of the truffle wafting towards us. 'Go on, fetch,' I encouraged. Looking down I discovered that Snuffle was asleep.

Half an hour later the session continued inside. Tanya held the ball out in front of her for Snuffle to see. I then put my hands over Snuffle's eyes and Tanya hid behind the sofa.

'Find the ball.' Snuffle padded around the house, nosing in cupboards, eating the odd crumb from the floor and then eventually encountering Tanya.

'Well done, good boy,' we both encouraged, handing Snuffle some cheese as a reward. We repeated the exercise, this time hiding just the ball.

'Find the ball, Snuffle, find the ball.' Snuffle immediately jumped up on the sofa and began to scratch vigorously, pawing at the covering and circling aggressively. Putting his front paws down, he raised his head, wagged his tail and barked vigorously. It was a textbook way of indicating that he'd found something. Unfortunately for us, whatever was hidden under the cushion wasn't a truffle. Maybe a previous tenant had had a cocaine habit.

Over the next few days we continued to devote long periods of time to training. The tennis ball, we decided, wasn't effective, and so we tried truffle-laced saucisson and truffle-laced cheese. Nothing worked. At the beginning of one session I forgot to slice the truffle and instead just played hide and seek with a piece of plain old Gruyère. Inexplicably, Snuffle's level of interest was much higher. That evening I offered him a small plate of leftover truffle risotto. Snuffle sniffed the dish and then turned and walked away, curling up in a distant corner of the house.

In desperation the following night I prepared what I believe is a culinary one-off, a dish so extreme that not even the most experimental of chefs could ever have conceived it: *poulet fermier de Bresse aux croquants de truffes.*

To encourage Snuffle to eat, I'd starved him all day, and shortly before I presented the dish he was circling the house, nose to the ground, desperately trying to find even the smallest portion of food.

'Snuffle,' I called, clanking the dog bowls together to signify supper time. First I introduced small slithers of lightly poached free-range chicken. Then I took out the cheese grater and shaved copious amounts of fresh truffle over the top, before completing the meal with a handful of high quality dried dog food. *'Voilà,'* I cried extravagantly as I placed the meal before my salivating pooch.

Snuffle sniffed the bowl, looked plaintively up at me, and then began to whine as if in genuine distress. It wasn't difficult to read his thoughts – why the hell had I wrecked a perfectly good meal, a meal he'd been waiting for all day, by shaving truffle all over it? I looked disdainfully back at him as well – of all the dogs in the world, why did I have to get lumbered with the one stubborn enough to resist the supposedly irresistible scent of truffles?

A week later I happened to be in southern Luberon delivering wine and I stopped off at one of my favourite villages, Cucuron. Offer me a chance to have a glass of wine or a coffee anywhere in Provence, and I would renounce the glitz and glamour of more celebrated villages such as Gordes and instead opt for the simple pleasure of sitting beside the plane-tree-lined *étang* in Cucuron. The play of the light on water and the arrangement of the chairs, so that dappled sunlight teases the face, has combined to produce the most harmonious place to sit and contemplate life – out of high season, of course.

As I toyed with the ends of my coffee I felt refreshed and upbeat about life. I'd just sold a couple of hundred bottles of wine, the house-building project was finally coming together, Manu had nearly finished the renovation of the new apartment in the farmhouse, Elodie and Tanya both seemed happy – all I needed to complete the positive picture was to show a little more patience with Snuffle. Lost in my thoughts I didn't notice Eric Sapet, the chef of the adjacent restaurant, La Petite Maison, pull up a seat next to me. Years ago I'd written a review of his restaurant for a local magazine and we'd been friends ever since.

'*Salut, Jamie.*'

'*Salut, Eric.*'

Over his shoulder, through the open side door to his kitchen, I could see his *sous-chefs*. One was methodically working his way through a tray of lobsters, picking the meat from each of the claws, another was glazing an army of lamb chops. Shortly after my review Eric had gained a Michelin star. The accolade hadn't changed him and he remained very much a chef's chef. Small and round with a hunchback from bending over too many pots, his physique declared his love of his chosen profession. For the quality of the food, prices at La Petite Maison remained low. The best thing about Eric, though, was not his cooking but his jovial, friendly nature.

For a few minutes we sat and exchanged news, and talked a little business. Almost as an afterthought, I mentioned my truffle dog training and getting ahead of myself a little I asked where he bought his truffles and at what price.

'We pay around nine hundred euros per kilo before Christmas and New Year and about six hundred euros thereafter. I offer truffle dishes until the end of February; after then I find the taste declines.'

I'd feared that the truffle trade might work like the wine business, with restaurants demanding large discounts and then marking up the product for sale three or even four times. According to Eric, though, the truffle traders were able to set and maintain a price. Demand for the Provençal truffle was intense, with orders coming in from restaurants across the world. Moreover, top chefs only used the fresh product, unwilling to sacrifice the crunchy bite which disappeared on freezing. The season was therefore three months long and truffles were always scarce, with demand outstripping supply and the price per kilo rising consistently with the years. If I could just find some truffles, it appeared selling them would be easy.

'One thing, though – I only buy from wholesalers.'

My vision of the easy life, sitting on my terrace, piles of truffles around my feet, taking ever higher bids from international chefs ('Sorry Heston, there's nothing I can do – it's nine hundred euros a kilo or they're off to Gordon') vanished.

'Why?' I asked in an embarrassingly plaintive voice.

'First, there's theft; if I buy from just anybody, I have no way of knowing where the truffle has come from; secondly, I only buy truffles with a certificate of origin. I don't have time to examine them all, and eventually some shark is going to slip some Chinese ones in a batch.'

'Are all restaurants the same?'

'If they were, nobody would steal truffles.'

'But the reputable truffle hunter sells to a wholesaler, who presumably takes a cut?'

'Exactly.'

At least with truffles the price could justify a middleman, whereas with wine it often couldn't. Before I even had to worry about these issues, there was still the problem of training Snuffle.

'What have you tried?' asked Eric.

'Saucisson, cheese, risottos, eggs, salads, you name it – if it's got truffle in it, he won't touch it.'

'And yet you say he's a high-maintenance dog.'

'Very,' I said, a little too assertively.

Eric grinned. 'There's one thing you might like to experiment with; mind you, it's not going to come cheap.'

He took a pen from the top pocket of his chef's whites and began jotting down a recipe. To read was to salivate.

Cooking with truffles is so simple that even a child can master the art. First, wash the truffle and scrape away any excess mud. Then, cut the truffle in half and slice or grate over anything from salad to scrambled egg. There are, of course, a few tricks of the trade; for example, if cooking a risotto, it's best to leave the rice and truffle in the same jar for a couple of days. This way the individual grains release the infused flavour during cooking, which is then highlighted by the grating, moments before serving, of fresh truffle over the risotto.

It's also important to be generous – at least 10 grams of truffle per plate is necessary, 15 if you are feeling rich or courting a partner. Apparently, the effect of excessive consumption is so pronounced that for some orders of monks eating truffles is inconsistent with their vow of chastity, so try 20 grams if you have misplaced the Viagra and want to pep up your sex life.

The fact that truffles are often married with the most basic ingredients means that despite the price tag they are accessible to all. The most famous truffle chef in France is Bruno, who runs an eponymous restaurant near the village of Lorgues in the Var. One might expect his signature dish to be flamboyantly expensive, perhaps a *filet de veau aux truffes*, but instead its base is one of the most prosaic foods in the world. Served in company canteens topped with anything from prawns to chilli, microwaved in desperation by drunk students, the humble baked potato has no gastronomic pretensions, until, that is, it gets into the hands of Bruno. With a sprinkling of truffle and the secrets of his kitchen he transforms something typically coated in baked beans into mouthfuls of pleasure, where the earthiness of the truffle momentarily blends with the ethereal.

There is one golden rule of truffle cuisine – never ever expose truffles to high temperatures. Baking, frying, poaching – anything other than scattering them over a prepared dish will kill the flavour and your investment. Rules, however, as Eric Sapet explained, can always be bent. The Provençal truffle, unlike, for example, the Italian white, can sustain a degree of heat and Eric's recipe, which he explained was an old classic of French cooking, took full advantage of this fact. It was, he claimed, an unsurpassable gastronomic experience.

We tried the recipe that evening. Snuffle, who usually disappeared at the barest whiff of truffle, sat on the floor with his tail wagging and his nose quivering. Reaching for the oven gloves I checked the colour of the pastry. It was just off the required perfect golden brown. I returned the dish to the heat, noting Snuffle's annoyed bark. There was a chance that we'd found the dish that would cure his phobia.

Tanya laid the table and poured two glasses of wine. The smell of the truffle was almost unbelievably strong. Our open-plan kitchen/diner/sitting room was suffused with a heavy earthy odour.

'It's like living in a cave,' I said as I pulled the dish from the oven, trying not to trip over Snuffle as I did so.

If the pastry had served its purpose, it would have shielded the truffle from the heat, allowing it to gently season the other ingredients during the baking process. With the point of my knife I punctured the protective shell and dodged a jet of steam pungent enough to send a monk scurrying for sanctuary.

'Here goes...' I cut into the millefeuille of truffle and foie gras, serving three thin slices. Tanya and I tasted. A silence followed.

Then both of us helped ourselves to another mouthful. Tanya looked up at the ceiling. Judging by the flavours in my mouth she could only be offering thanks to the heavens.

'This is quite unbelievable. It feels like I'm not tasting truffle, I almost am a truffle,' she finally said.

'It's like they fed the goose truffle for its entire life,' I added, shaking my head in amazement.

'It's a shame to give it to the dog.'

'A real shame.' Both our forks met in mock battle.

'The French would think it sacrilegious.'

Tanya mastered her hunger and put the dog bowl on the floor.

Snuffle padded over, paced in a circle, and sniffed the air. Glancing up at both of us he feigned indifference and turned away, chasing his tail in a circle until he once again faced the bowl.

'If he's not going to eat it, then I am.' I reached for the food.

Snuffle was quicker, diving forward and landing like a pouncing cat with both paws either side of the bowl. Momentarily he inhaled and then with a delighted bark he ate his portion in one bite, before repeatedly licking the bowl and begging for more.

Chapter 14

The day had finally arrived. To celebrate we decided to have breakfast in the village cafe. The winter had been mild and the tables and chairs basked in the March sunshine. Stray dogs ambled past, delivery vans left their hazard lights winking in the street, and high above our heads flaking wooden shutters were thrown open. There was a pleasing hum of activity in which to sit and soak up the medicinal warmth of the sun. A messy dusting of pastry fell across the table as I opened the bag from the *boulangerie*. The croissants were still warm to the touch and neither of us had the willpower to wait until the coffee arrived.

I'd put on my best shirt and trousers and Tanya had also chosen something a little more dressy than usual. There would inevitably be photos, and in years to come we would look back at this moment. Elodie, probably to her future chagrin, had been forced into a sailor outfit from a smart boutique in Avignon. I thought it looked ridiculous, but Tanya assured me it was very à la mode.

'Nice day for it,' said Tanya, pulling her sunglasses down.

'Couldn't be better,' I agreed.

'Feels like we're shipwrecked sailors finally sighting land.'

'Give me a palm tree, a pina colada, and a turtle to tow me ashore.'

Nerves had put me in a frivolous mood. At times over the previous ten months I'd thought the project would never start. Now we were ready I was overcome with relief. All the administration, the wrangling over prices, the scheduling of the work, the worry over the foundations had finally come to an end. Brick would be placed upon brick and the home we hoped to live in for the rest of our lives would gradually emerge.

The one reservation I still had was my relationship with Ange. In the musical *Chicago*, the lawyer Billy Flynn sings a song entitled 'Razzle Dazzle'. Flynn is defending a guilty client and he knows the only way to succeed is to distract the jury with a combination of magic tricks and fancy dancing. What follows on stage is an amazing combination of intricate footwork and sleight of hand.

As we sat in the cafe, waiting to make our way up to the building site, I couldn't help but feel that Ange had being singing his own version of 'Razzle Dazzle' the morning he'd threatened to resign. Instead of being called to account, he'd left with an insouciant whistle and a click of the heels. Even now with the bulldozer waiting to go, there were still some grey areas on costs. However, we'd accepted we were in Provence and that pricing would never be as tight as we wanted.

'Darlings, did I forget your anniversary?'

Delphine pulled up a seat and the waiter instantly disappeared to fetch her regular espresso. We must have looked confused.

'The finery, dears – I've never seen the two of you look so resplendent.'

'We're starting to build today.'

'Well, congratulations.' Delphine crumbled a sugar cube into her coffee, clapping her hands together and dusting the remains onto the floor for Fifi.

'Why don't you come along, watch the ground being broken?'

'Delighted.'

'We're going down, rather than up; six metres of foundations.'

'I'll need about the same for your tooth.' Sitting nearby our perma-tanned dentist had overheard our conversation and couldn't let the opportunity to remind me of the root canal I was putting off pass.

'You said wait until the house was finished,' I stalled.

'No pain?'

'No.'

'I guess we'll keep waiting.'

I made a mental note to book myself in around the new year, just after we'd moved in. By then my tooth would be throbbing enough for me to justify contributing to the dentist's annual St Barts trip.

The caffeine from the coffee kicked in and cleared my mind. We needed to be on site before ten so that I could take the confirmatory call from the bank and officially give Ange the go-ahead. Tanya and Delphine were busy catching up on village gossip; meanwhile, I mentally ticked off the bank's requirements – quotes for everything the mortgage covered, insurance certificates for all the builders, and life insurance for Tanya and myself. In all, I'd sent them one hundred pages, having checked and rechecked the bundle. Nothing was missing, so why was I getting increasingly worried?

The sun illuminated another couple of tables, and a local vigneron pulled up a chair. His face was red and cracked from the early morning chill and the mud on his kneecaps and fresh scars on his hands attested to the hours of hard work.

'*Salut.*' He waved.

'*Salut,*' I called back.

'How about repeating that wine tasting, only this time in the summer?'

'Why?'

'Nobody will have flu.'

The English-French wine tasting had occurred during what was now remembered as one of the worst outbreaks of the virus ever. If anybody disputed the severity of the epidemic, the tasting was referred to as proof: 'Imagine it, people even preferred the English wine.' The joke never seemed to tire. People were so fond of the gag, it continued to introduce new customers.

Across the road a couple entered the *notaire*'s office. They kissed as they pushed through the door and the golden plaque denoting the lawyer's office glinted above their heads. Quite possibly they were about to buy a house. I hoped for their sake they weren't trying to build one. How naive we'd been that spring day as we made the purchase, with the suited government official soothing any nerves with jokes he must make on a daily basis: 'I have to warn you, Provence is an earthquake zone – it's not like LA but once a whole *champ de lavande* was destroyed… I know there's no house, but *c'est la France*, you still need a termite inspection.' Each gag was accompanied by an apologetic chortle. At least they'd broken up the monotony of the hour-long appointment during which each line of the contract was read out loud.

I took the last sips of my coffee and fumbled in my pockets for some euros. Tanya clipped Elodie into the pushchair and we strode confidently up the road. We were off to build a house.

Up at the *chantier* the full glory of the day revealed itself. The sky was, in the words of one local painter, 'almost absurdly blue'. At this time of year, he argued, it was too clear and brilliant to paint, obtaining a luminosity that defied the imagination and which would ruin all but the most impressionist of canvasses. To me, the lack of blemishes, the absence of a stray cloud, or the white plume of a distant jet, just the rich, luscious, unending blue was uplifting, but also somehow unexpectedly disturbing, leaving a nagging feeling that life could never be this perfect.

As we got out of the car our feet dispersed the remains of a delicate dew. The mild winter meant that already the first trails of blossom floated by and the grass beneath our feet was lush and dotted with wild flowers. The land resonated with the smell of new growth, of shoots disturbing wet earth and buds breaking through bark. On the far side of the plot the engine of a JCB digger was whirring, churning out clouds of black smoke that drifted towards us like miniature thunderstorms. A few metres away a series of orange markings showed the footprint of the building.

'Did someone murder a house?' joked Delphine as she lit a cigarette and took in the view. 'You guys are going to love it here. The space, the view and, from what Ange tells me of the build cost, not a bad investment.'

'Let's hope so.'

Ange clambered down from the distant digger, his trademark cap falling to the ground as he did so. Scooping it up, he hurried across the field towards us. I'd half feared that one of his frequent last-minute emergencies would have pulled him off to another *chantier*. But here he was, and if he was true to his word, our project was now his priority.

'*Salut, Ange.*'

'*Salut, Delphine.*'

Ange kissed all the girls, and then almost as an afterthought included me. Our stubble grated uncomfortably together. His aftershave was so strong that just a little more friction would have lit a fire.

'Do you have the cheque?' Ange was referring to the 5 per cent payment which we'd agreed should pass over when construction began. I tapped my jeans pocket. Without thinking my hand reached for the envelope. Instinct stopped me; better to wait for the bank's final confirmation. In France, once a cheque had been handed over it couldn't be cancelled.

Together we stood staring at the view, our eyes tumbling with the fields towards the village. I bent down and picked some grass, tossing it into the air to check the wind and then watching as it dropped listlessly to the earth. Ange lit a cigarette and tapped his foot impatiently against the ground. Tanya wrapped her arm around my waist and gave me a hug. Only Elodie seemed happy rolling in the grass and pushing herself back up again.

'Shall I take a photo?' offered Delphine.

Tanya, Elodie and I hunched together, grinning obediently as we were snapped from all angles. From the twenty or so Delphine took one would surely make the coffee table of the new house. The faint chimes of the village clock rose from the valley below. In a land where time was elastic it was appropriate that the hour was always struck twice, five minutes apart. I wrapped my fingers around the phone in my pocket, waiting for the ring.

'What's the plan?' I asked Ange.

'See the squares?' he said, pointing to the markings on the ground. 'We'll dig down six metres until we hit solid soil and then lower in the steel and set the concrete. Should take a week, then we can start going up. You'll see, from there it will be quick.'

Ange fell back into silence, once again tapping his feet on the ground. The churning engine of the digger made me want to forget the call from the bank and just get started. Thankfully, my phone rang before my will weakened. As expected it was the loans department.

'Mr Ivey?' said a female voice.

'Yes.'

'The documents are all here, and I've been through them all thoroughly.' Her tone was not positive and the fear that I'd inadvertently omitted something resurfaced.

'Go on.'

'It's the insurance. Your project manager's insurance covers building work but not managing others to do work.'

'Presumably all he needs to do is extend the cover?' I looked up at the blue sky, fighting the rage that was slowly overcoming me.

'Yes, but comprehensive insurance is expensive, that's why usually we deal with house-building companies.'

'I don't understand.' I cut her off in mid sentence. The conversation quickly degenerated, with us both interrupting each other. Unfortunately for the girl at the bank, I had nearly a year of frustration to vent. The call ended abruptly with me demanding that the money be released and the bank refusing.

'What's gone wrong?' Tanya demanded. I related the conversation and watched the bitterness creep into my wife's face. 'Stupid pieces of paper, why can't you do anything in this country...?'

'It's all nonsense,' interjected Ange, 'pass me the phone.'

Hope returned as he called the bank. Perhaps I'd misunderstood a key part of the conversation, or hadn't argued enough. Ange walked away with the phone pressed to his ear and we stood and waited. The day remained perfect; clear sky, warm sunshine, panoramic views of Provence, all reminding us what a peerless place we lived in. Delphine too felt the need for some distance and wandered off towards the trees.

Insurance was a notorious problem in France. The industry was out of control, revelling in the endless stream of employment law churned out by Paris. A book I'd been reading – *Sixty Million Frenchmen Can't be Wrong* – explained how many of the country's problems dated back to the French Revolution. Unbelievably, the ruling classes were still terrified of the provinces and the spectre of the guillotine. To guard against a repeat, the government micromanaged, demanding to know in an almost totalitarian way what every member of society was doing. Types of work were categorised and divided and then re-categorised and subdivided until it became almost impossible to do anything legally. Nothing made the Parisian mandarins happier than the fact that everybody was a crook; it gave them the perfect excuse to employ an army of tax inspectors to make everyone's life miserable. No one had yet thought up a tax on wiping your bottom but surely it was coming. Squeezing into a WC near us would be someone from the *fisc*.

'Surely Ange can sort it out,' encouraged Tanya, dragging me from depression.

I shook my head. 'The woman at the bank didn't seem to think so.'

'What'll we do?'

'Find someone else. Ange will help,' I said, trying to be optimistic.

Delphine and Ange intersected each other halfway across the plot and turned back towards us. The expressive shaking of heads and shrugging of shoulders seemed to convey the worst.

'It's nonsense, Jamie, nonsense. I've never come across a bank like it. They're idiots, nothing will ever get done if you borrow money from them. Find someone else.'

'We've already tried everyone.'

'Try again. I'm telling you, if they're this difficult now, what's it going to be like when something changes mid project? Better off starting again.'

His language quickly became too expressive for these pages. 'You can't sneeze in this country without some ******* official examining the bogey and slapping a tax on it.' On and on it went, with Ange's anger escalating out of all proportion to the situation.

'Nobody from here carries that type of cover, you need a new bank,' he said, finally running out of bile.

I nodded.

'Darlings, we must all go and get very, very drunk,' announced Delphine, who had clearly forgotten the time of day.

'See you in the bar at midday?' Ange shook my hand and headed back towards his digger.

There was nothing to do but leave. Delphine gave us a parting hug. 'I am so sorry my babies. Don't worry, it'll work out soon. Trust Ange.'

Over the next few days we tried to figure out what had happened. Our instinct to lash out at French bureaucracy had been wrong. Annoying though it was, everybody knew the rules and it was hard to understand how somebody in the building trade had made such basic mistakes. Surely Ange must have realised he couldn't just divide up the work as he pleased? The worst interpretation of his behaviour was he'd known all along it was unlikely he could do the job, but had decided to push his luck to see what happened. Once again Ange had done a Razzle Dazzle dance to shift blame away from himself. This time round, though, I'd already seen the performance and the necessary sleight of hand was harder to pull off.

A more generous view was that the people we'd chosen to work with were small town tradesmen, used to renovating houses, but with, despite their protestations, no experience of building a house from scratch. Wrongly, Ange had assumed that the job would be simple and gradually his lack of knowledge had been exposed. All the excuses and the delays were explained by the basic fact that this project was a first for him.

The biggest fools, of course, were us. We'd been blinded by the fact that we'd lived in the village for three years and knew everybody. Working with friends, we'd naively reasoned, would make our building project different from all the other disaster stories. Rather than challenge Ange over all the delays we'd accepted his explanations, largely because we knew that we would never behave in such a way, even to complete strangers, let alone to people we saw on a daily basis and with whom we'd shared drinks and meals.

Gradually, it became clear to me and Tanya that there was no point in trying to find another bank. In the first place, it was unlikely that we would be successful, but more importantly we couldn't build a house with a group of people with whom the relationship was already so sour. At least if we stopped now, there was no question of anyone being to blame. The bank had simply said no, and we could all get on with our lives and see each other as we had always done, without any sense of enmity.

The biggest sadness for us was having to deal with yet another delay in the project. We reminded ourselves that we'd not actually been actively looking for a house and that until we'd seen the plot we'd envisaged spending at least another decade in Manu's rental farmhouse. We'd always liked the place. Granted, there were some idiosyncrasies to put up with, but essentially it was a stunning location in which to live.

As often as we repeated this to each other, both of us knew that neither of us quite believed it. The farmhouse was beginning to fray around the edges and the addition of a dog and a baby to our family had made it increasingly difficult to live in. We needed to find a new builder as quickly as possible, because from signing to completion would conservatively take a year.

Four days after our ill-fated meeting at the building site, I picked up the phone to call Ange. Normally he answered immediately but this time it went straight to answerphone. I left a message explaining that we'd decided to stick with the bank and find a company that met their insurance requirements. I thanked Ange for all his hard work, enquired whether I owed him any money, and finally asked if he could let me have my copies of the plans and the engineering report for the foundations. My feelings were mixed as I put the phone down. On the one hand I'd wanted to challenge Ange to explain why it had taken so long to reach this point, on the other hand I was relieved that we'd taken the time to let our tempers cool. By being polite and conciliatory we'd preserved a friendship, or so I thought.

Chapter 15

At the end of the truffle season the town of Uzès holds one of the region's largest *fêtes de la truffe.* Every year its central square is scattered with sand and used as an arena for truffling (*cavage*) demonstrations. The event has become an unofficial testing ground for truffle dogs, with the evolution of different categories of competition according to breed and experience. Entrants come from as far as Italy and for a day at least the most successful dogs are worshipped like star footballers. Full of confidence in Snuffle's newfound love of the truffle I phoned and entered him in the novices' category.

The trials had the added bonus of taking our minds off the construction. A week had passed, and I'd left two additional messages but there was still no reply from Ange. The incident with the bank had apparently bruised his pride, and for now at least, he didn't want to talk. I phoned the architect and asked for an additional set of plans. In passing I also enquired how long it would take to complete the house if he took over the management of the project; the last ten months had shown me that a professional was needed. The reply was alarming – a minimum of fourteen months, possibly up to eighteen months, and his fee was 12 per cent of the build.

Our other alternative was a house-building company, offering a turnkey solution. According to the bank they would always have the necessary insurance. However, rumours abounded of half-completed jobs, poor workmanship and materials. Ange had even told us how one gullible client had paid half up front, only for the builders to suddenly disappear. 'Don't worry, Jamie, you know where I live,' he'd laughed. We really needed another recommendation, but the problem was there was no one to ask.

Frustrated by the lack of activity we headed for Uzès. Returning to the town was, for Tanya and me, like going home. Years ago we'd explored the possibility of opening a wine bar there, and had partnered with a local restaurant – La Renaissance – to test our unique concept of offering a wine list composed entirely of different rosés. For a month I'd bumped boxes of wine along the cobbled streets, pausing to mop my brow and admire the medieval architecture: the Tour Fenestrelle, a steepled French version of the leaning tower of Pisa, and the old dukes' residence, with the crest of arms of the duchy embossed dramatically on the roof. Nothing, though, surpassed the Place aux Herbes. This central colonnaded square, planted with plane trees and dotted with fountains, was a sight to make even the most seasoned tourists check their stride and take a surprised breath.

We arrived just as the bells of the church chimed ten and pulled up seats in the Renaissance cafe. A few other customers huddled under blow heaters drinking strong black coffee and smoking. Nearby a staff member tended a large iron skillet. I'd seen paella made in these dishes before, but today, judging from the smell of truffles drifting by, the dish was *brouillade*, the delicious spiked scrambled egg I was first introduced to at the Rognes truffle market. La Renaissance was offering baguettes filled with the mixture for €5 and also a more complicated six-course truffle menu, including novelties such as *crème brûlée à la truffe*. The square was already busy with people gathering for the *fête*, many of them accompanied by eager looking dogs.

Annie Cellot, the flame-haired owner of La Renaissance, came rushing to our table. On days like this she did everything in a hurry. The restaurant seated over fifty people and yet, as a result of the outrageously high nature of French social security contributions, remained an entirely family affair.

'Bah, Jamie, Tanya, et oh là là un bébé, comme elle est belle.' Annie hugged us all and did her best to ignore Snuffle, who was chewing excitedly on the bottom of her jeans.

'Michel, Ju, Alexandre – c'est Jamie et Tanya,' she called out, summoning her husband and sons.

'What brings you back?'

'The dog trials,' I said, scratching Snuffle's ear. 'We want to try him out against the best.'

Drifting along the street was the sound of monastic chanting.

'Here they come,' Tanya announced, as round the corner marched members of La Confrérie de la Truffe. The men wore the usual flowing robes and kept stride underneath a large banner decorated with images of Provence's black diamonds. Hoisted in the air, balancing between two heavy wooden poles, was an enormous silver dish containing mounds of truffles. It was the type of contraption more commonly used to carry religious effigies.

The procession was on its way to the church, where a truffle mass was to be conducted. For one day only Christ would magically transubstantiate into a truffle and a glass of wine rather than the more traditional bread and wine. The first time we'd come across this type of mutation of the traditional mass was in Patrimonio in Corsica, where, to celebrate the arrival of the new season rosé, a service was held using pink rather than red wine in the communion cup. The Pope might not approve of such bastardisations of the prayer book; however, they were undoubtedly good for attendances because following the *confrérie* up the streets of Uzès was a trail of hungry looking worshippers.

A microphone screeched across the Place aux Herbes and there were three dull thuds as the sound was tested.

'*Bonjour* and welcome to the *fête de la truffe*. We'll start proceedings with the auction and then move on to the dog trials.'

The auctioneer clambered onto the stage and held a black truffle the size of his fist above his head, commencing the bidding in rapid French.

'A 250-gram *Tuber melanosporum* from an irrigated *truffière* just outside of Richelieu.'

For professional buyers the provenance of a truffle is an important indicator of taste. Size is the other factor. As a rule of thumb, the larger the truffle, the stronger the flavour.

'Let's start the bidding at two hundred euros.'

We sat, drank coffee and exchanged news with Annie as the auction continued.

'So what happened to the rosé bar?'

'We could never find the right property. Instead, we ended up in the markets.'

'And it's still just pink?'

'We sell a little of everything.'

Annie laughed. At one stage Tanya and I had been so evangelical about rosé that we refused to drink anything else.

Up on the stage the auctioneer was taking a telephone bid, presumably from a Parisian restaurateur.

'Any advances on three hundred and fifty euros? No? Sold.'

The crowd, which was now sizeable, sighed in disappointment. A prize truffle was on its way north.

'And now something of a rarity – a Kalahari Desert tuber, weighing nearly a kilo.' The auctioneer held aloft a light brown truffle the size of a ruler. People gasped and pointed.

'Found by a nomadic tribesman. Who'll give me a hundred euros?'

Nobody raised their hand. The price fell to €75 and then €50. A man near the front raised his hand and there was a polite round of applause. Clearly nobody had a clue what the truffle was going to taste like.

'Sold for fifty euros.'

Burgundy and then Italian white truffles cheered the auctioneer up by reaching more elevated prices and the auction closed.

The novice dogs were scheduled to appear in minutes and my confidence in Snuffle was quickly fading. He might be able to successfully find truffle-spiked cheese in our garden but how would he react to the crowd? And could he find real truffles? I'd yet to test Snuffle in our *truffière* because all the advice was to wait until I was sure there were truffles. A hard frost was needed to stimulate the growth of the tuber and recently the weather had been too warm. To develop into a good truffle dog, Snuffle had to feel the thrill of success rather than the deflation of failure. Today was the first step in a long journey.

Tanya, Elodie and I made our way across the square to the funnelled entrance reserved for competitors. We joined a queue of nervous, excitable young dogs. Long, short, big, small, black, white, blotchy, thin, overweight, cross-bred, pedigree – there was no unifying factor, apart from the propensity to bark. The trial organiser, a heavyset man wearing a deerstalker hat and cape reminiscent of Sherlock Holmes, paced up and down the line examining the dogs. He crouched down and held out his chubby paw of a hand to Snuffle, who sniffed greedily.

'Good, you'll go second.'

'Best to get it over with,' encouraged Tanya.

The microphone screeched again.

'Allez – on va commencer les chiens.'

All the dogs moved forward to face the arena – an expanse of sand dotted with branches to symbolise truffle oaks. Somewhere in the great beach in front of us were five truffles. A good dog could find them all in under one minute.

'First it's Victor and his owner Patrick,' announced Sherlock, as I'd mentally dubbed the organiser.

Victor bounded into the ring, but was immediately called to heel. He was a small, short-haired cross-breed. Clearly excited, he was still self-possessed enough to look up at his owner for instruction.

'How old is Victor?' asked Sherlock.

I realised with dread that every entrant was going to be interviewed.

'Seven months.'

'And how long have you been training him?'

'Since birth. We rubbed truffle oil on the teats of his mother.'

'Good, good, let's see how he gets on. *Allez*.'

The crowd was now three deep. Victor trotted across the sand, nose to the ground.

'*Allez chercher,*' cried his owner and Victor was off, walking in ever decreasing circles, before pawing a spot in the sand. The dog's work was so fast that his owner did not have time to uncover one truffle before Victor indicated the resting place of the next. The clock stopped on forty-nine seconds. Everybody applauded and Victor was rewarded with an enormous piece of saucisson. The truffles were collected and hidden again.

'And now, we have Snuffle, trained by Jamie.' We walked into the ring. Tanya and Elodie followed just slightly behind. The moment should have been a special one – the surrounding medieval buildings, the fluttering pennants, the festival atmosphere. However, I was about to be interviewed in front of 500 people in French and I was terrified.

'How old is Snuffle?'

'Seven months.' So far, so good.

'Ah, the same age as Victor. Do you think he'll do as well?'

'Let's see.' Trying to hurry through the interview, I crouched to release Snuffle.

'And how have you trained him?'

I meant to say that we'd started by putting truffles in socks and letting Snuffle play with them, but my mind momentarily went blank.

'We put truffles in our shoes,' I confided, to raucous laughter. The French words for shoes – *chaussures* – and socks – *chaussettes* – are confusingly similar.

'Typical English, so rich they can afford to let their dogs chew their shoes.' The interview concluded to more laughter. I flushed red. I needed a great performance from Snuffle to redeem some pride.

'Go on Snuffle, find the truffles,' I urged, 'find the truffles.'

Snuffle charged into the ring, nose to the ground. He hit the central area where Victor had so successfully located most of his finds, and kept going, full tilt.

'He's found one,' said Tanya excitedly.

'I wouldn't be so sure.'

Snuffle was now 20 metres away and still going fast. Sniffing away he came to an abrupt halt as he rammed into one of the crash barriers that held the crowd back. Looking up he began to nibble on a lady's shoe.

'That's the problem with using shoes to train your dog,' joked Sherlock to yet more laughter. 'Seriously, though, sometimes you think you've trained your dog, but the scent he's following is yours, not the truffle's.'

It's often said that dogs are sensitive to human emotions. If their owners are ill, they curl up at the end of the bed, or if there's an ongoing family row, they make themselves scarce. To date,

Snuffle had not demonstrated any ability to interpret people's moods. However, as the laughter continued, he looked around the crowd and bolted as fast as he could for the exit. Ears back, tail elongated, paws bounding forwards in a blur – it took a diving rugby tackle to stop him. Everybody applauded loudly. Perhaps there were some sports fans in the audience. Then I noticed that rather than pointing at me and Snuffle, the crowd was focused on Elodie and Tanya.

Somehow, Elodie had wriggled free of Tanya's grasp and in messing around in the sand had uncovered a truffle. I was immediately convinced it was a total accident but the French in the crowd didn't seem so sure.

'I've heard of a child in Périgord who can do this.'

'Extraordinary ability,' concurred the man's neighbour.

'Raised in a family of truffle hunters, though – this one's English.'

'A sense of smell like that is God-given.'

We hurried away before anyone kidnapped our child and forced her into a life of slavery on their truffle plantation.

Part 3

Gendarmes in the Garrigue

Chapter 16

In August in Provence, here are some of the things you can do: go hot-air ballooning, order delivery sushi, eat white summer truffles, visit a chocolate factory, dine in a Michelin restaurant, stay in a campsite, sleep in a five-star hotel, play golf, visit a market, drive bulls through the Camargue, drink wine, enjoy a spa, fry in the sun. The choice is as endless as the tourist dollar.

Don't be fooled by the rustic feel of the place: if you have the money, then some smart concierge company can make pretty much any wish come true. Why else would Brad and Angelina, the celebrity burlesque act of Provence, forever be flirting with expensive properties, helicoptering through the hills, teasing estate agents with the seductive sheen of their black Amexes, before clamping the wallet shut and settling for a chaste château on a long lease?

There's one caveat, though, one thing you can't do. Don't request a tradesman. 'Live wire in the bathroom, Mr Pitt? It'll have to wait until the first of September. Overflowing sceptic tank, Miss Jolie? The truck is at the mechanic's and the mechanic is on holiday until, you guessed, the first of September. Why don't you stay with the Depps?'

Occasionally in life, there is an opportunity to rewrite the rules, to attempt the Provençal equivalent of landing on the moon, to achieve what even Brad, Angelina and all their millions can't; to find not just one tradesman, but a whole team of them, and not just to fix a problem, but to start building a house.

While the rest of the world was cursing bankers who'd gambled away the wealth of nations, Tanya and I were quietly grateful. Right at the moment when we were casting around for new builders, *La Crise*, as the French called the credit crunch, was in full swing, decimating the economy and crippling, in particular, the construction sector.

Since the debacle with Ange, we'd approached a number of house-building companies. For some it was too late; the tumbleweed was already blowing between the desks, the shutters clapping a funeral march on rusty hinges. Others had only a skeleton staff and usually they'd been turned delirious by the financial storm. Manic laughter drove us from such offices. 'Build a house? We haven't even got money left for lunchtime baguettes, let alone to pay suppliers for materials!'

Finally, though, we found a company near Aix-en-Provence with staff still in their right minds, albeit playing with paper clips and nervously eyeing the closed door of the owner's office. The diggers waited in an idle line outside and stockpiles of bricks threatened to become historical monuments. When we knocked on the door, it was almost too late; the company was scrambling for breath. Only by doing the unheard of, the almost profane, could the business be saved. However, this was no ordinary construction company. In the office, perfume, not sweat, was the dominant smell, and on the desks nail varnish replaced the usual pictures of naked women. The place was run entirely by women, and the owner was savvy enough to recognise salvation when it walked through the door. We could pretty much name our price – our house would be built, and what's more they'd start tomorrow.

Thus, precisely five months after our last failed attempt to start the construction, Tanya and I were once again standing on site. The digger's engine was turning over, the same dark storm clouds of diesel were floating towards us, but this time there was one important difference: everything had been approved by the bank. At my signal – handing over the cheque – France would never be the same again. The unheard of would become reality. Atoms might collide in the particle accelerator but no scientist or social anthropologist ever thought the day would come when a *chantier* was officially opened in Provence in August.

Of course, there was an explanation – the workmen we were introduced to were not native French, rather immigrants from Africa, probably Tunisia. Cheque in her handbag, company saved, the French *directrice* of the building company would be off for her usual month in St Tropez, punctuating the lazy days by the pool with the odd lunch at Club 55. Before she could head for the beach, though, she had one piece of bad news for us.

Madame Roland spread the plans out on the bonnet of her black Range Rover. It was early in the morning and the sky was still a benign pale blue. The sun which had crept over the tops of the trees provided a soft light, the warmth of the rays revitalising rather than burning the skin. A soft scent of pine drifted in the air.

'Monsieur Ivey, I need to show you something.' The words were almost smothered by the pneumatic squeal of the digger's arm clawing into the hard earth.

'*Regardez*, these are the architect's plans and these are our execution drawings.' Her heavy make-up glinted in the sun.

The second set of drawings was covered in markings giving measurements for everything from the windows to the staircase. The writing was tiny, the detail precise. As we hunched over the plans Madame's dyed blonde hair swirled into my face, carrying with it the smell of peppermint shampoo.

'Don't you see the living room? It's designed for Corsicans.'

Corsica was notorious for its vendettas, its cured meats and its inhabitants' love of knives. Momentarily, I couldn't place what these attributes could possibly have to do with our living room. Then I thought of Napoleon.

'It's a major problem – jump in the air and you'll hit the ceiling.'

'What do we do?'

Earth rained noisily to the ground and the arm of the digger swung hungrily downward.

'We just build it higher.'

The words were drowned by a fart of diesel.

'Can we do that?'

'There's a small risk.'

'A risk of what?'

'That the *préfecture* will inspect and demand rectification work.'

'What, knocking it down?'

A landslide of soil tumbled earthwards. The digger had already created the 6-metre deep square for the first concrete foundation.

'It won't come to that. Never does.'

'What's the alternative?'

'We stop work and you reapply for planning permission. It'll take you six months and there's no guarantee you'll get it.'

By my feet Elodie was digging away with a spade, creating her own foundation. We'd been explaining how we were going to build a house and gradually she'd embraced the idea. At home her toy chest was filled with diggers and men in hard hats, and her favourite programme was now *Bob the Builder*.

'There's one more thing,' said Madame Roland. 'If we add to the walls, that will put extra strain on the foundations. Should be no problem, but I thought I'd mention it.'

After anger, and then fury, comes despair. I'd already exhausted the two preceding emotions; instead, there was a calm emptiness, a sense of ceding to the inevitable. It seemed that however hard we tried, however thoroughly we prepared, researched and planned, we would never understand the construction culture. There was an unwritten set of rules, an inbred understanding of just how much cheating was permissible, that was anathema to the Anglo-Saxon mind. A Frenchman in my position would just stick two fingers up at the bureaucratic planning process and get on with building his house, confident in the knowledge that if the worst came to the worst, he could probably bribe his way out of the problem. Instinctively, it felt wrong to build a house for which we didn't have the permission, but that was the Provençal way. Our viewing trips with Eric had encompassed many weird and wonderful houses; most had grown organically into sprawling abodes and not a single one of them was legal.

'Trust me, it will be fine,' reassured Madame Roland, glancing at her watch. Unless she left soon the traffic into St Tropez would be hellish. The digger continued to carve out the second hole for the foundations.

I looked at Tanya. After nearly a year and a half trying to get started she knew better than to be surprised. 'Shall we just get on with it?'

More soil cascaded to the ground. A lorry laden with steel reinforcements for the foundations waited at the gates of the *chantier*. The driver was impatient to deposit his load and was revving his engine in frustration.

I reached for Tanya's hand and gave it a squeeze. 'I think it's too late to do anything else.'

Madame Roland smiled the smile of a woman whose holiday had just begun. Kissing each of us formally on both cheeks, she folded away the plans, and pulled herself into the cabin of the car.

The expensive engine purred. Madame wound down the window and chilled air blasted into my face carrying with it a hint of peppermint. 'See you in September.' She grinned and headed off for a month-long love-in with Ambre Solaire.

A small blue Citroën passed through the open gates of the building site. The car pulled to a halt opposite us, so that we had to step backwards as the driver's door opened. A grey-haired lady in her mid to late fifties stepped slowly out, using the door frame to take some of her weight. She wore a floral summer dress which her ample frame more than filled. Her hair was short and her mouth tight and small. Before she spoke it was possible to sense the anger in her demeanour, possibly from the way she'd nearly parked her car on our feet.

'What do you think you are doing?'

'We're building a house.'

'I saw the sign, but why here? You've the whole field, why not in the corner over there? Plenty of shade, by far the best spot, yes – you should build there,' she said, starting to walk to a distant corner of the plot.

'Madame.' I stood still, making her turn back towards us. 'We're building the house here.'

'We'll see.' She took out her phone.

'Who are you calling?'

'The mayor, he's a close friend.'

'He'll be on holiday, like the rest of Provence.'

'I have his mobile.'

The woman dialled. We were precisely thirty minutes into the work of building our house. We'd just agreed to the illegal walls, and already an unknown woman was on the phone to the mayor. Each ring brought with it a heightened feeling of nausea.

'*Oui, allo.*'

'*Oui, bonjour, Miriam à l'appareil.*'

'*Bonjour Miriam, ça va?*' The mayor sounded pleasantly surprised, as if hearing from an old friend.

Eavesdropping on the conversation, we learnt that Miriam lived across the valley from us and had done for the last twenty years. Like us, she'd purchased a plot of land and built. One of the guarantees that had persuaded her to put pen to paper was that nothing would be built on the hillside opposite. Miriam had paid for an uninterrupted view of nature and now it was being wrecked. According to her, she was quite within her rights to demand that our house wasn't built at all; however, since we were such a nice charming couple, she'd settle for us hiding the construction in the trees. That way everybody would be happy. Her voice was confident and her sense of righteousness undeniable.

Given our luck, the mayor's response was bound to be a crack squad of *chantier* police to shut down the project, leaving us houseless and penniless.

'I miss Ange,' I joked feebly.

'I don't,' replied Tanya.

The tone of Miriam's voice changed as the mayor took over the conversation. She nodded her head, looked at the ground and repeatedly said, '*Oui, je comprends.*' The digger continued its work, hauling the steel reinforcements towards the holes for the foundations. People had always reassured us that once the construction started the build would progress quickly. Tanya and I had longed for this moment. However, in all likelihood the huge and growing pile of excavated earth would simply have to be used as refill.

'So we'll see you in September for a drink. OK then, goodbye.' Miriam finished her conversation with the mayor. Their farewell was so cordial I feared a stitch-up.

'Apparently the plans have been available for the last year at the *préfecture*, so I have lost my chance to object.' Miriam smiled.

Her manner became calmer, less austere. 'I still think you'd be better off building nearer the trees, much more shade.'

I cut her off. 'We can't. Our soil survey is specific to this precise location. The same with our engineer's report for the foundations.' There was no way I was going to move the house anyway, but these were solid, convenient reasons to give for my intransigence.

'What's the soil?' asked Miriam.

'Clay.'

'*Oh là là, les pauvres,*' exclaimed Miriam, with apparent pity in her voice. 'You must come with me now.'

Tanya and I didn't speak much as we bumped our way across the valley behind Miriam's Citroën. Instead, I lost myself in a confused maze of thoughts. What should have been a happy morning was quickly turning into a disaster. Things would probably be fine, I reassured myself, but it was apparent that if Miriam had the slightest suspicion our building didn't conform to the plans she'd be straight back on the phone to her chum the mayor. Why did it have to be so hard to put brick on brick and build a house?

Miriam lived in a small villa perched on the hillside. The views of the village were, if anything, slightly better than from our plot. The iron bell tower of the church was just that bit closer and the curve of the dome acted as a frame for the fields beyond. Mature trees provided plenty of shade and the garden was filled with fragrant blooming flowers. A sprinkler lassoed water into the air and the droplets fell in a multicoloured rainbow onto the verdant lawn. Pebbles crunched underfoot as we headed up the path to the front door.

'*Regardez.*' Miriam jabbed a finger at a crack the width of a ruler which zigzagged from the roof, striking the top of the door like a lightning bolt.

'Come with me.' She ushered us into the large open-plan living area. The floor tiling was uneven, discoloured and split in places where the ground seemed to swell gently, like the sea on a calm day. Paintings filled entire walls, almost obliterating the plaster behind. Half-finished canvasses were scattered on the kitchen tops, on the sofa and on the central dark wooden table. A large picture window looked out across the village towards our plot of land. The digger moving across the hill was no bigger than one of Elodie's toys but it was instantly clear that Miriam would be able to observe our construction in minute detail.

'Look at the ceiling,' Miriam directed.

Waves of deep cracks fanned out above our heads. Individual pieces of plaster, some the size of chocolate bars, were dangling by fine threads and metal braces had been inserted at the top of the walls to try to stop the infection spreading. Judging from the fine fingers of blistered wall weaving their way through the paintings, these joists were failing. I began to wonder whether we should be wearing hard hats.

'This house was built twenty years ago on clay soil, just like yours, and now look at it. Whatever you paid for your piece of land, it wasn't worth it. Your house is going to fall down, just like this place.'

'Ah, but we've invested thousands in foundations and an engineering report,' I said, relieved.

Miriam wouldn't be halted, though. 'Foundations? I've seen your foundations. They're exactly the same as the foundations of this house and they'll be crushed just like my foundations. Clay expands with the heat and contracts with the cold. It moves and absorbs water like no other soil type. Concrete foundations are mere matchsticks when compared with the power of the earth.'

She pulled an A4 file from a long row that occupied a shelf in the kitchen where the cookbooks should have been. Crumpled well-used plans were spread across the table and Tanya and I looked at drawings of foundations remarkably similar to ours.

'See the rest of those files,' Miriam waved a hand along the line, ' – correspondence between my lawyer and the insurance company. They're refusing to pay to stabilise the house. I haven't got the money and so if I lose it will probably fall down.'

If the demonstration was part of a well-rehearsed plan to stop us building, it was extremely effective. I felt immediately sorry for Miriam, who was facing the prospect of being kicked out of a home she'd built. The inside might be falling apart but the garden showed how much she loved the place. And her argument about our house was persuasive. Did we really want to go through the heartache of building in the knowledge that the house would probably fall down? If the worst happened, the insurance company that notionally guaranteed the build would, rather than pay up, doubtless bombard us with disclaimer letters. Then again, what choice did we have but to go ahead? We'd paid the money for the land, we'd signed the contract with the builders, there really was no way out, other than accepting financial ruin.

'Thank you for showing us all this,' I said. 'We really must get Elodie to bed, it's been a long morning.' I got to my feet, reeling with shock, like a boxer who has taken one too many punches.

Miriam nodded and pulled on a painter's smock.

'Are these all yours?' I steadied myself and motioned to the coloured canvasses which were twirling like a kaleidoscope before my eyes.

'I have an atelier in Avignon.'

Sitting on a shelf by the door I noticed a collapsed golden telescope. It was of the type used by the captains of great sailboats in distant centuries.

'Does that work?' I blurted out.

'Have a go.'

I pointed the telescope across the valley, scanning the trees until my eyes settled on the construction site. The head of a builder was poking out from one of the foundation holes; another builder was resting on a pile of bricks smoking a cigarette. The magnification was such that if and when we built the house, Miriam would be able to see us get undressed.

'Belonged to my father, and his father before that; quite collectable, I believe. Good luck,' said Miriam as we opened the door to leave. Despite the phone call to the mayor, it seemed she genuinely meant it. Somehow we were now comrades in arms fighting the onslaught of clay soil. A summer of extreme heat and a winter of extreme cold would, according to Miriam, concertina our house before we even had the chance to move in. With her naval telescope, she'd be the first to know.

Chapter 17

At the beginning of September I organised a Côtes du Rhône wine tasting. The purpose of the event was to thank customers of our wine business but there was also a personal motivation.

Just over a year before I'd struck the village of Gigondas and all its satellite appellations from my wine list, vowing never to drink another bottle from the area. Clients still wanted the wines but guilt as fresh as New Zealand Sauvignon prevented me from selling them.

The reason? Just a sniff of a heavy Côtes du Rhône brought the following unpleasant memory tumbling back:

I am bouncing along in the back of the car belting out the last few verses of 'In the Navy' by the Village People – think 'YMCA' but more camp – believing I am quite possibly the funniest man alive. Tanya is heavily pregnant and driving. A vague sense of foreboding penetrates the misty veil of inebriation.

Next to me is my father-in-law, Stuart, who yes, just happens to have served in the navy. He's singing along half-heartedly but really he is wondering just why his son-in-law has the presumption to be ridiculing his military service.

Of course, it wasn't my fault. The evening had started convivially with a couple of Kirs in a small cafe. As the alcohol flowed so did the bonhomie, the conversation gradually became more raucous and my father-in-law and I ordered a bottle of Gigondas to accompany our main course.

Neither of us looked at the alcohol percentage until it was too late; at a whopping great 15.5 per cent, it was nearly a fortified wine. The effect was not so much to loosen my tongue as to unravel it and wrap it around a nearby tree, handily forming a noose for me to hang myself with after my bawdy rendition.

I sing the lyrics with gusto as the car bumps along the Provençal roads, giving my father-in a-law a mock salute.

And so there you have it; the explanation for why I received a pair of socks last Christmas rather than the usual jumper and for why Gigondas was removed from my wine list. However, at Tanya's bequest, I'd decided it was time to mend bridges with my father-in-law, hence the Côtes du Rhône wine tasting, for which he had travelled over from England.

Before the tasting, though, I had a very important meeting to attend – a dog training class. Following directions I headed through the industrial hinterland outside the town of Orange, passed the municipal dump and a low-slung office block, over a rattling iron bridge, into the middle of a barren field. Three other cars and a battered van were already parked in a line. There was a row of orange bucket seats which appeared to have been wrenched from a sports stadium, and a gate leading to a fenced-off area filled with bollards, hoops, rings and ropes. I opened the car door. The acrid smell of boiling chemicals, emitted from a nearby factory, drifted in the air.

Snuffle leapt from his seat and excitedly greeted his fellow pupils: an enormous bull mastiff with shoulders as high as my waist, restrained not by a lead but by a chunky rope; a prim, trim Airedale that danced skittishly away; and a golden retriever, groomed to perfection but with a nasty set of fangs. As we waited more dogs arrived – fierce Alsatians and two enormous cross-breeds.

'How's Rocky?'

'He was at the bins again.'

'And Hercules?'

'Went missing for a day.'

The owners so far were universally women and so I could only assume they were talking about their dogs. Their dress was certainly diverse. Rocky the bull mastiff's owner looked like a rock band roadie. She sported greasy dark hair, leather trousers and a leather jacket with cut-off arms. Unsurprisingly, she dripped with sweat in the autumn sun. Her jewellery, if it could be called that, consisted of leather bands studded with silver spikes. Hercules, an Alsatian, belonged to a petite middle-aged lady. She wore jeans, a T-shirt and a jerkin with the silhouette of a large guard dog on the back.

The dogs detected Gaspar's arrival first. All the barking and bottom sniffing stopped and they marshalled themselves into an obedient line, sitting, waiting, tails wagging, watching the ten-time champion trainer approach across the field.

'*Et bonjour tout le monde.*' Gaspar wore army trousers, boots, a sweat-stained T-shirt and a red baseball cap. He made his way along the line of dogs, holding out his hand to each of them.

'Have you been a good boy?'

'I see you've had a haircut.'

He reserved a compliment for each of his canine clients. Finally reaching us, he parted the hair that covered Snuffle's eyes and fixed him with a penetrating stare. 'Ah, my new student. *Allez, on va commencer.*'

The dogs trailed in a line through the gate. Rocky was a little slow to react and his owner took the end of the rope and whacked it vigorously across his nose, shouting a loud, aggressive '*Allez!*'

Her whole face went puce as she yanked on the lead, trying to command her lethargic dog to heel. After a couple more vigorous swipes with the rope, Rocky ambled into the arena and joined the other dogs. The golden retriever bared its fangs and leapt at Rocky's throat, nearly dragging its diminutive owner from her feet. Snuffle looked on in horror.

'*Au pied!*' cried Gaspar and we began a procession around the field. Most of the dogs pranced obediently at their owners' heels. Copying the women, I held the lead in my right hand, letting it fall across my body and grasping it lightly with my left to control Snuffle.

'Good, Jamie,' praised Gaspar, 'training a dog without a lead is like driving a car without the key.'

'*Tout le monde, demi-tour à droite.*' The women pirouetted on the spot. As one they turned, exchanging the leads behind their backs and walking briskly off in the opposite direction. I clumsily turned a half circle with Snuffle and rejoined the rear of the procession. This was more like a dancing class than dog training.

A latecomer made his way across the field. It was another man, thank God; perhaps his *demi-tour à droite* would be as inept as mine. His dress suggested otherwise – suede loafers, white trousers and a polo shirt. He wore a chain around his neck, had thinning white hair, and but for the pug dog trailing in his wake, I'd have been convinced he'd taken a wrong turn on the way to the yacht club.

'*Chiens, couchez!*' shouted Gaspar and all the dogs obediently lay down, with their long tongues panting in the heat. '*Bougez-pas,*' called Gaspar, and as one the women stepped away from their dogs, instructing them not to move. Rocky immediately disobeyed, taking a sudden interest in a dragonfly and gaining a sore nose for his trouble.

'That's what I used to say to my wife,' joked the newcomer.

I must have looked confused.

'*Coucher pas bouger.*' He gave a little lecherous laugh. 'I'd like to put her on a lead,' he added as one of the women paraded past with her dog.

The rest of the lesson drifted by in a flurry of misplaced double entendres. By the end of the hour I was pretending not to speak any French and the man had all but given up on me. Snuffle lay at my feet, exhausted. He'd managed to sit on command, but apart from that he'd expended all his energy on the nervous excitement generated by the presence of so many other dogs.

Gaspar came over to chat to Snuffle. 'Well done, little one. Next week, we'll work on walking to heel.'

The training session had lasted longer than expected, meaning I was late for the wine tasting. I'd booked a room in a vineyard with space for fifteen people. Each tasting station had a small silver sink cut into the desk and a pad and pencil to take tasting notes, as well as some dry crackers to clear the throat between wines.

The plan was for me to do a basic introduction to tasting and then encourage people to record their own reactions. I'd lined up ten different wines, sumptuous whites and mellow reds with the luscious depth I'd been missing so much over the preceding Rhône-less year. The alcohol in these well-made, well-balanced wines was, I believed, almost impossible to detect. The strongest wine on offer was 14.5 per cent and the weakest 12.5 per cent.

Entering the tasting room I expected to hear a pleasing hubbub of noise, excited chatter about the wines on offer, and anecdotes brought back from far-flung summer holidays. Instead, there was a still and dusty silence. Clean glasses winked under the spotlights. Trays of assorted antipasti testified to the absence of people. I glanced at the clock. It was already ten minutes after the appointed start time. Even in Provence this was a little worrying. The door opened and my father-in-law entered. He had wispy grey hair, a brow furrowed from years hunched over legal papers, and the rosy complexion of someone who was enjoying France just a little too much. His eyes registered the empty room.

'Might as well get going,' said Stuart kindly, 'the latecomers will just have to catch up.'

'I guess so.' I was in a daze. I'd run five such events in the preceding year and they'd proved increasingly popular. The clientele was usually an eclectic mix – educated locals keen to develop their palates, Parisian second homeowners looking for an easy way to keep their cellars stocked and groups of tourists, including, on one occasion, four octogenarian American women who drank so much they barely made it back to the tour bus.

The first few wines tasted bitter and confused. My palate was cold and my mind elsewhere. Gradually as the quality of the bottles improved I managed to blot out the strangeness of the situation. Five minutes into the tasting there was a knock on the door.

A bearded man and his diminutive wife entered. They both wore shorts and stripy T-shirts and although the clothes didn't quite match, the overall impression was of twins who'd been dressed in the same gear by their mother. The sun had burnt a tan line into the man's upper arms. The skin on one side of the line was pale and freckly, on the other side a raw red. The woman was plastered in zinc block and wore a baseball cap with a curtain of material draped from the rear to keep the sun from her neck.

'Do we have to pay?' At least they were English so I wouldn't have to repeat my spiel in a second language.

'No, no – it's free, come on in. How did you find out about us?'

'The tourist office.'

'Well, take a place. To recap, tasting is a personal experience. Don't be put off by the experts who claim to detect scents of mown summer grass or fresh wood chippings. Keep it simple. Say what you see and taste.'

'What's the bowl for?'

'Unwanted wine.' The man raised his eyebrow to his wife, as if to say 'hark at him and his posh ways'. The concept of tipping alcohol away was clearly alien to him.

In a show of support, Stuart upended his glass. The faintest of drops fell into the bowl.

'The next wine is a 2005 Châteaurenard, Boisrenard red; spicy, intensely purple, and explosive on the nose, the tannins just need some time in the cellar to soften a little. It's consistently been voted one of the top hundred wines in France.'

'Tastes like a packet of Worcester sauce flavour crisps,' said the bearded one.

'I agree,' said his wife, biting into a cracker, unconcerned by the crumbs collecting in her bra.

'Good,' I encouraged. 'That's the spicy notes. Can you taste the tannins in the back of the throat?'

'Kicks like a Paint-stripper.'

'I'm sorry?' I visualised the two of them lounging in front of the TV, sharing a tin of industrial cleansing fluid.

'A Paint-stripper – it's the happy hour special at the Prince of Wales,' clarified the man. 'The chilli-vodka peels the moisture from your mouth. Leaves your tongue like sandpaper.'

Stuart had tilted his glass and was busy studying the meniscus, examining the subtle variations in shade which were indicative of age. It was time to move onto the next wine.

'The 2003 Cuvée Florence from Domaine Les Goubert in Gigondas, a profound, complex and well-balanced wine matured for twenty-four months in oak – a dream with a Sunday roast, with the final glass being reserved for the fireside in the evening.'

'Reminds me a bit of Tizer.'

'You mean Dr Pepper.'

'That's what I said.'

'No, you said Tizer.'

In the circumstances, Stuart and I couldn't help but bond. After an hour of listening to more marital bickering and some of France's finest wines being likened to the pint glass cocktails at the Prince of Wales, we were relieved to clamber into the taxi home.

As we did so I heard some familiar notes.

'In the navy…' sang Stuart, who'd obviously been sipping more than he had been spitting.

I joined in, wrapping my arm around his shoulder, pleased that there would be no more socks for Christmas and welcoming the chance to concentrate on something other than the memory of the embarrassingly empty room.

Chapter 18

Shortly after Snuffle started school, Elodie also began her education. Her crèche was located in a neighbouring village, sheltering beneath centuries-old plane trees. The narrow cobbled road was impassable for cars. There was a cafe on the corner where the locals sat sipping strong black coffee and smoking cigarettes on the terrace. The *boulangerie* was only paces away and the smell of baking bread drifted down the street. Feng shui experts couldn't have created a more calming location. And yet on the first morning, there were tears in Elodie's eyes as we shepherded her towards the door.

Over the last few months she'd grown quickly and her trousers rode high above her ankles. Her hair, which until recently had remained stubbornly short, flowed in golden locks down to her shoulders, curling at the end into little ringlets. As we reached the entrance her little hand tightened around mine.

Now was the moment to leave her alone for the first time. The headmistress, a gentle dark-haired lady, took Elodie's hand and nodded to us to go. We turned and left, both of us sneaking a glance over our shoulders as our child, apparently inconsolable, shouted our names. Then, like a number of other parents we ordered a coffee in the nearby cafe, listening as the screams subsided. By the time we'd finished all that could be heard was the sound of children playing happily.

Within a week a routine had been established and by the end of September Elodie skipped happily into crèche. I'd taken to buying a croissant from the nearby bakery and enjoying a coffee in the cafe. The *boulanger* laced his creations with an indecent amount of butter, and the coffee was one of the strongest in the area. Sitting in the shade of the trees, with the blue sky visible through the mesh of arching branches, quickly became a treasured moment in my days. And it was here, with any income from the next truffle season still a couple of months away, that I came up with our next marketing idea for the wine business.

Ever since the two English boules players had invaded our garden playing their extreme version of the game I'd been thinking about adapting the concept into a tournament. A little research showed that boules had not always been heavily codified. *Pétanque* – which literally means stuck feet – originated in the port of La Ciotat, near Marseille, at the turn of the century. Unsurprisingly, the idea of playing a game where little or no movement was involved quickly caught on in Provence. However, throughout the rest of France different versions of the game survived. To my delight I discovered that in Normandy a rambling version of the game was still played in farmyards. From the description the concept was not dissimilar to my proposed extreme version.

Rolling back the years and holding a tournament without rules or boundaries should, I reasoned, appeal to the locals. Historical pageants were common and so why not an old-fashioned boules tournament? We'd get a team from our village to compete against a team from the neighbouring village and put up some wine as a prize. Spectators could be introduced to our wine business while they watched. Within a week of the Côtes du Rhône tasting I was sticking posters on lamp posts advertising Provence's first Tournoi de Boules Extrême, to take place in two weeks' time. All I needed was some players.

The village boules club consists of a sizeable dusty square bordered by wooden sleepers. Plane trees have been planted at regular intervals, but as yet they are relatively young and do not provide quite enough shade. In one corner there's a small hut with a sign declaring that the bar is open to members only. Except during play, an iron shutter is always pulled tightly down. Pinned to the wall are notices of upcoming *concours* (competitions) and a blunt pencil dangles from a piece of string to enable people to sign up. In the summer play takes place most afternoons and there's usually an audience – a nearby car park is heavily used by camper vans and rows of tourists sit on foldaway chairs picnicking as they watch.

When I arrived, late on a Saturday afternoon, the shadows were long and there were about twenty men waiting to play. Some members broke away and made practice throws, others chatted.

'*Eh bien, Eric a gagné le loto.*'

'*Combien?*'

'*Deux cent mille.*'

'*Bah oui. Il a de la chance.*'

The members were apparently men of few words. Over a third of them conformed to the stereotype of a boules player I'd created in my head – army-style combat trousers, a red hunter's cap, and a bushy moustache surrounded by stubble. A bit of a paunch seemed desirable but was by no means a prerequisite. The rest were a curious cross section: thin, diffident men who hung back on the fringes of the conversation, smartly dressed gentlemen sitting on foldaway chairs, others shuffling by in what appeared to be pyjamas and slippers. At least the club was open to all comers, and therefore hopefully new ideas, I reasoned.

The language spoken was French but with a strong and intimidating Provençal twang, the most obvious manifestation of which was a habit of punctuating every other sentence with the word *'Bah'*. Pronounced like the baa of a sheep, it meant very little, but was a reliable conversational crux to fall back on, indicating that one was still alert and hadn't succumbed to the soporific sunshine.

Urgency is not usually a word that figures in the Provençal lexicon, except perhaps behind the wheel of a car. However, in the final minutes before the game started there was a growing air of impatience, as more and more people arrived and started clacking their boules between their fingers. The sound was grating. At some point, when between fifty and a hundred boules were being banged together, the volume became too great to withstand – for the sake of all our eardrums, the game needed to begin.

On cue the shutter of the bar creaked upwards, revealing the man I'd come to talk to – Antoine Sublet, one of the most revered players at the club.

'Allez, on va commencer le concours.' He lifted a large silver bowl onto the counter and began drawing out numbers. The digits were written on small pieces of paper and Antoine's large fingers, swollen with the heat and curled inwards like a boxer's after a fight, struggled to unravel the crumpled balls. Each phase of the draw took a couple of minutes to complete, and the process was occasionally delayed by female passers-by who called out greetings to Antoine. Instinctively he stopped what he was doing and ran his fingers through his dark greying hair before shouting flirtatiously back:

'Isabelle, should anything happen to your husband, promise you'll call!'

'Sandrine, you were always the most beautiful girl in the class.'

The players who were lucky enough to have been drawn early retreated to discuss the merits of their pairings.

'*C'est vous encore.*'

'*Allez, on va gagner.*'

'*Sylvan, j'ai de la chance.*'

Each new pairing was met with laughter and jokes until the hat was finally empty. I approached the counter. Antoine was at the back of the bar holding a hurried conversation through the side door. I coughed loudly, but was ignored, and so I waited. Behind me there was the gentle clack of metal upon metal and the occasional exclamation of surprise at a particularly successful shot. The shadows were lengthening, autumn arriving, but it was still ferociously hot. The glare of the sun off the gravel created windows of fiery light in the canopy of the plane trees. Underneath my thick denim jeans I was sweating heavily and I could feel water droplets gathering in the creases at the back of my knees. The smell of garlic from a nearby home drifted on a rare gust of wind. Antoine's nostrils twitched and he turned to face me.

'Have you seen the posters for our boules tournament?' I asked.

'*Quoi?*' Antoine grunted, pretending not to understand.

'Le Tournoi de Boules Extrême?'

'*Non.*'

'Can I explain the concept to you?'

Antoine folded his arms defensively. He listened as I talked him through the idea.

'Play starts at point A, finishes at point B. In-between these two points players can go wherever they want – behind trees, in rivers, down ditches – and the winners are the team in the lead when the *cochonnet* crosses the finishing line.' I concluded.

Antoine unfolded both arms and rested them on the bar. '*Je comprends pas.*' He began to do the washing-up. Undaunted I began again, explaining that there really were no rules to understand and that in any event everything would become clear on the day.

'Plus the winning team goes home with a magnum of wine.'

'Which vineyard?'

'Domaine les Goubert, Gigondas.'

Antoine nodded, recognising the name. For the first time since the conversation began he smiled.

'Will you enter some teams?'

'Normalement, oui.'

In Provence a *normalement* is the most definitive answer you can receive. It means that barring earthquake, mistral, rain or an urgent need for a siesta, something is going to get done.

I drove to the neighbouring village, confident that I had at least one set of teams for the tournament. The headquarters of the second *club de boules* of the day was located in one of the most traditional bars in the area. The no-smoking ban was routinely flouted and a swirl of ash fluttered from the floor as I pushed open the door. At a table in the corner four men were playing cards. Their cigarettes burned in a central ashtray as they fingered gambling chips. The men unilaterally placed their cards face down and turned to look at me.

I'd heard that the cafe was the centre of 'black' labour in the area. If you wanted a job done for cash, then this was the place to come. At the bar chariot horse racing was showing on the television. A pile of screwed-up betting slips rested next to the nicotine-stained, shaking hand of another regular.

'I'm looking for Benoit.' My voice was unnaturally high. Explaining the concept of our boules tournament in my home village had been difficult enough; explaining it in this environment was daunting.

'You've found him.' The man who spoke swung around on his stool. His eyes were yellow, his hair greasy and he was so thin he looked ill.

'I'm holding a boules tournament at the end of the week,' I began, conscious of the hesitancy in my voice and the speed with which I was speaking.

Benoit managed to listen while keeping one eye on the racing. My mention of the magnum of red wine coincided with him ripping up another betting slip.

'Do you think you'll be able to send some teams?'

Benoit drained his pastis, and rocked from his seat, heading for the open door of the *urinoir*.

'*On verra*,' he said as he unbuttoned his trousers and began to pee.

Loosely and politely translated this meant, 'It isn't going to happen, mate, be so good as to get out of our bar.'

The morning of the tournament was bright and sunny. A gentle cooling breeze blew from the north and for the first time in months the air felt light and fresh. It was precisely the type of weather needed to entice people from the heavy shade of their houses. The grape harvest was still not quite finished, but the more forgiving temperature heralded the new season.

We marked out the start and finish points in the countryside behind our house. Manu had declined to take part, but had grudgingly agreed to boules being played through his fields. The course began on the dirt track driveway, meandered through the field of lavender, looped around an olive grove and finished in the vines underneath our kitchen window. After my experience in the boules bar we'd decided to make the tournament less formal and just organise games as and when people turned up. I'd be the roving rules referee, striding through the field, with Elodie safely secured in a rucksack on my back.

Outside the house we erected a blackboard on which to write the names of the competitors. On a nearby table we laid out open bottles of the wines for tasting. A pile of fliers and business cards were held down by several of the heavy local stones. Although we expected most of the competitors to turn up with their own boules, we'd begged and borrowed additional sets in case of need. Simon, a friend from England, was staying with us. He'd been looking forward to the tournament all week, reckoning that the uneven bounce would give him a chance against the more skilled locals.

Fabian, the geothermal millionaire, had arrived at precisely 10 a.m. and I'd endured a difficult half an hour as I tried to make the final preparations while discussing the benefits of using the latent heat in the soil to warm our new house. Glancing at my watch, I noted that competitors and spectators were now appropriately late. I gazed down the road looking for the trails of dust that arriving cars always sent spiralling into the air.

'The thing about geothermal,' Fabian continued, 'is that your electricity bill will be halved. Add a wind turbine and a couple of solar panels and you'll soon be selling power back to the grid.'

'But you can't even walk over the land after the pipes have been laid.' I was beginning to get worried and talking to Fabian was a pleasant distraction.

'It can be a problem, but with the amount of land you've got, there's no point worrying.' Fabian had never seen our plot, but in a small village people talked.

Deciding we might as well get started I paired Fabian off with Simon and sent them off into the field. Simon wrapped an arm around Fabian's shoulder. 'Now remember – it's just like golf,' he said as they headed off.

'Do you think anyone else is coming?' Tanya said as she came out of the house.

'Should get some more.'

'At least Simon's having a good time.'

'Hope he doesn't mind changing his heating system.'

An hour after the appointed start time there were seven cars on our drive. Two of them belonged to couples who'd seen the posters and turned up on spec, the other five to friends. We played some boules and then drank some wine. We even managed some sales. It was hard, however, to avoid the conclusion that the morning had been a disappointment. Holding an event in Provence is not difficult at all; offer a free glass of wine and a few nibbles and usually the whole village and their extended family will turn up. There are typically not too many events to go to and so the opportunity to have a chat while drinking at someone else's expense is all that's needed.

Normalement the fields outside our house should have resounded with the clack of boules. *Normalement* life in Provence is very social. But nothing quite seemed normal anymore. Perhaps it was *La Crise*. People were getting used to a simpler life and just not going out, begrudging even the cost of petrol. The lack of an invitation to Delphine's annual *fête des vendanges* implied that she too had succumbed to the new reality and seen fit to cancel.

Chapter 19

Madame Roland, the *directrice* of our building company, must have been back from the beaches of St Tropez for well over a month, but her skin still glowed with a rich golden summer sheen. Her nails, always long, were painted a deep ferocious red, and the dark roots of her hair had been bleached white, either by the sun or by one of the Riviera's skilful celebrity hairdressers. As usual, a bubble of overpowering perfume surrounded her. Today there was a strong citrus note, and a hint of musk.

We stood together on the *chantier*, regarding the progress of the building work. The foundations were in, and a raft of concrete had been laid on top of them. The idea was simple – the soil beneath the house could expand and contract, but because the house was built directly onto the foundations, and elevated a half metre or so from the ground, the bricks would never move. Already the first walls were climbing towards the sky, rising in uneven, ugly grey towers.

However, the concrete mixers were ominously silent and there was no sign of any workmen.

'The water went off yesterday – barely a trickle is coming up. Could be the pump's too small, could be the well's not deep enough,' explained Madame Roland.

'What do we do?'

'Here's the problem: if we pull up the pump and it's OK, then you pay, plus you pay again for a new borehole.'

'How much?'

'Ten thousand, maybe more. Best thing to do is find out how deep the well is, then we'll know whether there's water. If there is, then it's definitely the pump at fault.'

'I'll get on the phone.'

Madame Roland climbed back into the soft leather interior of her car.

'Oh, and Jamie, don't take too long – the cost of materials is going up and up.'

The deeds for the house showed that the well had been dug some fifty years ago, and that the land had changed hands twice since then. A quick search of the phone book revealed no entry for Rousseau, the name of the family that had originally owned the plot, and so that afternoon I sat down and tried to discover which company had dug the well. Family businesses tended to last a long time in Provence and there were only twenty *forage* (well drilling) specialists.

Hopefully the relevant company would still exist and hopefully their records would stretch back far enough to confirm the depth of my well.

With each company I explained the location of our house and the problem.

The response was always the same. '*Tout à fait*, one has to know the depth.' Then there was a shuffling of papers, perhaps a smoker's cough, followed by confirmation that they couldn't provide the missing details. After ten companies I was dispirited. We'd just have to pull up the pump and risk paying double. Whatever happened, the concrete mixers had to get going again.

I dialled one of the remaining entries for *forage* in the book. It was an advert rather than a listing and I didn't take the time to look at the address. Mechanically, I explained the problem.

'*Oui, oui, alors, on arrive vers seize heures.*'

I put the phone down astonished. Somebody was actually going to come out and try to help. No call-out charge, just an attempt to find a solution. I looked at the address: Marseille. I almost phoned back immediately and told them not to bother. The unofficial capital of the south of France had, in my experience, a well-earned bad reputation.

Before my only visit, some two years ago, residents had warned me 'hold on to your wallet, hold on to your wife'. Given the order of the advice it sounded like a misogynist's charter; still, I'd been keen not to prejudge the city.

First impressions hadn't been favourable. On the slip road from the *autoroute*, high on an electricity wire, I'd noticed a pair of trainers swinging from their laces and into my mind had come a vision of some unfortunate tourist, stripped of all his possessions, walking barefoot to the nearest gendarmerie to ask whether anyone had seen his wife. After all, this being Marseille, there would be no point enquiring about his wallet.

I'd also been warned about the driving. 'Remember that famous French film *Taxi*, where Marseille resembles a Formula One circuit? It's not fiction, it's fact.' Sure enough, at the first set of red traffic lights I'd encountered, the driver of a Renault Laguna decided to convert his car into an impromptu moped. David Blaine might struggle with this particular trick, but not, apparently, the locals. The secret is to hit the curb at the right pace and *voilà*, four wheels become two. Pedestrians, bins, cafe tables were all acceptable collateral damage for the Marseillais driver determined to jump the lights.

That day, virtuoso driving was apparently quite necessary because stretching the length of the visible *corniche* (coastal road) was a *bouchon* (traffic jam) capable of punching its own personal hole in the ozone layer. Exhaust fumes churned into the still air, obscuring the horizon and suffocating anyone unfortunate enough to be in a convertible. Rather than hitting the curb at pace and flipping my car onto two wheels, à la Renault Laguna, I decided to stop and have lunch.

The setting was beautiful, overlooking the old port. The Mediterranean gently rocked a flotilla of sailing ships, the bells on top of the masts clinked pleasingly and fishing boats chugged into port and unloaded their slithering cargo.

While I sipped on a glass of warm wine and took in the view, a waiter wearing a grease-stained shirt shoved various ill-conceived dishes under my nose, the lowlight of which was an entrecôte steak covered in a *sauce aux poivres* with the consistency of school custard. I paid in cash and waited for my change. After ten minutes, I was finally presented with a saucer filled with nearly fifty bronze five-cent pieces. It was the Marseillais way of thanking me for my custom. I collected every coin and left.

The city and I had had nothing to do with each other since, but right now, haring up the *autoroute*, was a truckload of *forage* experts, ready, once again, to treat me to the Marseillais version of service. Still, the well needed to be fixed and no one else appeared capable or willing and so I waited for four o'clock and headed to the *chantier*, taking Elodie with me for the ride.

Up until this point, day on day, I'd been able to watch progress. As far as I could tell the builders were on schedule and I'd been able to confidently tick off the days until delivery of the completed house. With no workmen, though, the place had a distinctly different feel. The *chantier* felt abandoned. It had – if only temporarily – joined the many derelict building sites across Provence. A loophole in the planning law meant that, provided some work took place every year, planning permission could be extended indefinitely. As a result, on some *chantiers*, only a single brick was added every year.

Rather like a thunderstorm, the Marseillaises could be heard approaching long before they came into sight. The sound of car horns followed their progress up the valley, through the village, towards the building site. Next I heard the engine and the creaking grind of metal on metal, quickly followed by blaring rap music. Finally, the truck swung into view. It was an old pick-up, with an oversized crane mounted on the back. The driver took the dirt track leading up to the *chantier* at a reckless pace. Bumps pitched the cabin to the left and the right, and the crane rocked this way and that. An iron cable with a hook on the end looped lethally through the air. A jobseeker would rightly think joining the army a safer bet than climbing aboard such a truck.

Abruptly the engine clicked off and the noise stopped. Dust fell to the ground, revealing two young men in battered jeans and faded T-shirts. They wore aviator sunglasses and pulled heavy industrial gloves from the rear of the truck.

'Where's the baby, then?' Their demeanour was rushed.

I presumed they meant the well rather than Elodie, who could not have escaped their notice. My daughter had started to choose her own clothes and, like her mother, she had something of a shoe obsession. Given that she only had two pairs to chose from this didn't usually present too much of a problem. However, recently she'd discovered Tanya's collection, which is how she came to greet the Marseillaises wearing a pair of furry boots/slippers that rose the length of her legs and engulfed her midriff. I'd tried to take them off her but in the end her tears had proved more durable than my perseverance, and she now greeted the *forage* experts with amused and determined eyes. Hesitantly she took small shuffling steps, as if to prove that her choice of footwear was not as ridiculous as we all thought.

I directed the Marseillaises towards the well in the corner of the field. One of them hoisted himself onto the arm of the crane and the other swung back into the driving seat. With bangs on the roof replacing language they manoeuvred the truck into position.

'Up she comes.' One of the men attached the hook to the cable within the well. There was a whirr and the truck winch, mounted on the crane, squeaked into life. Within minutes the pump was pulled into the light. Rusty and battered, it certainly looked defunct.

The Marseillaises didn't waste time on a diagnosis, slinging the pump into the rear of the truck and rummaging in a pile of boxes for a replacement. The winch whirred again, the cable was played, with protest, back into the well and the new pump disappeared from sight to begin its subterranean life.

'Give it a go.'

I turned the tap. A trickling smudge of water emerged. This was followed by a vicious vomit of liquid, then hissing air, and finally a constant gush. The pump was working. The Marseillaises raised their shades, removed their gloves, wiped their foreheads and presented me with the bill: 2,000 euros for twenty minutes of work. Even so, it was better than the ten thousand or more that Madame Roland had predicted, and so I signed the cheque. Within moments they were gone, bouncing off down the track, heading off to some other emergency.

Somehow Elodie had taken off one of Tanya's boots. She now wore it wedged on her head, the heel and sole dangling to one side like an oversized pompom on a Santa hat. Her expression was totally serious and all her attention was focused on filling the other boot with handfuls of mud. I tried not to laugh and I tried not to think what Tanya would say.

Instead, I called Madame Roland.

'It's fixed. You can start work again.'

'Who did the work?'

'A company from Marseille.'

'*Oh là là.*' I could imagine her on the other end of the phone, using that peculiarly French gesture, a vigorous shake of the wrist, to indicate that somebody had just done something very stupid.

Chapter 20

There is an etiquette to supermarket shopping the world over. Everybody enters, trolley empty, list in hand, hoping to whizz in and out as quickly as possible, praying they don't meet anyone they know. The bright lighting, the claustrophobic aisles, the chill of the freezer cabinets and the mind-numbing wait at the checkout combine to create an unpleasant experience. The shorter it has to be endured, the better.

However, particularly in a small community, the interior of a local supermarket is always filled with casual acquaintances. The aisles hide a delaying minefield of banal greetings and pointless conversations. A quick reconnaissance trip, skidding the length of the shop without putting anything in the trolley, is often essential. That way, problem areas can be identified, and gossips avoided. It's possible just by glancing at other people's trolleys to chart where they'll go next – after dairy it's always the drinks aisle and after cereals it's usually the chilled cold meats. The crafty shopper who plots his course can, with a little luck, avoid all interruptions.

The optimum moment for weekly groceries in France is lunchtime. The aisles are empty apart from expats scooting around sheepishly stocking up on Marmite and baked beans.

It's my favourite time to shop. Even so, I'm forced to deploy a full array of conversation-halting body language. The vegetable section is the most likely place to spot a familiar face. If eye contact is made, a wave of acknowledgement is necessary, but then one can quickly become distracted by the urgent need to fill a plastic bag full of lemons. If there's no eye contact, then there's always a handy pile of melons or pumpkins to dive behind and wait until the aisle clears.

Outside the vegetable section it's harder but still possible to avoid conversations without appearing rude. The secret is to adopt an air of being under overwhelming time pressure. A nuance of supermarket behaviour is that people don't actually have to believe your charade. The majority of shoppers don't want to talk either. They'll be grateful if you glance at your watch, run your fingers in a hassled way through your hair and indiscriminately chuck articles into your trolley. A pantomime performance is quite sufficient.

Sometimes, though, even a skilled operator deploying all the right body language can get caught. In my case there's a fatal flaw in my nature that means for just one small moment I'm vulnerable, a sitting duck, prey to any sick, twisted blabbermouth who labours under the misapprehension that the supermarket is a meeting place, a chance to catch up on news and enquire after the family. My weakness? *La Provence*: I always flick to the back page to check out the weather.

The newspaper rack in our supermarket is located right next to the quick 'ten items only' checkout. It's a zone fraught with danger. Shoppers in a queue are happy to stop and pass the time of day and the usual rules of etiquette do not apply. Yet it's always important to watch the weather. Among the joys of living in Provence are the glorious warm October days. Working for ourselves, it's possible to ditch the day job and head to the coast. At this time of year the French seaside is an absolute joy. The Mediterranean sparkles, it's still warm enough to swim, the restaurants are all open, and the ambiance is one of leisurely enjoyment. The harsh heat and the crowds of the summer have disappeared and the feel is of a bygone era. In other words, it's well worth the risk of checking *La Provence* for the forecast.

It was just after one o'clock. The safest time to shop. The typical Frenchman would be at the table indulging in a glass of wine, having a *courgette farcie* starter, salivating over the smell of the *grillade* (grilled meat) to follow, with half an eye on the tarte Tatin for dessert. Expats would have just finished their sandwiches and be searching for the car keys. Normally the next half an hour would be clear. As was my habit, I picked up the paper. On Thursday the skies were clearing, the temperature rising and the only worry was the mistral, predicted to rise to 20 kilometres per hour by the afternoon. Could we risk a beach trip?

I flicked the pages and my eye was caught by an article about an unusual festival. A local boutique owner was organising Provence's first, and in all probability the world's first, *fête du string*. Entrants were invited to customise their G-string with bangles and handicraft designs, and the results would be displayed on mannequins in the village hall.

I shook my head, lowered the paper, folded it and put it back in the rack. Turning around I came face to face with Ange. We'd not spoken since the rendezvous on the *chantier* six months ago. My phone messages had remained unanswered and in the end I'd simply given up. We'd passed each other in the car. He'd kept his eyes on the road and not noticed me. There had been no chance meetings in the village to clear the air and resume our steak tartare recipe exchange.

Now we were so close that with a slight lean forward I could give him the customary kiss. No amount of supermarket savvy body language could save me now. In fact, I was grateful for the opportunity to try to kick-start our old relationship.

'*Bonjour.*' I held out my hand, unsure whether we were still on kissing terms.

Ange looked the same as ever. Baseball cap pulled low over his head, clothes stained with brick, plaster and paint, hands dirty and covered in grime, fingernails chipped and broken. There was the familiar smell of garlic and if he accepted a kiss the prickly bed of his perma-stubble would greet me.

Ange looked up. He fixed his dark eyes on me, holding my gaze for a long second.

Finding a use for my outstretched hand I pointed at his shopping. 'What are you having with the confit?'

A smirk cracked the corner of Ange's mouth. He then turned, put his shopping basket on the floor and walked out of the shop. The inference was clear. My presence revolted him so much he was even prepared to forego his lunch. I was left standing, arm held out, head half stooped for a kiss, so that I overbalanced and had to grope for the trolley to balance myself. The shock of someone being quite so rude was extraordinary. It was like being slapped in the face, hard, twice, and then once more for good measure.

Mechanically, I completed the weekly shop, but my mind ranged over all our actions. I'd offered to pay Ange for his work but he hadn't called back. How can you pay someone who won't even give you an invoice? No fault there. We'd employed other builders only when the bank had refused to release funds. No fault there. Why, therefore, was he so angry with us?

Perhaps he'd told people we didn't have the money to build the house, and then suddenly been made to face the embarrassing reality of us opening the *chantier*. Potentially there was also an element of xenophobia. Anyone outside one's immediate village was considered a foreigner. And we'd employed a company from distant Aix-en-Provence to work for us. Not only that but it was a company that used Tunisian builders – men who were prepared to work for cheaper wages and break up the comfortable monopoly enjoyed by the local artisans.

Could Ange's anger be justified? Perhaps we could have fought harder to find another bank, but after all the excuses, the broken down cars, the clampings, the stray wild boar, we'd lost confidence. But what if the litany of accidents had actually occurred? What if, as Ange had maintained, local practice was to give estimates rather than firm quotes? We'd felt so strongly that we were being misled but perhaps there was an alternate truth that fed Ange's bitterness.

I was still working through possible explanations as I crunched back up the drive. The vines glowed a ripe orange in the sunlight, the leaves on the oaks were a bright luminous yellow, and the cherry orchard opposite a polished burnished brown. Wisps of cloud skidded across the hills so that shadows and sunlight hid and then illuminated the vibrant colours. I gathered the shopping bags together and the plastic bit uncomfortably into my fingers. Taking deep breaths of the cool air I cleared my head.

I opened the door and Tanya placed the phone back on the hook. She looked a little disconcerted. Elodie was sitting at her high chair covered in spaghetti. Snuffle was licking up a pool of sauce from the floor. Crayons and miscellaneous toys were scattered across the room. During my absence carnage had been visited on the sitting room.

'Who was on the phone?' I placed the bags on the floor by my feet.

'Oh, only Fabian.'

'Still trying to sell us heating?' I realised too late that Tanya's tone was serious.

'He wanted to know why we weren't at Delphine's.'

'I thought it was cancelled.'

'Apparently not, went ahead as usual.'

'Where was our invite?'

Tanya shook her head. 'I don't know.'

Delphine was extraordinarily liberal in handing out invites to her *fête*. She'd once told us that there was no point in having a grand old property unless you shared it with people. Every year the guest list grew, the terrace became more crowded and the pleasing bubble of voices lingered ever later into the starlit night. The jazz band would have been bigger than the previous year, another loop of lights would have been added to the plane trees and an extra table to the buffet.

'Anyway, I've got something to tell you.'

'Hold on. I saw Ange in the supermarket.'

'How was he?'

'Wouldn't even speak to me. Walked out of the shop.'

'Jamie, it doesn't matter.'

'The wine tasting, the boules tournament and now Delphine. It's like there's a blacklist.'

'I said it doesn't matter.' There was a tear in Tanya's eye. 'I've got something to tell you.'

I took her hand, expecting the worst. Perhaps a malicious rumour being spread about us, or news that the *préfecture* had discovered our illegal wall. The firmness of her grip was painful. The wind blew the front door open, scattering a pile of invoices into the air. As the door clapped shut the paper drifted to the ground, settling with the silence of snow. The radio in the background announced a series of train strikes and the timer on the microwave pinged.

'I'm pregnant again.'

'You're what?' I gave her an enormous hug. 'That's fantastic, when did you find out?'

'Just now while you were out.'

'And there's no doubt?'

'No.'

'Have you called your parents?'

'No, I was waiting for you.'

'How many months?'

'One.'

'Do you want to wait for the scan?'

'I'll tell them now.'

We hugged again. Buoyed by the change in mood, Elodie started laughing and clapping. There was a bang from the cellar as Manu ripped the door from another old car. I leaned on the wall for support. I was going to be the father of two. What a responsibility, what a delight. I couldn't wait. Then came the realisation – getting the house built on time was suddenly more important than ever. We now only had seven and a half months.

Chapter 21

Throughout October and November I was a regular at the dog training classes. The lessons were undoubtedly good for Snuffle. He calmed down and learnt to tune himself in to the sound of my voice. On our morning walks he obediently returned when called, and gradually we began to develop a genuine bond. He shadowed me all day and I enjoyed his reassuring presence. For the first time in my life I began to appreciate why some people were so mad about their dogs. Snuffle, like a child, had his own personality – playful, affectionate, forgetful and slightly dotty.

Despite my new found enthusiasm for dogs I still felt an outsider at the training classes. My gender (95 per cent of the other attendees were women) and nationality obviously marked me out as different. I also felt conspicuous because I had such a small dog when compared with the majority of the women, who manhandled great beasts.

At times it looked an unequal battle, with the dogs the obvious winners. Lightweight, nail-varnished, made-up women with spangles on their tops would yank on the thick ropes they used for control. The dogs lazily obliged. The tempers of the women were remarkably short and at the slightest hint of disobedience they would be wrapping the rope around their hands and beating the dogs on their haunches, screaming 'Non!' at the tops of their voices. Since they'd all opted to buy male dogs, I couldn't help but think that some form of anger transference was going on. A particular dog's transgressions might only be small, but perhaps because the husband of the owner had just started an affair, the dog got a blast of concentrated, unforgiving female anger.

'Non!' The word was screamed, at times almost spat out. It wasn't much of a leap of the imagination to picture these women at home in the kitchen, rope in hand, beating their husbands in a similar fashion. Putting them all together in a field seemed to feed their righteous indignation at the male species. The more aggressively one of them corrected their dog, the more the others nodded in support. If their husbands were indeed having extra-marital dalliances, they were wrong to choose male dogs as pets. The average man might think about sex ten times a day, but the average male dog thinks about nothing else.

The other reason I felt excluded and different was my inability to perform the basic turns and manoeuvres that Gaspar demanded. I'd always had two left feet and felt inhibited whenever I stepped on a dance floor. Now I was being asked to twirl in time with ten to fifteen Frenchwomen. It would have been hard enough to do without a dog, but with Snuffle in tow it became a simple exercise in limiting the embarrassment. My particular bête noire was still the *demi-tour à droite*. When the women did the *demi-tour*, there was a blur of motion, a swivel of the hips, and a little jazzy kick as they set off in the opposite direction, dogs seamlessly following. There was one lady who did the whole class without a lead. When she moved, her dog followed, and her *demi-tour* was a thing of beauty, while mine was a confused mess of lead and dog that often ended in me stumbling forward onto the grass.

My presence at the dog training sessions ruined the marvellous synchronicity that these women had achieved. As one they anticipated Gaspar's commands, forming criss-crossing choreographed patterns in the arena. Occasionally, a spectator would occupy the row of orange bucket seats, and spontaneously burst into applause after a particular complicated set of moves had been flawlessly performed. Needless to say, whenever there was any clapping, I was taking a break.

This being France, the highlight of every class was food. The exercise was initially a simple one. Gaspar would take a handful of sliced-up saucisson and offer it to each of the dogs. Meanwhile, the owners would say a firm 'Non!' and the dogs would obediently turn away from the food. Needless to say, the women were excellent at this exercise; their 'Non!' could not have been more vehement had it been one of their husbands pawing at the cleavage of a lover. My initial efforts were rather timid, but I was soon mirroring the female owners with a loud firm 'Non!'.

One week Gaspar forgot the saucisson. Hercules' owner volunteered to contribute a *chausson aux pommes* she had in the car, however. Spiced with ginger and nutmeg, the sliced stewed apples had been encased in light pastry. It really was too good for the dogs, she said, but just this once she would make an exception. As owner after owner shouted a firm 'Non!', the group became distracted discussing the precise quantities of each ingredient needed.

The classes were never the same again. After that, everybody agreed that to train the dogs properly they had to be really tempted. Saucisson was fine, but a dog might behave completely differently if, for example, he encountered a juicy *poulet roti* (roast chicken). Thus began the tradition of each member of the class bringing in some home-cooking to tempt the dogs. In the space of a few weeks we had a *roti de porc*, a *daube de boeuf*, a *blanc de veau* and a *fricassée de poulet*. Each recipe was lovingly prepared and then described, and for a while it felt like I'd signed up for a cooking course. The tradition came to an abrupt end when Rocky got loose, leapt into a car boot and devoured an entire casserole. If dogs could talk, he would have said, *'Oh là là, c'est bon.'*

At the end of each lesson Snuffle and I spent a little time with Gaspar honing our truffle-hunting technique. We used an artificial substance bought on the Internet called Canitruffe, to simulate the smell of the truffles. With more and more success Snuffle located the Canitruffe and Gaspar was convinced that he was following the truffle smell, not my smell. He had one caveat, though. Before I could be sure that Snuffle would turn into an effective truffle dog, Snuffle had to accept the *couche* command. For a dog, complying with a 'lie down' command is the ultimate act of submission. So far Snuffle had resisted, growling in anger when I'd tried to encourage him into a prostrate position. Towards the end of October, Gaspar decided that it was time to force the issue.

When I arrived, for once people were not discussing their dogs. The previous day France had gone to the polls in the local elections and the right-wing President Nicolas Sarkozy had received a terrible beating. Everybody was delighted and there was an impromptu sing-song.

'Au revoir, Monsieur Le Président,' the women joined hands and chorused.

Such a response was surprising. Despite the humble surroundings, the *'club canine'* was like a golf club, a haven of middle-class respectability. The annual fees were high and the members treated the weekly lessons as social occasions. It wasn't unusual for people to invite the family to watch and bring along a picnic. These were people who should support the government. Anyone might own a dog, but only the rich could afford to teach it how to dance.

'*Au revoir, Monsieur Le Président,*' they chanted.

The problems for Sarkozy had started on the night of his election when he chose to host a dinner at one of Paris's most expensive restaurants, drinking champagne, eating foie gras and hobnobbing with wealthy industrialists. Making matters worse, he then headed off on holiday on a friend's yacht, demeaned the post of president by ambling up the steps of the Élysée Palace in his jogging kit and, horror of horrors, ditched his wife and married an Italian model. Was it any wonder that these women now had a new hero, or heroine, Marine Le Pen, daughter of Jean-Marie Le Pen, who had succeeded her father as leader of the French National Front? Orange had been one of Le Front National's traditional strongholds and there was no need for me to ask for whom the members of the club had voted.

'*Allez, on va commencer,*' said Gaspar, putting an end to the politics.

We paraded around the arena. As usual, we started with *au pied* and Snuffle trotted obediently to heel. We executed an early *demi-tour à droite* which, apart from the fact that we dropped two dogs in the line, was nearly perfect. We criss-crossed the field, weaving in and out of the other dogs, and Snuffle showed not the least bit of interest in playing with them, focusing on keeping step with my stride. The saucisson came out and I didn't even feel a tug on my lead as we paraded serenely over the temptation. It was hard to avoid the conclusion that Snuffle was now a very well-trained dog.

'*On va essayer le couche,*' said Gaspar.

Taking Snuffle's paws he gently moved him forward from the sitting position, saying '*Couche!*' in a loud, strict voice. All the women watched. This moment was the most pivotal in the training of a dog, similar to the day a horse is finally broken. Gaspar, as head of the pack, had the most chance of success. Snuffle had watched all the other dogs submit to him, and would probably feel inclined to do the same.

'*Couche!*' Gaspar repeated.

Snuffle's body tensed, but slowly, ever so gradually, he edged forward onto his paws. He was lying down on command.

'*Pas bouger,*' instructed Gaspar.

How long would Snuffle hold this position of subservience? I counted slowly to twenty. A grin spread across Gaspar's face and he congratulated Snuffle with some saucisson. Snuffle returned to the sitting position.

'Now you try.'

'*Couche!*' I moved my hand forward slowly towards the earth, in the same manner as Gaspar. Snuffle appeared distracted.

'*Couche!*' I repeated. Snuffle looked at me, he looked at Gaspar and then miraculously he obliged, lying down on request. My dog had formally recognised my leadership.

As well as Snuffle's acceptance of his position in the family pack, another important development in our lives was slowly becoming part of the community of parents at Elodie's crèche. It was hard to imagine a more idyllic location for a child to begin her education. The classrooms formed a quadrangle around a shaded courtyard in the centre of which was an olive tree. There were slides, swings, toy cars, pretty much anything a toddler could desire.

Although heavily subsidised by the state, the crèche was run as a cooperative of parents, and people were expected to volunteer for small DIY jobs – fixing stair gates, putting up fences and matting, and generally ensuring the environment remained safe. I spent a couple of Saturday mornings working with some of the other dads. Most were farm labourers or artisan craftsmen and the quality of their *bricolage* was far superior to mine.

Thankfully, there was a young electrician called Franck who looked after me. I followed him around fetching hammers and nails when necessary and handing over supportive coffees. The arrangement seemed to suit both of us. Although he looked like a typical Provençal – short, dark eyes, dark hair – his working catchphrase *'c'est vite fait'* would have been anathema to most of his countrymen.

'Did you see OM last night?' Franck asked.

Like everybody else in the region he was a fanatical fan. To live in Provence and not be aware of the fortunes of Olympique de Marseille was almost impossible. The day after a match conversations in bars, *tabacs*, post offices and newsagents always revolved around the football team's results.

'It was great.' OM had beaten Paris Saint-Germain 3–2 with a goal in the last minute. The rivalry between the two teams was one of the fiercest in France, and the Provençaux would now be happy for weeks.

'Come over and watch the next game.'

In any other country, this would have been a perfectly normal thing to say. In France, it was socially daring on an almost unprecedented level. Traditionally, only relatives and long-standing friends were ever invited into the home, and yet here was Franck casually asking me over.

I nodded, delighted, and we moved onto the next job: repairing all my work from the previous week.

Chapter 22

The morning after the OM game I awoke with a heavy head. The evening had started with pastis and concluded with a lot of La Cagole beer. Outside my bedroom window the sound of the mistral added to the pain of my hangover. The shutters were closed but it was easy to imagine the destruction outside. Pine trees bent into boomerangs, branches sliced from oaks, and saplings uprooted. Pots, tables, chairs, the paraphernalia of human life, tossed into the air and carted to the corner of a distant field.

I listened to the unique howl of this fiercest of winds, the shrill warlike scream, as an angry fist of energy thumped into the walls of the farmhouse. In the Alps, cold tentacles of air would be winding themselves tighter and tighter around the peaks, before they plunged down snow-filled crevices, uniting into a gale as they hit the funnel of the Rhône valley. Unhindered the wind would gather pace, the rippling river belying the strength of the air thundering onwards, learning to speak, and then to howl, before hitting the Camargue delta and spreading like a virus across the south of France.

Experience had taught me to wait for the lull, the unnatural peace, the humanising pause for breath, the seconds – even minutes – of hope before the next onslaught. Casting open and quickly pinning back the window, I was greeted by a resplendent blue sky. A gentle breeze stirred the gravel drive. Brilliant sunlight warmed the terrace. Only an upturned chair blown from the garden of some neighbouring house hinted at the abnormal force of the wind. Yesterday's puddles had already been sucked from the ground, devoured by the dry air. A whirling devil of dust chased up the driveway and moments later a sledgehammer gust nearly forced the window from my hands. Leaning back, I set my weight against all those kilometres of bitter cold anger that stretched back along the Rhône to the Alpine peaks. I yanked the latch shut.

Pulling on my jeans and jumper I entered Elodie's room. She stood, hands resting on the top bars of the cot, having a conversation with the wind, interjecting a noisy babble in-between the howls. I noticed that a small pool of water had formed on her window sill and that condensation ran up the inside of the glass. The cause must have been the central heating which I'd turned on for the first time the previous evening. We'd had no trouble before and I ran my finger along the frame to see whether the hot summer had warped the wood.

Picking up Elodie I made my way along the dark corridor – an electrical fault meant light bulbs were continually blowing – to the colder air of the sitting room. I turned on the television and selected the children's programmes. Then, cautiously I opened all the shutters, on each occasion waiting for the wind, like a searchlight, to sweep momentarily onwards. Two more panes of glass were covered in water and pools collected on the floor underneath. Dark stains ran down the paintwork and a draught of air from the ill-fitting front door carried a spectral chill.

I went to fill the kettle. There was a hiss and a cough. Fat globules of warm water spat from the end of the tap. Another hiss and a cough, and then nothing. During Manu's renovation project such interruptions of essential services had been all too common. Today, though, there appeared to be no explanation. The wind had yet to knock the electricity out, which meant the pump from the well should still be running. Manu's building work was complete and so it was unlikely that a plumber was fiddling with the pipes. I called for Tanya, put on my coat, and headed out into the mistral to find our landlord.

At first it was fun. A little like an attraction at an amusement park. I'd throw myself recklessly forward, only to be blown upright by savage gusts. Turning around, I allowed myself to be taken in the direction of the wind. My legs tumbled over each other, propelling me at sprinting speed down the drive. Thrill seekers paid for this type of ride. In fact, the last time the mistral had blown, the world speed record for windsurfing had been broken on a canal in the Camargue. Unfortunately, though, this mythical wind of winds never visited only momentarily. Local folklore had it that it either blew for three, seven or fifteen continuous days. Imagine being on a fairground ride for that long.

As expected, Manu was out and about. A huddle of men were standing next to some sort of digger. The wind seemed to have shrunk them. Their backs were bent, their heads swallowed by their jackets and their knees straining against an invisible force. The slow ponderous movements of their limbs reminded me of the polar expeditions I'd seen on TV. Puffs of diesel plumed into the sky like a distress signal. I shouted a greeting, but the words were snatched from my mouth. Bending my neck and head down, I clawed my way across the field.

'*Bonjour.*'

The men grunted.

'*Salut.*' Manu removed a pair of industrial ear mufflers and managed a smile of greeting.

'We've no water.'

'I know, should be back on by the end of the day. We're drilling another well.'

Ever since we'd lived with Manu he'd been obsessed with the possibility of running out of water. His precious fields of olive trees consumed vast quantities and then there was the new apartment to supply. I'd observed him meandering across his land with divining sticks, hands twitching in search of an elusive aquifer. He'd met my sceptical teasing with a believer's stoicism and a top-up of moonshine. Magnetic fields would guide him to the water. It appeared that today was the day of truth.

'Our windows are leaking.'

'What?' The drill started hammering into the ground.

'Condensation.'

'That's normal, it's hot in the summer, it's cold in the winter. The windows are wooden, they expand and contract. It'll settle down. You'll see.'

I nodded. 'And we still can't shut the front door.' Manu had an answer for everything and so I always pursued him on several fronts. That way he could usually be persuaded to come and at least have a look at a problem. Invariably, though, due to some quirk of French lettings law – I think it's called the foreigner's caveat – the responsibility for, and cost of, repairing fell on us.

'OK, I'll be over.' Grey oozy mud splurged out of the top of the drill, seeping over the ground like volcanic lava.

'It's a good sign,' confirmed the foreman, increasing the power of the drill.

Manu appeared content. 'Might as well look at the door.' Together we trudged back across the field. Conversation was impossible. Instead I hid in Manu's slipstream. The treetops swayed elastically, performing a contortionist dance. The disturbed barks of Manu's hunting dogs filled the occasional silence left by the screaming wind.

'Let's get this door off and see what the problem is.'

'In this wind?'

'Come on.'

Tanya and Elodie were still in their pyjamas and they quickly fled to a warmer part of the house. Invoking the foreigner caveat, Manu levered the door from its hinges and had me bend and take the weight. The wind immediately invaded the house, knocking knives and forks to the floor and sending a mug teetering to the edge of the table.

'Il est descendu.' I've never known anything wooden in Provence not *'descendu'*. It's the universal excuse for things that don't fit.

Manu reached for his drill. My fingers burned with the strain of holding the door. I could feel splinters working their way slowly through my skin and a dull throb in my lower back.

'Have you found water on your *chantier*?' I'd been delaying telling Manu about our building project, reasoning that it was hard enough to get repairs done anyway, let alone if we told him we were moving out. I didn't let my surprise register.

'There was an old well.'

'I'll come and divine if you want, always best to have a second source.'

'It's OK, we're sure there's enough water.' For some reason I didn't want Manu snooping around our building site.

'You'll be needing some more olive trees, though, and I've got some to spare.' Manu's drill whirred and a couple of new screws alleviated the weight. At this point warning bells should have gone off in my head. The Provençaux are notoriously frugal and are always slow to do anything and yet Manu seemed to be offering me some of his trees.

The economics of *oliviers* had always perplexed me. Provence is full of them, yet a mature tree can cost upward of 5,000 euros. The countryside near Maussane-les-Alpilles must hold at least ten thousand. To the locals the olives are a valuable source of income and the region makes some of the best golden peppery oils in Europe. However, the real cash cow is selling mature trees to second homeowners. What pad in the sun is complete without an ancient olive tree by the swimming pool? The thick knotted trunks, to the northern European mind, epitomise the south. A glass of rosé in the shade of an olive tree is what a summer holiday is all about. And so, as with their properties, the Provençaux simply wait for the outsider with a fat cheque book.

Manu's potential gift was therefore unusually generous and completely unexpected, particularly since he was the proud owner of some of the most beautiful trees in the region. Each year he spent weeks pruning his grove into perfect symmetrical shapes. The aesthetic result always had passing photographers reaching for their cameras, but the real motivation was money: a pruned tree produced a larger crop the following year. I'd helped Manu harvest one cold January day and we'd retrieved nearly 10 kilograms of olives per tree, which at the price paid by the mill gave him a substantial annual income from olives alone.

A year ago all but a few of Manu's young saplings had been ripped up by thieves who'd attacked in the middle of the night. At first light the field had looked like it had been visited by an army of moles. I don't think I have ever seen Manu as angry. He strode back to the house, grabbed his shotgun, slung his most vicious hunting dog into the car and headed off to find the perpetrators. Swear words as ripe as an August melon trailed down the drive but the manhunt was unsuccessful. After a couple of days ruminating over the crime, Manu was back out in the fields, paint pot in hand, covering the trunks of his remaining young trees in lashings of vandal-proof paint. The stuff was supposed to become less effective with age, but a year and a bit later, it was as vibrant and virulent as ever.

'*Un, deux, trois!*' We heaved the door back into place.

'Do you want to look at the windows as well?'

'It's just condensation. It's normal. See you on the *chantier* in an hour and we can work out where to put the trees.'

In the three months since construction began I'd learnt to expect frequently interrupted days. To keep to the build schedule, my working life had to take second place to problems on site. Prevarication being the enemy of progress, a week rarely went by without instant decisions being needed – location of the sceptic tank, location of the pump to heat the house, a decision on some cheap but cracked stone tiles for the bathrooms, etc.

Our Tunisian builders might have been reviled by the locals but the speed with which they worked was impressive. Already the exterior walls of the house were up, and today for the first time it was going to be possible to climb the staircase and walk on the first floor. Together we would see the view from our bedroom window, provided, that is, the wind didn't knock us to the ground. I'd planned to visit at the end of the day, but as always things had changed.

The cement mixer was churning when I arrived on the site and the builders were using a pulley system to haul the bricks up to the first floor. The impression was of extreme danger. The men weren't wearing hard hats and as the bricks edged their way higher the bundle swung like a wrecking ball. It appeared only a matter of time before man or wall was taken out by a thudding blow, but I was no expert and so I kept my mouth shut.

The house looked stark, ugly, small, a blot on the beautiful countryside. The walls were hidden by piles of different materials. Bricks, timber, mounds of sand, reclaimed roof tiles – the place was an embarrassing mess of noise and junk, but there was always industry. Normally a fire burnt continually, consuming as much of the waste as possible. Today, old, sodden, wind-slung ashes slapped into my face as I approached. Levering myself up onto the concrete raft on which the walls floated, I saw that the staircase had been set in place. There was no handrail, just a fairy-tale spiral which seemed to defy gravity. I would wait for Tanya before climbing to the first floor.

Two hoots of a car horn attracted my attention. Manu's pick-up truck rattled through the gate. The vehicle drew up by the side of the house and I leapt down to greet him. Somehow I had to hide my disappointment. Normally, transporting olive trees is an almost industrial endeavour. Picture Gulliver pinned to the beach by hundreds of Lilliputian cords: this is what an olive tree in transit usually looks like. Their roots are beasts, almost doubling the size of the tree, a mechanical winch is needed to haul them onto the transport trailer, then rope after rope is used to secure the writhing behemoth. I'd expected Manu to arrive with helpers.

Instead, the back of his truck was empty.

'Salut, Jamie.' Manu leapt proudly from the cabin.

'Now, let's see, where's the best place for olive trees? An avenue down the drive?'

I nodded my assent. It was becoming apparent that Manu saw his role as an advisory one only. If there were to be any olive trees transplanted from his field then I would have to pay for them. Pausing by the well, he kicked over a stone and discovered the discarded box for the new pump.

'Building a swimming pool?'

I shook my head.

'Don't tell me someone's put this down your well.'

I nodded and Manu shook his head ruefully.

'It'll maybe last the year. Look at the box – it's meant for a pool-house. How much did you pay for it?'

Before I could answer, two hoots of a horn signalled the arrival of another car. It was the blue Citroën of Miriam, our neighbour from across the valley.

Miriam strode over, chin out, jaw set. She wore a knee-length fur coat from which the hem of her thin flowery summer dress protruded, flapping recklessly in the wind.

'Glad I caught you. What have you done about your wall?'

First the pump, now the wall. Warm saliva flooded my mouth. Could she already have spotted the extra centimetres of height? I played innocent, ready to deny all knowledge. In the worst case scenario, this being France, perhaps I could bribe her. A crate of wine might be an appropriate starter. A dozen Domaine Tempier from Bandol to begin with, keeping the big battalions, even the odd Bordeaux first growth, for when things got truly desperate.

'What wall?' I stalled.

'Well, the falling down one, of course.'

'Falling down?'

'You mean they haven't told you? Come with me.'

Miriam led me round the side of the house. An ugly smear of fresh concrete was plastered over a 10-metre stretch of bricks.

'I thought you knew. They covered it up yesterday. It was as wide as your arm. Big enough to see on my telescope.'

I rested the palm of my hand against the wall, as if by feel I might ascertain the truth of her story. Certainly something had been quickly hidden from view. The smooth bricks were now ridged and uncomfortable to touch. A brittle tear of concrete came away in my fingers. Underneath I could see daylight. Beneath my feet I imagined the clay soil sighing with relief after the taut, dry summer and, as it relaxed, dragging our expensive foundations downwards, mercilessly cracking anything that rested on them. The folly of building a house on such soil was all too obvious.

'Do you want the number of my lawyer?' Miriam was delighted, hopping from one foot to the other in excitement. 'He's very experienced at this sort of thing. At the same time he can sue whoever sold you the pump.'

'I'll call the building company first, see what they have to say.'

So far the builders had done everything on time, using good materials. They'd responded quickly to all our queries and adapted the shapes of some rooms on request. It was important that we trusted them. The crack must be immaterial, otherwise they would surely have informed us. Despite her professed expertise, Miriam's knowledge of construction had to be as limited as mine. Anyway, how could I rely on the opinion of a woman who spent all day glued to her telescope watching our *chantier* with the mindless loyalty of a soap opera addict?

Manu, I'd noticed, was treating himself to a tour of the house. I'd seen his head poking out from the half-finished roof, but with the fierceness of the wind he'd quickly ducked back down, only to reappear in the sitting room.

'Nice place you're building. Three bedrooms, two bathrooms, kitchen – she's going to be big.' He stood regarding the house, weighing up the quality of the bricks and tiles. 'Good views, not far from the village.' Manu nodded his head. It didn't appear he wanted any response from me, he was almost talking to himself, probably working out how many luminous orange olive trees he could sell me.

The village clock chimed eleven. It had already been an eventful day.

Chapter 23

I am sitting in the small stone *borie* overlooking our truffle trees. It's nearly midnight and the cold has already penetrated five carefully planned layers of clothing. Underneath the fleece, the jumper, the two T-shirts and the vest, my skin is perspiring. The sweat brings a dank chill to my bones. By shifting position I temporarily find comfort, my vest pulls upwards and for a moment at least dry fabric rests against my skin. Jagged stones poke into my back, lodging themselves uncomfortably between my shoulder blades. On my lap is Snuffle, head forlornly pressed between my knees. My hands are sunk underneath his chin for warmth and occasionally I scratch him. It's been two hours now and his movements have gradually become more lethargic. It will be no problem for him to wait like this, semi-alert all night, but for me, the boredom has already crept in.

It's December already. Time usually passes quickly in Provence. It's to do with the strong seasonal differences, the intense blue of summer, the burnished gold of autumn, the white blanket of winter, and the drifting pink blossoms of spring. Nature's clock does not allow the mind to tarry or dwell, instead thoughts are driven ever forward by small changes in the surroundings; the first buds of spring, the heavy late summer grapes falling from the vines, the first pumpkins of autumn, and the heady smell of fires in the hearth heralding winter. Tonight, though, the clock has slowed.

The dead hours until dawn loom. There's nowhere else to look, there's nothing else to see. With my torch I've examined every notch, mark and scratch on the interior walls. The crumbling dust of erosion, the etchings of lovers' names, even what looks like the remains of a swastika. Some of the stones are stained. Water, grease, oil, blood – the rock has imbibed them all. The shelter smells of centuries of agriculture, of rotting wooden implements, rusting iron, stale grain, mould-eaten clothes, wet crumbly rock, of decay, of another, more industrious age. It also smells, if such things have smells, of hardship, of flight, of war. Finally, undeniably, like an undertone in a fine perfume, it smells of truffles.

I imagine my predecessors in this conical structure of stone. First the farmer, who day by day constructed himself a shelter. Every time he overturned a suitable rock in the fields, he would have carted it to this high plateau, and lodged it in the walls of the nascent building. The ridges in the ground show that the land up here was once ploughed, but the main purpose of this lookout, high above the village, must have been for shepherds. Generations of the same family sheltering from the wind, rain and heat, repairing and maintaining when necessary, subsisting on flatbreads studded with olives and tomatoes.

Then, the more recent history. A family of Jews fleeing the narrow streets of the village. Climbing, always climbing, as the torches of the Germans waltz below, the barking dogs becoming more distant and intermittent as they make good their escape. Finally, the relief as they find the promised shelter and huddle inside, all five of them, with their backs curled against the stone walls.

A year or so later, rifles are lined against the wall, a box of grenades, a radio and some explosives. Resistance fighters visit periodically, stocking up for distant raids, speaking in hushed whispers as they fasten the leather straps of the guns and ammunition belts, transforming themselves from peasants to soldiers. Then the last incumbent of the war, a German deserting his comrades in the village. Allied warplanes circle overhead. In irony, in desperation, the soldier carves the swastika into the stone.

Next comes a Frenchman returning from war-ravaged lands, longing above all else to create and to grow. Fingers that once visited destruction now gather the acorns from other truffle-infected trees and sow them in a line in front of the *borie*. Like me, he is summoned to this spot by the first frost of winter, sitting and waiting, determined that no scavenger will beat him to the truffles.

Outside the moon is full and ripe, bright enough to cast shadows. Each branch, each twig, each leaf finds its twin stretched on the ground beneath. The stars are visible in their thousands, with the constellations obvious to all, and the North Star resplendently dominant. There is near silence. Only the sound of leaves fluttering through the branches and settling on the ground. The noise is gentle, and calming, like fat flakes of snow nestling onto a landscape already muffled by a heavy fall.

Underground, I imagine the earth trembling. As the temperature drops the fungus awakens, called by the moon and the cold into life. The gossamer threads that connect the spores to the trees hum with nutrients and the truffles swell and bloom, inexorably pushing the hard frostbitten earth aside. Their ripe infectious smell recalls the heavy spring rain, and the life-saving August storm; pungent and irresistible, the tubers will double and then triple in size. By morning, the field in front of me will be alive with black diamonds. And just like me, every truffle hunter in the village will be waiting for first light to rush to their favoured spots. The purpose of my vigil is to ensure that nobody gets to my trees before me.

This year, the truffle season began with blood. The weather to the north of us has been more extreme and the first truffles are already on restaurant tables. In this initial greedy flurry of activity one man lost his life. A plantation owner, who'd endured a catastrophic drop in his truffle harvest the previous year, decided to take matters into his own hands. He waited up all night, with the cold metal of a rifle resting across his lap. A sound in the field alerted him. Only the accused knows whether the shot was intended as a warning but it certainly wasn't fired into the air. If the court is generous, they'll find he was aiming at a nearby tree; the reality might be he was aiming where he hit – the heart.

In the context of such an event I am hopelessly underprepared. Here I am, armed only with a corkscrew, accompanied by a dog so vicious he once fled a cat. I'm not after revenge, or out to scare people, I just want knowledge. Last year we didn't find a single truffle. Is there a possibility that the trees have stopped producing, or could somebody be getting there before me? I am determined to find out. If a competitor comes, I hope a simple shout will be enough to scare him off.

Snuffle leaps from his resting place, tail in the air, head low to the ground, fur bristling with aggression. I fumble for the torch. I know it's somewhere by my foot, but in the dark of the *borie* my fingers struggle to locate it, ranging over dust and stone. Finally I have it. I swing the beam onto the orchard and all is quiet. The leaves are still falling silently like heavy snow.

With Snuffle to alert me, I can afford to sleep. I roll out a camping mattress and snuggle into my sleeping bag. I close my eyes and realise that I am nearly warm. I wait for sleep to envelop me, but my brain is still working fast. Every day I fight with the building company over some unforeseen element of the construction. The extra charges are mounting up and we are at their mercy, captive clients desperate to get their house built. I'd never appreciated that the construction process would make me feel this hounded.

We are building a home, concentrating on the tiny details that we hope will bring us joy, guarding some money for a fireplace, to tidy the garden, to buy the paint for the shutters and the interior. The boss of our construction company is building her balance sheet, attempting to pass on as much as possible of the rising cost of materials and labour. Each day is a stressful tug of war between these two conflicting aims. Just when I need to spend more time on my wine business, to develop new sales, to finally get our website up and running, I am assailed with the minutiae of construction. Nearly two years after we started, it still isn't clear whether we will have enough money to finish the project.

This week the roof is due to be finished. According to French tradition, we are going to host a party for the builders and some friends. Only part of me feels like having the *fête*. People have promised me that it will get easier once the work starts on the inside. There will be fewer surprises, fewer unexpected costs. I hope they are right. At the back of my mind I am still worried about the illegally large wall. The additional centimetres have brought with them endless angst. We've sunk everything into the project and yet, come completion, the planning office at the *préfecture* could force us to knock it down. Then there's the chance the foundations will not hold, and that the clay soil will triumph. As yet there have been no more cracks, but I check the walls every day.

I drift into truffle-filled dreams. The *borie* becomes a sauna. The coals hiss steam. Someone adds more water. I look again at the coals and realise that they are actually truffles. The aroma of the tuber is so overpowering it becomes difficult to breathe. I cover my mouth with a towel to avoid choking on the fumes. I wake with a start to find Snuffle sitting on my face. He whimpers for food. Outside the leaves still fall. Underground, the truffles are expanding. I can sense it. I look at my watch: it's 4 a.m. The poachers will be leaving their warm beds, making their way to their preferred trees, waiting for the first chink of dawn. I close my eyes and hope that sleep will come again.

This time it's the truffles I can't get out of my mind. All the literature says my orchard is perfect for truffles. The study from the bank confirmed the trees were infected with the spore for *Tuber melanosporum*, the black diamond, the second most expensive truffle in the world after the Piedmont white. The trees are planted the ideal 10 metres apart. The oaks are the recommended mixture of the three producing species. Last Easter, under the light of the full moon, I climbed each oak and pruned the largest branches to ensure that plenty of summer sunlight hit the soil below. Heat, moisture, aspect, soil type, the cycles of the moon – I am as obsessive as a vigneron. It isn't about the money, though; the determination stems from a desire to prove we haven't been duped into buying the plot of land by the myth, rather than the reality, of a truffle harvest.

Once more sleep comes, disjointed and filled with unpleasant dreams. In the Bar du Centre, my locals' beer glass – a wine glass, a tumbler, whatever receptacle is to hand – is replaced by the standard 25-cl serving and then, horror of horrors, by the litre mugs reserved for the Dutch and German tourists. In the corner Serge titters unpleasantly, chewing on tobacco that drips like black tar onto the table. He crosses and raises a saw, chopping each of the legs from my stool in turn, until I am squatting on the floor, trying to reach my drink, which is still resting on the bar. Somebody knocks the glass onto my head and beer hisses through my hair like boiling water through a colander.

I wake. The sky is hovering between night and day, the stars have disappeared, and smudges of watery grey dissolve the black. The moon is still visible, but paler, disappearing by the second as the sky brightens. Snuffle is on his feet by the door of the *borie*. He's quiet, but his posture makes me think he's heard or seen something. His head snaps to the left and he barks fiercely with anger. He's gone, chasing into the bushes, tail outstretched behind him. I kick my legs like a drowning man, forcing the sleeping bag from my body. I grab the torch and then discard it, realising it will be useless. I follow Snuffle, tumbling down the hill away from the truffle trees. Down I go, pulling up my belt-less trousers as I run. Snuffle is still barking. Unbelievably, I am catching up with him. Perhaps he has them cornered. He comes into sight, all black, big paws scrambling at the bark of a tree like a baby bear. Catching my breath, I look up. Rather than the dark eyes of a Provençal peasant, there's a cat. I shake my head in despair.

'Come on Snuffle, let's go and find the truffles.'

It's cold, really cold, back up by the oak trees. The ground is solid and white. The fallen acorns are encrusted with ice. Their cups resemble the frosted rim of a cocktail glass. The flat light is lifting, the trees emerge from amorphous dark shadows. The pale leaves on the evergreen oaks are visible; seconds later, so is the crumpled tinder-brown foliage of the other trees. Wet air carries the smells of the night, the combined rasping, rooting breath of hundreds of animals and the shivering perspiration of the undergrowth. An anaemic sun offers only the memory of warmth.

'Over here!' I call to Snuffle and crunch my way over branches and twigs made brittle by the freeze, snapping them like ancient bones. I change the tone of my voice. It becomes gruffer, more commanding. We are at work. This is what we have waited the whole night for, defending our patch. The truffles are now ours by dint of our ownership of the land and our ceaseless vigil. One tree at a time, we mustn't miss them by hurrying.

Snuffle is alert and focused. His small feet scurry across the ground, taking him first in one direction then another. There is no pattern to his movement. It is so random and haphazard that an observer might think him deranged. All the time, though, Snuffle's nose is to the ground, his brain working hard to filter the multitude of scents and isolate the black diamonds. In my pocket I have his favourite treat of small chopped-up pieces of saucisson. He knows the food is there, he's seen it and smelt it, and he knows what he has to do to earn the reward. The work is exciting, exhilarating. I watch my dog's every movement, anxious not to miss his signals.

The first three trees have not produced and we move on. There's no need to panic yet. Truffles appear erratically. These same barren trees might in following weeks be surrounded by the tubers. All across the valley, this scene is being repeated. Dogs scampering across the ground, pausing, and pawing at the earth. Their owners following closely behind, alert to the dog and any untoward sounds that might indicate they are being watched. It could be the owner of the land, or worse still, a rival hunter trying to identify truffle-bearing trees.

Six trees down and Snuffle's enthusiasm is waning. He looks plaintively at me, demanding recompense for the work he has done. I withhold the saucisson and he returns to work, but at a reduced speed. A suspicion grows in my mind that he knows there are no truffles. He's going through the motions for my sake, but the telltale smell is just not there. Another two barren trees and we are at the far side of the orchard. The *borie* where we spent our cold night is only just visible. My limbs feel suddenly stiff, and tiredness assails me. I rest a hand on the trunk of a tree. Snuffle has finished searching. He's lying on the ground panting, looking patiently up at me. I offer him some saucisson, which he gratefully accepts.

Perfect conditions, no possibility that someone was here before us, and yet still no truffles. After all the training and work, it's incredibly disappointing. The chill is oppressive. I cross to the *borie* and gather my possessions, folding the sleeping bag away and quickly shoving the remains of my belongings into a rucksack. The tips of my toes sting with pain. I'd remembered layers of clothing but foolishly only worn one woolly pair of socks. My feet are heavy and unsteady as I traipse back through the pines, stumbling where the gradient is steep. Wisps of cloud shroud the village. The clock tower spears through one such puff, and the iron framework from which the bell hangs hovers weightless in the air, severed from the body of the building. It's a strange and beautiful view. One to be treasured and added to the rich repository of sights and smells that make up our life here.

Chapter 24

At the front of the room three gendarmes are scanning the gathered crowd. These officers are not the slick, sunglass-wearing, motorbike-riding, fag-smoking, gun-toting youngsters that hang around roundabouts eyeing up the girls. No, they are *sérieux*, older, wiser, with guts that testify to a working life of two-hour lunches and complimentary wine for the boys in blue. Their paunches hang over their belts and bars of fat collect under their chins. Heavy bags slouch from their eyes. Haircuts are universally short, trimmed right back to the scalp, like a football hooligan or a boxer. There is an air of fatigue crossed with despair. It comes from the way they stand, all drooped and despondent, going through the motions for the sake of form.

I can't really blame them. The audience this evening is a group of local *trufficulteurs* called together in response to the shooting. Even Dan Brown couldn't conjure a secret society as tight and impenetrable as this lot. They listen but they don't say anything. I am sitting at the back. In front of me are three rows of men. Bald spots alternate with cloth caps, ski jackets with leather jackets. The smell of truffles is wrapped around these men like a cloak. A forensic examination would find shards of the tuber under their nails, and in their hair. It's cold in the hall. Outside it has begun to snow. It's a few days before Christmas and people are anxious to get home before the roads close. As darkness falls the luminous green exit sign becomes prominent. There's an emergency door with a push-bar handle that'll take me straight out onto the streets.

So far there's been a lot of talk from the police. They only have so many cars, so many officers, the amount of land to cover is vast, expecting them to provide round-the-clock protection to *truffières* is unrealistic. However, and this is why we are all here, there mustn't be a vendetta. People must not take justice into their own hands.

'Every time you see a suspect car, you must give us the number plate, the time and the date. Even if the plate is false, we can do something. And if a suspect is apprehended a number of times early in the morning, or late at night, he better be able to justify his presence.'

There was silence. People stared at the paint on the walls, the ceiling, mud-stained boots. They shifted in their seats, and the legs of chairs squeaked on the cheap plastic floor. It appeared the meeting was breaking up without any progress having been made.

'What happened could have happened to any of us.' The speaker wore a blue jacket and had a silvery-white crop of hair. 'He was a good man, and we will do all we can to help his family. Justice is badly served to consider such a man an assassin. All he was doing was protecting his property. Next time, you won't find the body – it'll be leg irons and the Rhône or a hole in the ground.'

The police officers stood, arms crossed, lips pursed. Unwittingly, they'd multiplied their work. Wheel clamping was beyond their remit, let alone digging for dead poachers.

Another man stood – cloth cap, patches on the arms of his jacket, and trousers that sagged around a large derriere. 'We are armed because we know the robbers are armed. Go to the

Carpentras market, and speak to the buyers; if we are robbed, it's not to make omelettes.'

The inference was clear – if the *voleurs* had been gourmands rather than businessmen, lining their stomachs rather than their purses, they might have been forgiven. However, it was obvious that the stolen truffles were destined for the world market, rather than the table of a hungry peasant.

'Last year I was robbed three times in a week,' shouted an angry farmer. 'I fenced off my trees – the next night they came with wire cutters.'

'And you,' an accusatory finger was jabbed at the police, 'you call us here, and you've never caught a single person.'

Tempers were raised. An uneventful meeting was suddenly transformed. People clamoured for their turn to speak. Fists and arms were waved in wild gestures, prescribing full circles in the air. The gendarmes looked on, impassive.

'Everyone knows who the robbers are,' shouted another man.

The lead gendarme had had enough. He stepped forward and slowly removed a notebook and pen. Flicking through the pages, he found his place.

'Perhaps you would like to give me their names.'

The hall went quiet. Snow drifted past the window. The engine of a car was revved and revved again. The rear door to the room swung open and a latecomer entered. The man leant against the wall and folded his arms. Cold air seeped into the room and I shivered. Nobody spoke.

'Come on, if you want this to stop, give me names.'

The men looked at each other, waiting for someone to break the code of silence. Ears were rubbed, hats taken from and then replaced onto heads, jacket collars raised and then lowered, scarves wrapped in ever tighter nooses.

'Why don't you help?' The gendarme snapped his book shut.

'I once made a police statement and accused a robber. What happened? Nothing.'

'*C'est vrai.*'

'*Il a raison.*'

Men muttered to their neighbours and the tension left the room. The reason none of them were speaking was police incompetence. It had nothing to do with the fact that in tough times, with truffles scarcer and scarcer, they each suspected the other. Far better to blame the police than name a neighbour.

On my way out I was accosted by a young man in a business suit. In his hands he held a pile of pamphlets for his security company. He thrust one of the leaflets into my hand. The title read, 'Laser protection, the only way forward for the truffle industry.' A photo showed a line of truffle trees criss-crossed by a mesh of beams. 'Anyone breaks the beam and our armed response team will be with you in minutes,' said the young man in a cheery manner, as if he was promising the swift delivery of a pizza, rather than the arrival of a collection of Uzi-wielding ex-servicemen.

Fires blazed in a circle around our new house, punching a hole in the snowstorm. Someone played a jaunty tune on a violin. The music, when mixed with the snow and the flickering light, gave the scene a surreal, almost theatrical feel. The smell of roasting meat drifted on the air.

Snuffle heard my car arrive and came roaring towards me. Leaping up on two feet he resembled a performing circus bear. After the requisite minute of patting he lost interest and flung himself around in the snow. His favourite game appeared to be springing into the air to try to catch the falling flakes. Given the vicious abandon with which he snapped his jaw shut, he might have been trapping leaping salmon rather than particles of frozen water. For variation, he charged around in a circle and then at full speed headbutted the gathering drifts.

Inside the house a group of about fifteen people were gathered. Coffee cups and a bottle of wine were balanced on pieces of brick and wood. A concrete mixer had been filled with snow and was in use as a temporary fridge. A kettle suspended over the fire whistled. Tanya was sitting in a camp chair, wrapped in a warm blanket. One of the builders was rolling a ball towards Elodie, who was whooping with delight. Another builder was perched on a window sill with a violin on his lap. The face of Madame Roland, the *directrice* of the company, was hidden by an enormous fur hat. Such was its size and squashed aspect, it appeared a raccoon or similar animal had fallen from a skyscraper and plastered itself onto her head.

'*Et alors, Jamie, vous êtes content?*' She waved her hand dramatically in the direction of the new roof.

I nodded my assent. In fact, I was troubled. The meeting with the gendarmes had disturbed me. When we'd bought the plot of land the truffle trees had seemed an added attraction, an opportunity to share in the mystique of Provence. The stories we'd heard in the bars made *cavage* – the practice of hunting for truffles with a dog – seem like a romantic profession. Theft was involved but the fact that the object being stolen was effectively a mushroom made the whole crime seem trivial. To the English mind, at least, it had been amusing – so redolent of the Provençaux, always thinking of their stomachs.

The meeting had changed my perspective. The readiness with which everybody had admitted to carrying guns was scary. My midnight vigil had seemed a slightly eccentric way of ensuring nobody got to my truffles before me; unbeknown to me, it had also been dangerous. The atmosphere among the *trufficulteurs* was sour. Shoot first and ask questions later, was the repeated refrain. The thieves would presumably take the same view. Did I really want to be involved in this? Did my family? All for the sake of a couple of thousand euros a year.

Adding to my concerns was the lack of guests at the party. We'd invited most of the people we knew in the village but only a scattering had turned up. All right, it was snowing, but the house was scarcely a kilometre away and there was under an inch on the ground. In my head our falling popularity was inextricably linked with the story of the construction of the house. My relationship with Ange was still terrible. Ange and I saw each other maybe once or twice a week, passing on the street or in our cars. Neither of us bothered to even look at the other, staring stonily ahead. For a couple of minutes afterwards I always felt angry. Unwanted thoughts tormented me. What was being said about us behind our backs, and by whom? Would our life here ever get back to normal?

'Jamie, vous êtes content?' Madame Roland asked again.

'Oui, je suis content.'

'Well, you shouldn't be.' Miriam rejoined the party. She'd been nosing around on the first floor. 'Tiles are unevenly laid. The whole thing will probably collapse under the weight of the snow. There are more cracks in the walls, the building's being tossed around like a boat – surprised if she'll see spring.'

'Perhaps you'd like to point the problems out,' said Madame diplomatically, cleverly leading Miriam away. I'd already formed the impression that Miriam was a pathological doom monger. If she'd been on the passenger list of the *Titanic*, she'd have disembarked, having imagined some problem or other prior to departure. Doubtless she'd have told all the other passengers, but nobody would have listened.

I rejoined Tanya. The early stages of her second pregnancy had been particularly uncomfortable. Every morning she was assailed by waves of nausea. Stoically she refused to let me look after

Elodie, insisting I concentrate on the construction and the wine business. In the firelight her skin looked pale and her face drawn. The blood had drained from her lower lip and whether from the cold or otherwise she gave an involuntary shiver. The construction of the house was taking its toll. In some respects it was harder for her. Relationships with people in the village which she'd worked hard on were suddenly and inexplicably severed.

For the first time in a long while we'd begun to reminisce about England, about what we missed, the convenience of being able to form friendships with people in our own language, without the inevitable cultural misunderstandings. Conversations like this had been relatively common when we first moved to France. However, they'd quickly faded as we became more and more immersed in life in Provence. Their re-emergence was perhaps a sign of the vulnerability we both felt. Perhaps it was also the pregnancy. It was only natural for Tanya to want to be with close family in a secure homely environment.

Our hearts were in the new home, but every night we slept in the rented farmhouse apartment which was showing increasing signs of wear. In the morning we awoke to swimming pools under the windows and a strong draught seeping under the warped front door. Every couple of weeks or so I complained to Manu. He simply shrugged and said it was natural condensation. The damp had begun to affect all our health, with colds lingering longer than normal. Poor Elodie was suffering the most and her nose was streaming on a semi-permanent basis.

Squatting down next to Tanya, I took her hand. She smelled of cough sweets.

'Everything OK?'

She nodded.

'I'll drive you home if you like.'

'No, I'll stay, time you carved the lamb.'

Earlier we'd fashioned a table out of breeze blocks and some wooden planks. The meat smelt of charred rosemary, roasted garlic and crackling fat. The leg glistened in the firelight, its skin attaining a reflective sheen. As the snow fell outside, the builders, their boss, Miriam, Tanya and Elodie all huddled around, drawn over by the siren smell of the lamb. Together we were an odd bunch, brought together by the endeavour of building a house. As I sliced the meat onto plates I realised that despite these men working for us for nigh on four months, we'd hardly spoken. During my visits to the site there had always been a distance. The pace of their work would slow, they'd observe me, we'd say hello and goodbye and that was it. Normally there were two men working, sometimes three, exceptionally four. Superficially their features were similar to the Provençaux – dark eyes, dark hair, dark skin – however, they were taller, leaner and their colouration just a subtle shade deeper. The locals summed this all up in one word. *'Arabe.'*

I ate next to the man I judged to be the oldest. His stubble was flecked white, his skin creased, particularly around the eyes and on the backs of his hands. Eschewing the proffered knife and fork, he dissected the lamb with his fingers, pulling away strips of meat and dangling them into his mouth. He drank water rather than wine.

'Is it OK, the work?' I asked.

'It's not bad.'

'Do you go to the village?'

'Never.'

Our conversation was punctuated by long intervals of silence and made harder by the fact that our French accents appeared mutually unintelligible.

'Why not?'

'Here we have wood for a fire, we have food, we have beds, we have music, what more do we need?'

'Do you miss home?'

'A little, we send the money back.'

'And after this job?'

'Maybe home, maybe another job.'

The man ate his food quickly. Sitting with me made him uncomfortable and he was glad when he was finished and was able to reach for his cigarettes and head outside.

I noticed that Snuffle had isolated a late arrival at the party. It was Franck, the electrician and parent at Elodie's crèche. Snuffle's eyes never left the man's plate. His tail wagged as if it were clockwork. Occasionally, the electrician tossed him a piece of lamb which disappeared in an instant.

'Can I offer you some more wine?' I crossed the room.

'Thanks! What's the breed?'

'Petit chien lion.'

'I've got a poodle.'

'A poodle?' Surprise must have registered in my voice. I'd not seen a dog at Franck's house and the breed seemed wrong for this butch workman.

'They're the best for truffle hunting.'

He was right. Hypoallergenic with a turbo-charged nose, a poodle would have been perfect, but for my vanity. An idea occurred to me. 'Would you like to see our trees?'

'Already have.' Franck took a mouthful of food, seemingly enjoying a personal joke. 'But there aren't any truffles.'

It took me a moment to digest the implication.

Franck winked and stroked Snuffle. 'Maybe you'll have better luck next year.'

'You know he's in training.'

'Seems to prefer meat.' Franck dangled some lamb into Snuffle's mouth. 'He's a lion dog, after all.'

We both stared into the fire. How should I deal with the fact that Franck had been scouring the *chantier* for truffles?

'Tell you what,' said Franck, putting his plate on the floor for Snuffle to clean, 'I'll take you with me one day, show you how it's done.'

'Really?'

I was as excited as a puppy in snow. If I'd been outside, I would have headbutted a drift to check I wasn't dreaming. A truffle hunter offering to share information. Tradition had it that Franck, on his deathbed, should have whispered the location of his trees to his chosen successor. Yet here he was, bold as anything, offering to take me on a tour.

'Too much snow at the moment,' Franck peered outside. 'I'll give you a call when conditions are right.'

The offer was a lifeline. The more a dog finds truffles, the better he becomes. Success breeds success, and the dog comes to associate rooting around under trees with his or her favourite treat. The converse, of course, is also true. Failure breeds apathy and boredom.

During the autumn, under Gaspar's tutelage, Snuffle and I had had plenty of success with the Canitruffe; however, we'd yet to properly unearth a truffle. The more we tried, the more uninterested Snuffle became. I'd even noticed that oak trees had begun to induce lethargy in him. On a walk he'd hang back and pant with feigned exhaustion rather than risk the farce of another unsuccessful hunt.

'Where's your *truffière*?'

'You misunderstand.' Franck winked and I began to fear the worst. 'I just know some places.'

Right now was probably the most dangerous time to hunt for truffles in a decade. Both the police and the *trufficulteurs* had used the word vendetta. At the moment Provence had more gun slinging peasants than a small African republic and an American Bible Belt state combined. What's more, trigger fingers were as itchy as a bad case of venereal disease.

'Have you ever been shot at?'

Franck nodded.

'Just the once.'

He rolled up his sleeve to show me the scar and firelight flickered over the ugly red welt.

Chapter 25

Christmas approached and as a special treat, we did our festive shopping in Aix-en-Provence, meandering along the Cours Mirabeau, marvelling at the lights draped like expensive jewels between the rows of plane trees. Traders in temporary wooden huts stretched from the statue of King René, opposite the Deux Garçons cafe, to the tumbling fountain in the middle of the roundabout at the base. These opportunists sold nativity figures, lights, plates, linens, and of course, this being France, food. The finest foie gras, seafood glistening on trays of ice, free range *chapons* with golden corn-fed sheens, mulled wine, roasted chestnuts and champagne.

Later in the day we celebrated Elodie's second birthday by buying the Christmas tree and inviting children over from her crèche to festoon it with decorations. A crisp layer of frost coated the countryside, the skies were cloudless, a perfect regal blue, and wisps of pungent smoke drifted from the chimneys of the village houses. The drive filled with cars, and our house with the sound of children's voices. Once the tree was finished, the children donned coats and gloves and wrapped tinsel around the lower branches of the nearest olive trees. I drank an inordinate amount of champagne and Tanya rested her hand on her belly with a contented smile. Although it was too faint for me to feel, the new baby had started kicking.

On Christmas Eve, we attended the crib service in the neighbouring village, climbing with the rest of the inhabitants to the small church that rested on a rocky outcrop. The procession was torchlit, and the tight cobbled streets forced people and animals together. Elodie sat on my shoulders and the steaming breath of a nearby donkey wafted in front of her face. Amid the crowd I could see Franck with his daughter, Coralie. The snow from the previous week had melted, and yet it was still cold. The conditions were perfect for truffles and the call might very well come in the next day or so.

The arrival of Tanya's parents on Christmas morning spared us the debate of whether to go to the village bar or not. Instead, we feasted on *coquillage, chapon* with grated truffle, brie laced with truffle and – a trick learnt from Annie in Uzès – *crème brûlée à la truffe*. Outside, Provence shone under clear skies and for the next few days we walked amid the vines and olive trees. Elodie sat happily in a rucksack on my back and we ambled through the surrounding countryside, discovering new tracks.

By New Year my stomach felt as swollen as Tanya's. January started with a diet and a long anxious wait for a call from Franck. Snuffle and I scratched unsuccessfully away at the base of our oak trees. Frosts, full moons – nothing made any difference. There were no truffles. Meanwhile, each week was punctuated by a visit to one health advisor or another.

France spends 11 per cent of its GDP on its health service, the UK 9 per cent. I was never aware that 2 per cent could make such a difference. While friends in England were lucky to get one or two scans during their term, Tanya visited the *centre de radiologie* every month. Instead of waiting all morning for the machine to be free, she was called through within minutes of her appointed time.

Often she saw the gynaecologist immediately after the scan. The whole experience was quick, efficient and incredibly thorough. Blood tests were another monthly event. Everything from glucose levels to signs of toxoplasmosis was measured and monitored.

And, of course, there was the inevitable visit to the dietician. The questions were personal – how much weight did she put on during her last pregnancy? On the hips? On the stomach? How quickly did she regain her shape? Did her husband appreciate the speed of recovery? This last question was tantamount to asking how soon we got back into bed together, but according to Tanya it was delivered with a completely straight face, in a totally professional manner.

The list of what she could and couldn't eat was exhaustive. Its compiler was presumably a misogynist gourmand who liked women to suffer – foie gras, *coquillages*, *fromages*, *jambon sec*, *saumon fumé*. The notes went into extraordinary detail. For example, the dried ham section ran to about ten different varieties; Parma, Serrano, Pata Negra, etc... Clearly the umbrella term would have sufficed but someone wanted pregnant women to dwell on what they were missing.

The speed of progress on the house was uplifting. The windows had been installed early in the new year, and once the place was watertight, workmen scurried all over the interior. Plasterers rendered the interior walls, pipes for the underfloor heating were laid and covered in a protective foam, great fistfuls of coloured wires were yanked into gaping sockets, and the bath tiled into place. Suddenly, from a concrete shell, the house was transformed into somewhere we could envisage living.

The completion date was still months away, but as the essential services were connected, the first drop of water fell from the taps, and the first bulb pinged into life, it became more and more frustrating not to be able to move in, particularly since our problems with Manu and our rented accommodation showed no signs of abating. On a weekly basis a swarm of flies hatched in our living room. The warm humid atmosphere created by the condensation was apparently the perfect incubator and the chemical warfare which I waged on a daily basis ineffective. Mould grew in the bathroom, swallowing the carcasses of dead flies, and no amount of cleaning products could halt the progress of nature. Manu simply shrugged and said, 'C'est la Provence.'

Towards the end of February the weather changed. An unseasonably hot sun heralded an early spring. Trees budded, wild flowers coloured the fields, and the Provençaux emerged from their houses, attacking the rampant weeds which threatened to overpower their gardens. Truffles vanished from menus and it seemed another season had passed.

Daily life continued, the pungent Provençal mix of paradise and problems, heady black coffees on the terraces of cafes, early evening walks through olive groves and oak woods, discovering hitherto hidden fountains in nearby villages, delays on the *chantier*, falling sales in my wine business, trips to the doctor with Tanya, and sleepless nights with Elodie as she succumbed to damp-induced colds.

I forgot all about finding truffles. Then, in the middle of March, the temperature suddenly dropped, hovering near freezing. I looked at the cycle of the moon: it was perfect. The mistral swept in from the Alps, driving the gauge down still further, until I awoke one morning to a fine silver dusting. The landscape shimmered and shivered in the morning light. Underground, for one final time, tubers stirred, gossamer threads hummed with nutrients, and the black diamonds began to grow. In response to this final call to the fields, Snuffle the Truffle Hound retreated deeper into our house, barely poking his nose beyond the door. A couple of forays into our *truffière* produced nothing but despondent empty-handed returns.

Unsurprisingly, Franck the electrician disappeared from the morning drop-offs at crèche and unsurprisingly my phone didn't ring. His offer of help had probably been genuine at the time. A few glasses of wine and a convivial environment had induced a rare crack in the *cavage* code of secrecy. However, he'd doubtless woken up the following morning and thought better of his proposal. Why should he reveal hidden truffle locations? Part of me was relieved that the phone hadn't rung. Although no more shootings had been reported, the papers were still full of news about the ongoing war between *trufficulteurs* and poachers. Tensions and tempers were high. Franck's invitation was to go poaching, to break the law and to risk being fired at. Better he didn't call. Yet part of me still itched to find my first black diamond with Snuffle.

Chapter 26

Frost still lay heavy on the ground when I was summoned to an electrical emergency at the building site. The power had gone out and obstinately refused to go back on. My presence was required to OK an *augmentation de puissance* from EDF; essentially, pumping more juice down the line to keep all the heavy construction equipment running. I'd called Franck for some impartial advice on what was and was not necessary and he'd kindly dropped around to the *chantier*.

Technicians from EDF surrounded him, irate workmen denied power made their excuses for the delay in the work programme, and everyone waved their arms dramatically. Something as simple as flipping a switch and adding some more power became a half-hour argument. As the denouement approached and the EDF technicians shrugged their shoulders and claimed it was more than their job was worth to do anything before lunch, Franck looked at me.

'*C'est le bon moment pour aller chercher les truffes.*'

Off guard, concentrating more on electrical problems than *trufficulteurs* with shotguns, and answering instinctively, I said, '*Pourquoi pas?*' Why not?

Franck's car was a little old Fiat. The worn cloth of the seats, the dusty floor mats, the plastic trim, the entire interior reeked of truffles. On the dashboard was a curious device which is perhaps best described as a spirit level for cars. A line ran through the centre of an image of a car, and as the gradient increased so the line moved perilously near to the roof of the car, which, as Franck explained, was tipping point.

'It comes in handy when parking in strange places, or making a run for it.'

I consider myself quite an expert on the local roads. If I see a track I haven't been on, I take it just to find out where it goes. Before I got into the car with Franck I had proudly boasted that I'd been on every road in our village. No longer. Franck opened my eyes. Chains across dirt tracks: simply lift them up and pass underneath. Bushes blocking the way: drive through them. No entry signs: ignore them. There was nowhere Franck's little Fiat couldn't go. A maze of undiscovered trails charted the hillside, and a driver with no concern for the undercarriage of his car and one of Franck's spirit level devices could pass from Provençal village to village without the need for main roads.

On occasions we came dangerously close to tipping up. I formed the impression that Franck was taking the scenic route to his truffle trees. After half an hour in the car, the village was still in sight, but we'd weaved along such an intricate pattern of tracks that there was no chance of me finding the way again. Franck's dog sat on his lap as he drove. It was a miniature white poodle called Fred that belonged in the handbag of a Parisian grandame rather than rooting around in the Provençal *garrigue*. Snuffle sat on my lap wagging his tail enthusiastically at his new friend, unaware that he was about to be given a master class in *cavage*.

'*Et voilà, nous sommes ici.*'

Franck brought the Fiat to a juddering halt, driving it deep into the undergrowth. It was a struggle to open the door, but eventually I prised it open. Snuffle and I slipped out.

'Quiet.' Franck raised his hand. 'Can you hear something?'

I shook my head.

'Helicopter, Lyon to Marseille, commercial flight, nothing to worry us.'

We stood still. The surrounding pine trees swayed in a gentle breeze. It was cold and damp, the shadows long, and the atmosphere uninviting. Still Franck held his hand in the air to keep me from moving.

'OK, on my signal, run as fast as you can towards the clearing. Don't look back. Go.'

Snuffle and I set off at a sprint. I could hear Franck and Fred the poodle pounding the earth beside us. The subterfuge seemed ridiculous. We were in the middle of a wood, miles from anywhere. We'd listened for a good five minutes to check there was no one else around and now both of us were sprinting like we were being chased by a pack of Dobermanns.

'Good, that went well.' Franck was panting from the exertion. 'See those vines over there? Go.'

Up we sprang. I felt like I should have been wearing camouflage clothing and have smeared my face with warpaint. To keep Franck happy, I crouched as low to the ground as possible when running, coming to a skidding commando crawl finish.

'Is all this really necessary?'

'You'd be surprised. Right now there'll be at least five other truffle hunters on this hill. Everybody knows it's the last weekend of the season. They'll be checking the trees they know produce and watching for signs of movements. If they get lucky, they can capture another hunter's tree. Some people just hide in the woods, and wait and watch, changing location with every moon. Eventually they always get lucky and discover other hunters' trees.'

'But who does this land belong to?'

'Parisians – they're only here in July, no idea they've got truffles.'

'At least we're not going to get shot at.'

'Not here,' said Franck. 'Let's get started. Fred'll show the way.'

Franck's first truffle-hunting site was in the corner of a field of vines. A row of oak trees ran alongside. As we approached, a cloud of flies rose from the ground, making it almost impossible to breathe without inhaling a lungful of insects. The earth between the vines was littered with heavy stones and still covered in the crisp frost. I fumbled in my pocket to check I had Snuffle's treats. The ends of my fingers were already numb and heavy with cold and the tips of my ears burnt a bright red.

'Allez Fred – cherche! C'est où? C'est là? Cherche!'

Franck spoke hurriedly to Fred as the poodle zigzagged between the vines, nose to the floor. Each time the dog paused Franck would ask *'C'est là?'* but then Fred would move on and Franck would repeat his previous mantra, *'Allez Fred – cherche! C'est où? C'est là? Cherche!'* The words were whispered under his breath, presumably in case there were any other truffle hunters nearby. The tone of voice, the urgency and the repetitive nature of the command reminded me of farmers and their sheepdogs as they tried to round up livestock into a pen.

'Allez Fred – cherche! C'est où? C'est là? Cherche! Bien, c'est là.'

Fred had stopped and was pawing vigorously at the ground. Franck moved the poodle aside, took a large screwdriver from his pocket and began to dig furiously. As the hole became deeper he took large handfuls of earth, pushing them right under his nose, so that soon his nostrils were caked with mud.

'There's one here,' he said handing me some dirt and encouraging me to sniff. Franck was right – the crumbling cold soil smelt unmistakeably of truffle. He continued to dig, always smelling the earth to work out whether he was getting closer or further from the truffle. Eventually the tuber emerged, caked in mud, pockmarked, and smelling as strong as a teenage boy's bedroom. The first person to ever eat a truffle must have been desperately hungry.

Fred the poodle continued his search. In the next quarter of an hour he unearthed six more truffles. Each time Franck rewarded him with a small piece of saucisson, and then the hunt continued.

'Allez Fred – cherche! C'est où? C'est là? Cherche!'

Snuffle sitting by my side, watching attentively, reminded me of a substitute at a football match, nerves mounting, his side losing, desperately trying to get the coach's attention so that he could get onto the pitch. Franck moved us on 50 metres or so. I took Snuffle off his lead and pushed a recently unearthed truffle under his nose. We were off.

'Allez Snuffle – cherche! C'est où? C'est là? Cherche!'

Compared with the more experienced Fred, Snuffle's progress was much slower. He frequently doubled back on himself, sniffing the same piece of ground. Eventually, he stopped and scratched away at the soil with his paws. Franck swooped in with his screwdriver, quickly excavating a hole.

'Bien, Snuffle.' I enthusiastically patted my dog and handed over a small piece of cheese.

Franck handed me the soil to sniff and I inhaled deeply. 'Nothing.'

'Rien,' Franck confirmed. 'Never give your dog a treat until you are sure he's found a truffle.'

'Allez Snuffle – cherche! C'est où? C'est là? Cherche!'

Snuffle started again, working his way between the vines. Within a minute he was scratching away with his paws. This time I took Franck's screwdriver, ramming it into the icy ground and levering away the soil. Deeper and deeper I went, pulling at a great clump and holding it to my nose. I smelt nothing at first, but then very faintly I thought I detected the odour of truffles. I handed the soil to Franck and dug away.

'It's there, but it's deep – try a little to your left,' guided Franck as I handed over more soil. I put the screwdriver down and used my fingers to push away the soil. Bent double, peering into a hole in the ground, I felt like an archaeologist trying to prise a rare find from an earthy tomb. With my nails I probed away, grating them across the dimpled surface of a truffle. Franck bent next to me and used the screwdriver as a lever. Slowly the truffle emerged, breaking free from the ground, until in the palm of my hand I held a great big, delightful, malodorous lump of black diamond. My heart thumped with pleasure.

'Well done, Snuffle!' I fished an enormous piece of cheese from my pocket. Snuffle wagged his tail with delight.

'Allez Snuffle – cherche! C'est où? C'est là? Cherche!' We were off again, riding a giddy wave of success. In the next five minutes we unearthed another two truffles and for the first time I began to appreciate what it was to be a true truffle hunter. It wasn't about the money or the secrecy, or even the seductive taste of the truffles, it was about the thrill of the search, working at one with your dog, putting into practice all the training, and then the elation of the find. It was addictive, adrenalin-fuelled fun. Base jumpers should give up throwing themselves off buildings and get truffle dogs instead.

For the next hour we snaked through the hills in Franck's Fiat. A few times the line on his spirit level teetered on the tipping point, but somehow, miraculously, we always rocked back down onto all four wheels. We stopped at three other locations and each time the routine was the same: park the car in the bushes, wait for five minutes to check nobody else was around, then scurry as fast as possible to the truffle trees. On occasions we saw the cars of other truffle hunters between the trees. Franck recognised the make and model of each car and could even tell me the breed of dog of each of the hunters. Once another hunter had been spotted there appeared to be a code of conduct that dictated both parties should go their separate ways. Franck kept the truffles we discovered in an egg carton in the glove compartment of his car. We'd quickly accumulated nearly two dozen truffles. At this time of the year they tended to be small but Franck estimated that he could get about 250 euros for the lot in Carpentras market.

The last site we visited was closest to the village and for the first time we'd parked the car on a tarmac road, several hundred metres away from where we'd ducked into the undergrowth. We were walking back down this road, dogs trotting happily at our sides, four more truffles for the egg box in the car, when it happened.

Warm fingers of light crept through the gaps in the hedgerow, stretching along the tarmac and engulfing the little Fiat. The running and ducking, digging and scraping had made my limbs weary and I moved with the satisfying heaviness of a good morning's work. The problems at the *chantier*, the *augmentation de puissance*, the intransigence of the EDF engineers seemed distant worries, easily solved. I was alive with the joys of living in Provence, at having finally successfully drawn back the curtain and peeked in at the secret world of the truffle hunter. Already I couldn't wait till next winter, when surely our *truffière* would start producing.

A branch jutted across the road and I reached up to move it away. As my fingers stretched towards the tree, one of the leaves was sliced in half. My hand was only centimetres away as it happened. There was a distant bang and a rift simply opened up in the centre of the leaf. The two halves floated silently to the ground. Terror must have registered on my face.

'Run!' shouted Franck.

'But…?'

'Run!' Franck was off, sprinting towards the car. Ducking inside he quickly popped the lock on my side and started the engine. The car was already moving as I launched myself through the open door. The dogs chased after us, leaping into the air like dolphins chasing a boat. After a minute Franck stopped to let them catch up. They barked excitedly as they climbed in and we rested, looking out of the window at the postcard-pretty village and checking every now and again that we hadn't been followed. The palms of my hands ran with sweat. Somebody had just shot at me.

I glanced at Franck. He seemed perfectly calm, a seasoned veteran of such incidents, able to put them behind him in an instant. A smile slowly crept across his face.

'Could it have been a mistake?'

Franck shook his head.

'A hunter after wild boar?' I pressed on.

Franck began to laugh. Gently at first, but eventually his whole body was overcome with giggles.

'What?'

'Your sniper,' Franck paused for breath, 'was a tractor engine starting up.' Franck covered his head with his hands and rested his convulsing frame against the dashboard.

'And the leaf? You saw the leaf?'

'Leaves fall from trees, it's nature, insects, the wind.'

Franck's face was red with amusement. My face was red with embarrassment. I'd behaved like a child who'd read too many ghost stories.

Chapter 27

The following week, out of curiosity, out of habit, perhaps even out of desperation, I was back by our oak trees. As I'd learnt, it was best not to feed Snuffle before going hunting. That way, he would be as eager as possible to earn treats.

Buoyed by his recent success Snuffle set off at a pace, sniffing and scratching, bouncing from tree to tree at such velocity that I struggled to keep up. The weather was much warmer and yet according to Franck there was always a chance of the odd later growth. Mid hunt, Snuffle skidded to an abrupt halt, digging all four legs into the ground, and sending up a cloud of leaves. Reaching for my tools I hurried to the spot.

There was no time for me to excavate the earth. Such was the intensity of Snuffle's digging that a small chasm had already been opened up – a rift into which his nose was firmly planted. I tugged, Snuffle resisted and eventually I pulled him away from his prize. A small brown dusty ball was firmly wedged between his teeth. I held his jaws tight to prevent him swallowing it. He regarded me angrily. A piece of saucisson finally broke the impasse. I reached down to collect what I thought was my first ever black diamond from our trees. All the effort, the hard work, had been worth it

– I'd finally managed to train Snuffle. I brushed the mud away and small particles dusted my fingertips. Out of curiosity, out of instinct, I raised a hand to my mouth. The taste was dry and slightly bitter, reminiscent of a familiar flavour – cocoa.

Stepping back, I looked into the hole in the ground. There was a small pile of truffles, perhaps ten. I'd never heard of them growing so close together. No wonder Snuffle had been keen. Truffles, apparently, were like buses, you wait all winter and then... At precisely this point I realised someone, that someone doubtless being Franck, had played a joke on me. My first truffles were in fact chocolate ones.

Back at home, verdant new growth plumed from the vines, yet the relationship with our landlord was far from spring-like. From outside the apartment I could see Manu's enormous frame looming over my wife. As usual with the Provençaux, there was a great deal of exaggerated arm waving.

It was now only two months until the baby was due and a week later we were moving house. The timing was far from ideal, but we couldn't govern nature. As a result of our impending *déménagement* (try saying that after a few glasses of wine) Manu's mind had been increasingly turning to getting new tenants and a visit, ostensibly to mend the front door, had turned into a full inspection.

Admittedly the house had fallen into a dreadful state of repair. The window frames were warped and buckled, and ugly black trails left by the daily incursions of water streaked down the paint work. In the shower room mould was growing on the ceiling. There wasn't a room without its personal colony of flies. Living in the place had become unpleasant, but with our new house nearing completion what choice did we have but to see it out?

'You see the problems,' I gestured at the walls.

'Your damage, yes.' Manu folded his arms and set his feet, apparently irritated that I had returned.

'What do you mean?'

'Well, look at all the water stains. It's going to cost thousands to repaint. The walls need to be stripped. A special damp-proof coating applied.'

'Hold on, what's that got to do with us?'

'You'll have to pay.'

Outside the window a lush field of poppies had sprung up and a family of frogs croaked deeply and repetitively. The air was fresh and fragrant and we'd opened all the windows to let as much as possible into the house. I swatted a fly away.

'I told you there was a serious problem. We've lived in terrible conditions for our health. Our child has suffered, we've suffered. All you could say was that it was normal, *"C'est la Provence."* You've made it almost unbearable to live here with the renovation next door. We should have asked for a reduction in the rent. And now, now you want me to pay for something that isn't my fault. No.'

Manu didn't respond at first. The frogs outside counted the seconds. Tanya pulled up a chair to rest her legs. Elodie wobbled into the room to see what was going on.

'Bien,' said Manu. He unfolded his arms and turned and left.

'What does that mean?' asked Tanya.

'I have no idea.'

We didn't have long to wait to find out. The following morning Manu was back. He appeared in conciliatory mood, explaining that when he let the house he'd taken out insurance and somebody would be coming around to look at the damage. We'd probably receive a letter telling us the date and time, but we really didn't need to worry about being there. He'd be taking care of things.

The atmosphere in the farmhouse returned to normal. Manu banged on his cars, and sprayed his olive trees with insecticide. The weather was warm and so Elodie spent a lot of the day outside picking small white snails from the blades of grass and feeding them to the chickens. A stream from the winter rainfall still trickled along the nearby gully and swathes of wild flowers lined the banks. Perhaps feeling a little guilty for his behaviour, Manu took Elodie up onto his tractor and gave her a tour of the field.

At the beginning of the following week the promised letter duly arrived. It wasn't at all what Manu had described. Our names had been set out at the top. We'd been allocated a case number and were required to be present at our rental property on Wednesday 24 April at 9 a.m. Far from a casual meeting with an insurance official, what Manu had in fact instigated was the beginning of a judicial procedure. And by telling us not to worry about turning up, he was attempting to win by default.

I sought Manu out in the fields the following day. He was bent double in a row of vines. A pair of wire cutters lay on the floor next to him. His hands were sore and bleeding.

'We'll be there on Wednesday.'

He shrugged as if it was of no consequence to him whether we attended or not. Reaching for his cutters he snipped another length of wire, bending it to the required shape with an expert twist of his fingers. The evenings we'd spent drinking moonshine, made from these very vines, meant nothing. Hours whiled away on the terrace dissecting the French political system had been redundant, wasted time. Like a pair of children we were now not talking.

I tried again. 'What's the format?'

'We present the facts of the case,' grunted Manu. 'The expert listens and then decides who is responsible.'

Manu turned back to his vines. As I walked back to the apartment I worked out exactly where the relationship had gone wrong. The moment he'd seen our construction site, something had changed. Rather than tenants, we were landowners. We suddenly had money. The flies, the damp, the mould – nothing was as unpleasant as the realisation that all the conviviality over the previous years had meant so little.

The afternoon before the expert's visit, we took Elodie for a regular check-up at the paediatrician's. She was nearly two and a half, a bright, vivacious, happy girl. A comic and a mimic, she delighted in repeating complicated words. Once she'd even managed to say 'rhododendron'. Thanks to crèche she'd started to speak a little French and occasionally, when she was particularly pleased with a toy, would exclaim *'Voilà!'* Over-proud parents that we were, we gushingly proclaimed that she was bilingual. Apart from her slightly hurried birth, we'd been fortunate – Elodie had had no major health problems in her life. Thus, all we were expecting at the doctor's was her final inoculation, a quick once-over and as a parting gift the usual prescription full of state-funded, totally unnecessary medicine. Instead we received a shock.

The paediatrician's office was large and welcoming. There was a Wendy house, a train track and miscellaneous other toys to occupy the children. Above the examination table was a mobile. It was home-made and consisted of a garden cane running the length of the table, decorated with the art of her patients. Each time we visited a new distraction had been added. Elodie loved it.

Dr Sami had been on duty the day after Elodie was born. Her relationship with Tanya had begun badly. Over-emotional, worried about me, charged with hormones, Tanya had decided that it was a good idea to check out. She'd been convinced that Elodie would be better off at home. Dr Sami had heard the rumour from the nurses and burst into Tanya's room, delivering – if we are polite – an old-fashioned telling-off, or – if we are impolite – a bollocking. The priority was Elodie and Elodie's health. She was premature and wouldn't be leaving the hospital until Dr Sami said so. Tanya cried, but once she'd gathered herself she discovered a great respect for the doctor.

These days, visiting the paediatrician felt like going to see a friend.

'*Et alors*, the house – is it finished?' Dr Sami offered me one of the chocolate biscuits she kept for the children.

'Another month or so.'

'About when the baby's due?'

We nodded.

'Have you got someone to look after Elodie?'

'My sister,' confirmed Tanya.

Dr Sami crossed to the examination table. A stethoscope covered in a fluffy giraffe toy swung invitingly from her neck. Her dark eyes smiled over the top of her half-moon glasses. '*Elodie, viens ici.*'

Any doctor who can persuade a child that a medical examination is fun, is a rare doctor, yet somehow Dr Sami had achieved this with Elodie. The train set was immediately abandoned, and Elodie began pulling at her clothes, anxious to get them off.

Dr Sami performed the usual checks – height, weight, eyes, everything was normal. She then rocked Elodie's head back to shine a light into her ears. She stopped. Her hands probed through Elodie's blonde hair.

'Have you noticed this?' Dr Sami parted Elodie's hair for us to look, revealing a bump about the size of half a squash ball.

'Any idea how it happened?'

We shook our heads. Children occasionally had bumps on their heads.

'*Ce n'est pas normal.*'

We gathered closer. First Tanya, then I, ran one finger gently over the bump, which was located towards the back of her head. There was no visible discolouration but it was slightly soft to touch, as if there was fluid trapped underneath the skin.

'It needs to be investigated.'

I nodded. The French health service was about to kick into action. No doubt we would be sent to a specialist, prescribed even more medicines, and eventually the problem would cure itself.

'First, an X-ray.'

This was slightly more perturbing, but even so I wasn't too worried. Elodie was happily playing with a toy train. She'd slept well, and been on excellent form all morning.

'I'll write a note for the doctors.'

The paediatrician sat at her desk and methodically wrote a letter describing what she had found. The giraffe stethoscope lay abandoned on the examination table. The chocolate biscuits were back in the drawer. I looked at Tanya and shrugged. Another case of French hypochondria – we'd go for the X-ray, and all would be fine. Elodie was leaping around with such vigour in the Wendy house that it appeared about to capsize. It was a wonder she didn't have anymore bumps.

'When shall we make the appointment?'

'I am afraid you must go now.'

'Now?'

'To the children's accident and emergency ward at Aix. It may be nothing, but it's better to investigate.' The paediatrician's voice was calm and reassuring. She wanted us to understand that she was being ultra-cautious and that there was probably nothing wrong. Yet we had to go now, not in a couple of hours, not tomorrow or next week. Now. The only possible reason for such urgency was that there was an immediate danger to Elodie's well-being. Usually, Tanya would be asking the paediatrician lots of questions. Her mother was a nurse and some of the medical knowledge had rubbed off on her. Instead she was quiet, sitting still, in shock, her face already a shade whiter. I reminded myself we knew nothing yet and that there was no need to panic. My mind was already plotting the possible outcome: half an hour to drive to Aix, then, given the efficiency of the French health service, an hour to see the doctors – with any luck we could be home for bath time, and the whole experience wouldn't be too tiring or stressful for Tanya.

Unusually, Dr Sami accompanied us to the car. She held the bags as we strapped Elodie into her seat. As we turned onto the main road I resolved to find my inner French driver. The journey from Pertuis to Aix would be covered in record time.

Chapter 28

I look at the face of my sleeping daughter. Everything is so young and fresh. Her eyelashes are dark and elongated, her cheeks rounded with health, her skin so soft and precious. She will never remember any of this. Sleep and forget. Tanya has gone home. I insisted. We will be here for the night. The results will be ready in the morning.

The room is dominated by a large yellow cot. The bars are made of iron rather than the customary wood and there's a pump to adjust the height. The place is odourless, antiseptic. I remember the moment we arrived.

A female doctor saw us; grey hair, glasses, studious, about fifty. Her manner was reassuringly professional. She parted Elodie's hair and examined the back of her head.

'When did you notice the bump?'

'At the paediatrician's this afternoon.'

'Not before?'

'No.'

'Has there been anything unusual about her behaviour – eating well, sleeping well, not tired, playing normally?'

'She's been fine,' I confirmed.

Lights were shone into eyes and ears, there was more prodding and poking and Elodie had begun to cry. The X-ray had been mercifully quick, an arm of a machine had hovered over my baby and 'click', it was done.

I look again at my daughter. She's been asleep for a couple of hours and it seems the night will be undisturbed. I close my eyes and try to rest but doctors keep coming in and out. Some of them check on Elodie, others ask me the same questions over and over. When did we first notice the bump? Did anything happen before then? A fall, perhaps? Did we leave Elodie in other people's care? Had they reported anything untoward? Only the identity of the doctor changes. Presumably it is routine; as people come on and off shift, they have to get to know the patients.

Staring at the blank wall in the dim light I suddenly remember we have the meeting at our apartment scheduled for the following morning. Tanya is in no state to deal with Manu. I phone. Tanya's voice is quavering.

'No, no more news. She still appears fine. She's sleeping now. One other thing; Manu's man's coming tomorrow, can you leave him a note from me?'

I dictate, leaving Tanya to do the translation later: 'In November I informed our landlord that there was a serious problem with his house. I told him he should call the builder who carried out the renovation. He refused, blaming the problem on the cold weather. Every couple of weeks during the winter I advised our landlord that the problem was continuing and getting worse. He did nothing. In the circumstances we take no responsibility for the damage.'

I care what happens, but I also don't care. It's a problem for another day.

'Give the letter to the expert and don't worry about it, try to get some sleep. I'll see you tomorrow. I love you.'

Elodie shifts in her sleep and I rise and brush the hair from her eyes. I wonder how she got the bump. There have been countless falls followed by short stretches of crying, but never the vomiting or the loss of consciousness the doctors keep asking me about.

I long to be speaking in English to understand the subtleties of language that might provide comfort at a time like this, the significant choice of word with which the doctor implies, although he or she can't say it, that everything is going to be all right. The French are very clinical, they are doing everything by the rule book, performing the required tests, keeping us in overnight, and I am grateful, but they are also providing no information. Despite the hours in the hospital I have no idea what the consequences of this mysterious bump might be; perhaps we are being saved the worry, because any negative outcome is too dreadful to contemplate. I just don't know.

Lights come on. Medicine is administered. Lights go off. I drift in and out of sleep. In the middle of the night Elodie is conscious. She starts to cry. I lift her up and pace the corridors of the hospital until day begins to creep into the ward, highlighting the thin layer of dust that covers the photos of smiling sick children on the walls.

The first doctor of the morning arrives. She is Indian, young, pretty even, but serious, carrying a file of papers. She takes out the X-rays and shows me the cracks they have detected in Elodie's skull. There is not one but two fractures. One historic, one recent, and we rehearse the same questions about falls and vomiting and loss of consciousness.

It occurs to me that this is a little like an interrogation. People are broken down like this, by incessant repetition of questions, until fissures appear in the story which can be widened and challenged at a later date. This young doctor opposite me is doing exactly that, noting down the answers, comparing them with the ones I gave yesterday.

The morning passes. Elodie sleeps and I speak to Tanya on the phone. We talk about the meeting with Manu, she describes what happened:

'He was so happy when I told him you weren't going to be here. Beaming. Started going on how it wasn't really necessary anyway. Then the guy arrives. Educated, in a suit, young, smart, driving a nice car, I never know what makes they are, but something like a BMW.

'Him and Manu immediately disliked each other and I handed over your letter.

'You should have seen Manu's face. The expert took it and read it, and asked Manu whether the contents were true. Manu said yes, but then started ranting on about us drying the washing inside. He pointed at all the walls, and jabbered on. They traipsed around the house. I couldn't be bothered to follow but then I got worried about what Manu was saying and so I eavesdropped.

'The expert was lecturing Manu, telling him his behaviour was unacceptable, it's his responsibility as a landlord to ensure the property is habitable. He'd had warnings, he hadn't acted on them.

'The expert then took me aside and explained we've no responsibility for the cost of repainting the apartment. The damage is not our fault. He was so nice and kind. Once he knew that you were in hospital with Elodie, he couldn't have been gentler.

'Manu left without saying goodbye.'

I hear Tanya's sister Claire arriving in the background. She lives in Nîmes and has driven over with her three children to help out. They arrange to come to the hospital later. It looks like we may have to spend another night. Elodie is happy. She's discovered an outside playground and is clambering over the toys. The other parents describe her as *'cascadeuse'* and they are right – she's hanging off the slide like a monkey, banging her legs and arms. At least if she falls she's in the right place.

There are more conversations with doctors. Older, greyer, more senior people, who ask the same questions about the origins of the fractures. Still nobody will tell me what the consequences are for Elodie's health. We wait and I worry. How long are they going to keep us here?

I turn on the television and discover a football match between African countries, former French colonies. Distractedly I watch the images; the ball pings across the turf, somebody hits the post, moments later somebody scores. My mind is elsewhere.

I am tired. The images on the TV screen glaze over. I try to sleep, but bleak thoughts tumble through my mind. Had Elodie hurt herself on the building site? All the concrete, the rough, hard, tough surfaces, the unexpected stairs, planks and bricks. She'd certainly tumbled a number of times. Was it my own hubris that had brought us to this hospital?

Building a house is such an arrogant thing to do. Most people look for somewhere they would like to live and then compromise because inevitably the money doesn't quite stretch. However, faced by this eternal problem we'd decided to build, seduced into thinking that professional property developing was an easy trade.

There's a cheer as one team scores. It reminds me of the current French political scandal: tall black athletic boys from the former colonies are allegedly being denied places in France's elite training camps. The purported reasoning? They are believed not to care enough about their adoptive country and when matches are close it's suspected they lack the requisite pride in the blue jersey.

Tanya, Claire and Claire's children arrive and I turn the television off. Claire's kids – Rosie, Tristan, Freya – rush to hug me. They smile, they laugh, they skip, their curls blot out the light. They charge over to Elodie, but the sight of the playground distracts them and they head outside. I kiss Claire and Tanya. The ordeal continues but for a few hours I have some support. I turn and see that the Indian doctor has been watching us. Standing in the centre of the corridor, arms folded against her chest, making a judgement. Minutes later she comes to our room. Claire looks after the children. Tanya and I sit on the edge of my bed and listen. The verdict is simple, clinical.

'Your daughter has two fractures on her head. There is fluid trapped between the bone and the skin. This will gradually disappear. There's no haemorrhaging, she's just fine in herself, there will be no long-term damage.'

Somehow I know all this already. Tanya sighs with relief and squeezes my hand in triumph. Claire and the children come bumbling into the room, full of descriptions of how marvellous the playground is.

The Indian doctor smiles at all the children. Her decision is made.

'*Allez.*' She hands me the file of X-rays and leaves.

Chapter 29

In May Provence was at its majestic best. Trees dripped with cherries, vines were covered in verdant new growth, village streets flowed with a pleasant trickle of tourists, and the produce in the markets hovered between seasons: asparagus from Pertuis and strawberries from Rognes, but not yet the melons and peaches of high summer.

We longed to be in our new house, opening the windows every morning to the vibrant countryside, noting the first drifting smell of lavender as the plant bloomed a cautious brittle purple, and admiring the riotous violet of the sage plants that always erupted with the heat.

On the *chantier* everything appeared ready. The floor was in, the lights were working and the rooms seemingly only awaited furniture and people to live in them. However, the construction company had a myriad of jobs to do before the house could be handed over. Among other tasks the pipes had to be checked for leaks and the modern-day plumbing of telephone and Internet lines had to be installed. Then in the final stages the floors needed to be cleaned and treated with a special protective chemical. This process was scheduled for the last week in May. After that we had to wait fourteen days while the chemicals dispersed and then the house was officially ours – exactly four days after Tanya's due date!

Most evenings we sat outside on the terrace behind our farmhouse apartment discussing the details of the move: where we would put specific items of furniture, which paints would work well on which walls and what colour we should spray the shutters. For the first time since we'd committed to the project, we were able to relax. The money had not run out, the work had not stalled and our dream house had become a reality. There was a certain satisfaction to be derived from just looking at the solid walls, and knowing that we had created them. The closer we came to completion, the more the pain and hardship of the process of building began to fade. Neither Tanya or I would ever build a house again, of that we were sure, but we also had no regrets. We'd learnt a lot about human nature.

I'd come to appreciate that truth was not the inviolate, immovable set of facts I'd previously assumed it to be. Everybody had their own truths, and when cultures collided these could be distressingly different. More than ever I believed in the influence of the climate. The savage summers and brutally cold winters of Provence bred a certain type of person – hard, frugal and fearful of outsiders but, like Franck, kind and generous when they accepted you into their circle.

In the end we'd been lucky. Take just a quick look at the landscape of Provence, and amid the lavender, olives and vines, it's easy to spot abandoned, half-finished projects, where the money has run out and the dream finished in acrimony and legal fees. We'd persevered and in the end it had been worth it.

One evening towards the end of May a car horn hooted at the end of the long drive that led up through the olive grove and around the back of Manu's farmhouse. Just a few days ago an American man had phoned and asked to meet us. He'd bought a second home near the village – in fact, it was more of a castle – and was about to start the renovation. Everything was lined up and in place, including the team of tradesmen to do the work. Today was his last day in Provence before he flew home, but an unpleasant rumour had brought him to our door. Despite the difficult timing, we'd agreed to meet.

The expensive car became stranded halfway up the dirt track. The man got out. He wore a beige suit and white shirt, and clutched a bottle of champagne in one hand. A woman followed. Wisely she took off her high heels and linked the straps with her handbag. The sequins on her light dress shimmered in the sunlight as she stumbled towards us. Together the pair looked perfect for a night out in a smart restaurant on the Côte d'Azur – quite what they were doing in rural Provence I had no idea. They came closer. The man was short and balding, with a pronounced paunch and an unfortunate sweat problem. The woman was thin, equine almost, with a hooked nose and the visible bones of someone who didn't eat enough. From the phone conversation we already knew his name was Dwight. The woman was an unexpected guest.

'So kind of you to meet us. This is my attorney, Beth.' He motioned to his female companion and with his other hand proffered the bottle of champagne.

'Would you like a glass?'

'Rude not to.'

I disappeared into the kitchen, searching for the box with the glasses in. Elodie was inside, clutching her teddy and watching a DVD. Excited about the move and chatting about our plans, we'd forgotten her bedtime. Pouring the champagne, I went back outside and handed around the glasses.

'Lovely place you have here.' Dwight took a large gulp of the vigorously fizzing champagne.

'Thank you.' I never tired of the view from the terrace, the rolling Luberon hills and the line of cypress trees spearing the sky. And from outside, the old farmhouse itself epitomised the Provençal dream – crumbling walls lit golden by the fading sun. Inside, things had improved with the new season, the damp had dried and the insect invasion had been temporarily repelled. For the moment at least, Dwight was right.

'And you've built a new place?' added Beth, attempting to cover her thighs with the scrap of material she was wearing that masqueraded as a dress.

'Worked a bit with our man Ange?' added Dwight.

'Yes.' I topped Dwight up. This must be the point of their visit. To ask for a recommendation or otherwise. 'Our man Ange' was already a worryingly familiar way to refer to a potential future employee.

Remembering Elodie, I excused myself. She was asleep on the sofa. I carried her into her bedroom and gently lowered her into the cot. I closed the shutters and patted Snuffle, who had padded after us and was now curled in a corner of the room. Parting Elodie's hair I gave her a kiss on the forehead.

'Sleep well,' I whispered and shut the door.

Back on the terrace the conversation had moved on. I assumed that Tanya had told Dwight and Beth of the terrible time we'd had with Ange. If they'd come for reassurance, they'd come to the wrong place. It was a shame their project would have to be delayed, but as we learnt to our cost, it would be better to start with the right people in the first place.

'And what's the village like in the winter?' Dwight's glass was empty and I poured him the rest of the bottle.

'We love it,' said Tanya. 'It's a lot quieter, but you really get to know the people. The weather's usually great, there are the Christmas markets, and of course the truffle fairs – it's so festive.'

Dwight glanced at his watch.

'If we're going to make the restaurant...' He left the statement trailing in the air.

Beth nodded eagerly. 'You're right, if we're going to make the restaurant.'

'Where are you going?'

'The *resto* on the road out of the next village.'

'Good, you'll enjoy it there.'

We kissed goodbye and they hobbled away across the field.

'Particularly tonight,' I added, once they were out of earshot.

Tanya looked confused.

'It's key-swapping night,' I grinned, 'and in that dress Beth's going to get a lot of attention.'

'Strange type of lawyer,' said Tanya.

We sat back down to our hardly touched glasses of champagne. Bats danced in haphazard flight as the moon replaced the sun. The air was still warm and the cluster of high village houses provided the first of many galaxies of light in the clear night sky. For a while we said nothing, listening to the animals, waiting as a blanket of stillness descended.

'So what did you say to them?'

'About what?'

'About Ange?'

'Nothing.'

'Nothing?'

'I told them we'd chosen to work with someone else.'

'You didn't warn them?'

'They didn't seem to want to talk about it anymore. Why stir up bad feeling? It's a small village. The man's got to work.'

Snuffle emerged from the house and flopped contentedly at our feet. I wasn't sure whether Tanya was right. I'd been ready to tell Dwight how Ange had treated us. And yet I could understand

Tanya's reluctance to discuss Ange. Firstly, Dwight was planning a renovation rather than building a house. This was Ange's professed area of expertise, so things should run smoother. And as Tanya pointed out, if they'd really wanted to know about Ange, they'd only had to ask. With his plans finalised and his flight home booked, Dwight had made his decisions and had not wanted to know. Our battle was not his battle.

Chapter 30

Franck's right leg stuck out from under the chassis of the hire van. His left leg was invisible, consumed by the engine. There was a problem with the gearbox, meaning it was impossible to find reverse.

'*Merde, c'est pas possible.*' It was hot already and in the confined space Franck was becoming frustrated. He'd declared the job '*vite fait*', only it wasn't.

'Pass me the screwdriver.' There was a sweaty pause and then more swearing.

Outside our rental apartment our possessions were ranged on the driveway: a fridge freezer, some sofa beds, boxes of files, photos, cutlery, clothes and paintings. Everything was ready and labelled. It was imperative we pulled off one of the slickest moves ever. Tanya was now two days overdue and her labour was imminent. We'd considered professional movers, but somehow with our limited goods it hadn't seemed worth it. Another error had been to relinquish our lease on the day we moved. Manu's team of painters had already arrived and were setting up inside. Tanya sat under an olive tree with Elodie, looking on anxiously. The heat of the day mounted.

Franck emerged from the bowels of the van. His face was smeared with oil and grease, his hands black from the work. '*C'est complètement tordu.*' He shrugged his shoulders. Loosely translated, this meant the van was buggered. In fact, we were buggered too: thirty minutes ago, as I'd crunched the gears and finally stuttered out of the car park, the manager had confirmed there were no other vans available.

'There's a farm lorry I could borrow,' confessed Franck. 'That's if it still works.'

I nodded and pulled up a seat next to Tanya in the shade. The sun was full of future menace. We'd arranged to start early with the aim of finishing by midday. With the delay, we'd be toiling long into the afternoon. Tanya shifted uncomfortably. Her belly was as oversized as one of the region's peerless pumpkins. For the last week she'd been having daily massages to try to provoke the labour. Acupuncture sessions had also proved ineffective. Truffles were unavailable and so the previous evening we'd tried a curry. Again, no effect.

'How are you feeling?'

'Been better.'

Such was our luck, I was privately convinced that today would be the day. The heat and the stress of the move would surely combine to kick-start labour.

'No sign of the contractions?'

'No.'

Tanya sipped nervously on a bottle of water and we waited. The countryside throbbed with insects. Inside our old apartment the painters were at work, their radio blaring France Bleu Provence into the countryside. The show was *Les Bonnes Affaires*, the inimitably Provençal swap shop.

'I have a panini grill. My boys loved it, but they've left home now. It can make four sandwiches at one time. Their favourite used to be ham and Gruyère, with a little mustard. *Oh là là, c'est bon*. The sandwich maker really needs a good home.'

'And what are you looking for in return?' The presenter was getting a little impatient with the life history.

'Well, my husband has always wanted one of those outdoor gas barbeques; four grills, hot plate, smoking chamber, spit roaster, complete with utensils. The phone number is 06 78 68 06 99.'

'I see, a panini maker, in exchange for a four-grill gas barbeque,' said the despairing presenter, switchboard doubtless flashing with hordes of callers ready to exchange their 2CVs for Ferraris. 'The number to call is 06 78 68 06 99. *Merci*, Monica.'

Where was Franck? A blaring horn, reminiscent of the sound made by a large ship, answered my question. Making its way up the drive, at about the speed of a docking passenger ferry, was an extraordinary looking lorry. The exhaust tank was fixed to the roof of the front cabin so that great puffs of diesel billowed into the sky. It gave the vehicle the appearance of running on steam, which at the current speed of progress appeared a possibility. The front window was coated in a thick film of grease, punctured around the windscreen wipers by two half-moons of semi-clarity. There was no bumper, no number plate, just an unprotected rusting engine that alternatively shrieked, whirred and clunked. However, none of this really worried me; what worried me was the rear, where we were supposed to load our possessions. The tyres already sagged like a sumo wrestler's belly, there was no roof, no sides, and a rotten floor through which the ground was visible. The contraption might be suitable for moving hay bales from a field to a barn, but it surely wouldn't take the weight of our belongings.

'Come on, what are you waiting for?'

Franck didn't seem to share my concern and so for the next hour we heaved beds and boxes onto the rear, strapping them down with elastic ropes, like sailors securing the hatches before a storm. Last on was the fridge. It wobbled precariously, there was a creak of wood and one corner pierced the floor of the truck, falling half a foot towards the ground before becoming wedged.

'Perfect,' said Franck, 'you're going to need to hold it.' He wobbled the fridge experimentally. 'Maybe two people. *Allez, on y va.*'

We hoisted Elodie into the cabin with Franck. Snuffle leapt in beside her. Tanya and I climbed onto the trailer and draped ourselves around the fridge.

'The lorry's not insured for the road, so we're going to take the truffle routes,' cried Franck with glee.

The first bump nearly pitched us off the side. After that we were more cautious, joining hands and hugging the fridge as if it were a safe full of gold. Our farmhouse apartment slowly receded. The terrace from where we'd watched the sunset was bare, the olive tree underneath which we parked the car bushy and already filled with tiny green fruit. The skylight out of which the countless visiting hornets had escaped was up. To help clear the fumes of the paint our bedroom windows were open. It was as if our essences and smells were being encouraged to flee the building and chase us down the drive. Our presence was being whitewashed.

Manu was working in a distant field as we rocked down the drive. He stood still and looked but didn't wave. If our hands had been free I am sure we would have given a farewell salute, but they weren't, they were clasped tightly around the fridge. Our last view of the farmhouse was down a long row of olive trees, under a stone arch, to the Roman fountain around which roses bloomed. It was a good way to remember the place.

Franck came to the main road. He dismounted, crossed the carriageway, unhooked a chain which barred access to a dirt track and gave a wry smile. Once a truffle hunter, always a truffle hunter, even if it was the middle of summer. Into the hills we went, passing into the deep shade of the pines, emerging into the brilliant sunlight as we skirted a field of vines, and ducking into the softer light under a row of *platanes*.

Up we climbed, leaving the village below us, the occasional pastel shutter visible through gaps in the foliage. The smells this deep into the *garrigue* were heady, rich, and all enveloping. I kept a careful eye on Tanya. She looked white and pained. All the changes in gradient, the little bumps and larger rolling waves of terrain were dizzying and confusing to the stomach. On occasions she winced and instinctively released a hand to clutch at her belly. My cries of concern were drowned by the deafening racket of the diesel engine and the crunching, bucking, screeching undercarriage. It became more and more difficult to cling onto the fridge, and in the end, high above the village, I banged on the roof of the lorry to call a stop.

'Let's rest a little while.'

'Good idea, I want to check the rear tyre. *C'est vite fait.*'

Snuffle and Elodie disappeared into the trees. Barks and screams of enjoyment told us they were still around. The shade was pleasant, and the sight of the lorry loaded with our possessions in such an incongruous setting brought smiles to both of our faces. Neither of us broached the subject that was really worrying us. Here we were in the middle of a Provençal forest, at least an hour's walk from a main road, with only a decrepit lorry for transport, a decrepit lorry which now had one defective rear wheel.

Franck had been gone for a disconcerting period of time. One rushed last-minute charge to the maternity ward was unfortunate; two would begin to look like carelessness. With a judder the rear quarter of the lorry collapsed to the ground, sending a couple of beds sliding towards the edge. The fridge, wedged as it was between the floorboards, now teetered like the leaning tower of Pisa.

'No contractions?'

'None, I'm fine. Will you stop worrying.'

'It's hard not to.'

There was another juddering, wracking, splintering noise and I turned. It sounded like the whole lorry had collapsed in a wheezing heap to the forest floor. Franck reappeared, a grin spreading across his face.

'I've raised the whole suspension, should be a little smoother on the way down. Shall we get going?'

The suspension might well have been higher, but the problem on the way down was that the brakes didn't work. Trees hurtled by like slalom posts, bumps became jumps, and the fact that we only lost one chair overboard was a minor miracle. Somehow we clung on, emerging into the field of truffles trees above our newly constructed house. The last vertiginous descent pitched Tanya and I forward against the dirty cabin window, and then rocked us backwards as the wheels found level ground. We'd arrived, and in what style.

Our new house lay before us, doors open wide, welcoming us in. The shutters were painted a delicate grey blue, the walls the colour of local sand. The roof was covered in aged tiles through which a small chimney protruded. The building was immaculate, clean, finished.

Later the same day, with the sun gently melting from the sky, Tanya and I sat on the terrace looking down at the village. It was a beautiful time of year. The lavender was blooming, sunflowers were at their radiant best, and the remnants of the spring streams still fed the fields, keeping them verdant if only for another few weeks. Inside the house, an afternoon of work had achieved a surprising amount. Our bed was made, Elodie's cot erected in her new room, tables, chairs, the basics of living were all in place. From now on our belongings could expand to fill the house, we could gather possessions as we lived, building a home from our experiences and the places we visited. It was a feeling of overwhelming satisfaction. The effort, the heartache, the rows, the disappointments and the disillusionment, all seemed worth it for the peace we had found. Elodie was sitting in a distant corner of the field, where some grass had survived the ravages of construction machinery. Snuffle was lying in the shade next to her.

On the table was the present Madame Roland, the owner of the construction company, had given us: a miniature wooden house with hooks inside for all the keys. In return I'd handed over the final cheque for the house. It was an unequal exchange, leaving Madame Roland grinning and me worrying whether I should have withheld the money. What would happen if things went wrong now? Would her company, as promised, intervene on request to deal with all the snagging? Tanya and I had decided to trust her. At times building the house had deprived us of faith in human nature. Yet in the end, we'd resolved that living a life where we suspected everyone and believed they were dishonest until they proved otherwise was no way to live. Far better to trust than be forever constrained by pessimism.

To do otherwise would turn us into Miriam, our telescope gazing neighbour. At the last count she'd identified eight potentially house threatening cracks in the walls and apparently she'd already spoken to her lawyer about representing us. To date I had declined the offer. The cracks had all been repaired and Madame Roland had explained that a little movement always occurred with new houses. Give it a year and things should settle down. Was I being naive in accepting this explanation? Only time would tell.

Snuffle came careering across the field, closely followed by Elodie. The two of them were inseparable. The dark shaggy dog and bronzed blonde two year old made an unlikely pairing, but wherever one went the other followed. They were so close that we'd caught Elodie sleeping in Snuffle's dog house. As Snuffle and Elodie approached I noticed they were both covered in dirt. Leaves had entwined themselves in Elodie's hair and a twig poked out of the toe of her sandal.

'What have you been doing?' asked Tanya.

Elodie grinned and Snuffle barked.

Tanya and I didn't need an answer. We both knew that Elodie's favourite new imaginary game was truffle hunting. Perhaps the onlookers at the Uzès dog trials had been right after all, perhaps she did have a special talent. Only the winter would tell; for now, we had to be content with a pile of muddy stones, and a filthy dog and toddler.

Epilogue –
Six Months Later

The car crunches up the drive. Inside are two French government officials, one male, one female. They are wearing heavy overcoats and carry intimidating, large briefcases. The woman checks her watch and they head towards our front door. This is it, then.

Elodie is at crèche and Tanya is sitting opposite Delphine, chatting away while feeding our new baby daughter, Sienna, who is the spitting image of her sister. Wide eyes, long lashes, chubby cheeks. In their passport photos the two sisters are impossible to tell apart. They couldn't have arrived in more different fashions, though. Rather than a truffle-induced dash to the maternity unit, Sienna bided her time, getting used to her new house, before emerging nearly two weeks late into the world. Lea, the same midwife who had delivered Elodie, was finally, after a prolonged labour, able to hand me my new daughter. Thankfully the time was eleven in the morning – another half-hour and Lea would have been looking at her watch and suggesting I pop out to the local cafe for a spot of lunch. Once more, steak tartare had been on the menu. I'd checked.

The government officials are nearly at the door. Sienna is giggling as her eyes follow a food-laden spoon. Fifi sits at her feet, also hungrily following the trajectory of the spoon. Sienna rocks back in her chair and cackles with laughter. The food misses her mouth and forms a trail down her bib. Fifi whimpers with dejection.

I kiss Tanya.

'You sure you'll be all right?'

'Sure.'

'OK.'

'You look like you've eaten a wasp,' says Delphine. 'Don't worry, I know how to deal with their type.'

I find Snuffle's lead and head out the back door, just as the officials knock on the front. The path is a familiar one. An embankment climbs away on one side, on the other there's a muddy field of arable land. We head into the mottled shade of an avenue of pines, and the path turns to our right at a steep gradient, making us scramble. The wood thins and we emerge into the prairie. Cold December air tickles my nose and a flurry of snow induces a sneeze. I zip up my jumper, enjoying the sensation of temporary warmth. Snuffle shakes his fur in disgust. The cycle of the moon is perfect and the truffle oaks await.

'*Allez, cherche, c'est où? C'est là? Cherche!*'

Snuffle starts working his way between the trees. I follow distractedly. My mind is on our house. The officials are from the planning office of the *préfecture* in Avignon. For six months after a new house is built they have the right to come and inspect the work to check it complies with the permit. Such visits are rare. This being France, everybody cheats a little and the government tends to turn a blind eye. Only if you are exceptionally unlucky, or if someone has a grudge against you, do you get inspected.

My heart had lurched when I read the letter. Life had been going so well. A new daughter, a new house, even sales in my wine business were on the up. Our future in Provence had seemed secure. However, just a few terse legally worded lines had changed all that. Somebody, somewhere had spotted our extra height wall and was going to make us pay. And, if the worst came to the worst, we'd have to sell the house because we simply did not have the money to carry out the remedial works.

For the last few weeks Tanya had held our family together, calmly going about the business of raising our two children. Meanwhile, I'd panicked. Every waking moment had been spent trying to conjure a way out of the mess we found ourselves in. My demeanour was nervy, guilty, embarrassed, and in the end we'd decided it was better I was absent when the officials came. Tanya would act the innocent and call their bluff. To the untrained eye, everything appeared to conform with the permit.

Of course, the man and the woman currently sizing up our house were far from untrained.

'Allez, cherche, c'est où? C'est là? Cherche!'

Snuffle rushes between the trees more in hope than expectation. Early signs are that this will be another barren season. We're deep into the grove now, moving onto the last half of the trees. A scattering of flies spirals into the air, their wings shimmering with the snow.

'Allez, cherche, c'est où? C'est là? Cherche!'

Snuffle stops on a spot about 5 metres from the final tree and begins pawing the ground. There have been too many false dawns for me to get excited. I squat to the ground and take out my tools, scraping away at the hard earth. I make a hole the size of my hand and grab a fistful of earth, pushing it to my nostrils. I smell nothing at first, but then very faintly I detect the odour of truffles. I wish Franck were here to confirm my find, because the scent is fleeting and disappears with a wisp of breeze.

I dig further to the right. Nothing. I dig further to the left. Nothing again. I dig deeper. The hole is soon halfway up to my elbow. I grab another fistful of soil and inhale deeply. Once, twice, three times to be certain. Another final scratch of the soil and then gently, gradually, with trembling hands, I prise the truffle from the earth. Snuffle wags his tail enthusiastically and I reward him with a large slice of saucisson. He barks gratefully. Scraping away the mud, I examine the marbling of the outer coating. I inhale. The aroma is pungent, fierce, and in the clean cold winter air, even beautiful. I am holding in my hand a *vrai Tuber melanosporum*, a black diamond. It's big, the size of a golf ball. Enough for a good risotto and several omelettes.

I turn for home. As I walk an idea begins to develop and a spring enters my stride. By the time we're back down the hill I am almost running. Snuffle is barking enthusiastically at my side.

Fate is on my side.

I have ten trees and a truffle dog and doubtless, being Provençaux, the officials are gourmands.

Acknowledgements

Many thanks to my agent Annette Greene for spotting the potential of the book and to Jennifer Barclay at Summersdale for her editorial guidance and belief in the project. Little did she know that her job would have been made a lot easier, but for the untimely death of my uncle, Alan Izzard, who has so kindly proofread my previous books. I have missed our discussions about the Latin stems of words and the correct use of the passive tense.

Thanks to Tanya, Elodie and Sienna and our parents.

Having a three-year-old bouncing on my lap as I type has been truly inspirational.